Reviews of the first edition of *Nations and Nationalism*

'Brilliant, provocative . . . a great book.' *New Statesman*

'An important book . . . a new starting line from which all subsequent discussions of nationalism will have to begin.' *New Society*

'A better explanation than anyone has yet offered of why nationalism is such a prominent principle of political legitimacy today . . . a terse and forceful work . . . the product of great intellectual energy and an impressive range of knowledge.' *Times Literary Supplement*

'Gellner's short book is an incisive, penetrating and persuasive discussion of how the nation-states of the modern industrial world differ from earlier states . . . Gellner uses this analysis to explain the force of nationalism in the modern world.' *International Security*

'Gellner's range is wide, covering the ideas of some modern thinkers from Marx, Malinowski and Carr to Heidegger, Hroch, Havel and Said.' Race and Class

NEW PERSPECTIVES ON THE PAST

General Editor
Constantin Fasolt, University of Chicago

Advisory Editors
Michael Burns, Mount Holyoke College
Pamela Kyle Crossley, Dartmouth College
R. I. Moore, University of Newcastle upon Tyne
Ian Morris, Stanford University
Heide Wunder, Universität-Gesamthochschule Kassel

PUBLISHED

David Arnold Famine
David Arnold The Problem of Nature
James Casey The History of the Family
Patricia Crone Pre-Industrial Societies
James Fentress and Chris Wickham Social Memory*
Ernest Gellner Nations and Nationalism, second edition
Ernest Gellner Reason and Culture*
David Grigg The Transformation of Agriculture in the West*
Richard Hodges Primitive and Peasant Markets*
Eugene Kamenka Bureaucracy*
Francis Oakley Kingship
Edward Peters Torture*
Jonathan Powis Aristocracy*
William Ray The Logic of Culture
I. G. Simmons Environmental History*
Bruce Trigger Sociocultural Evolution
David Turley Slavery
Merry E. Wiesner-Hanks Gender in History

IN PREPARATION

Michael Adas Locating World History

* now out of print

Nations and Nationalism

Second Edition

Ernest Gellner

Introduction by John Breuilly

First published in paperback, Blackwell Publishing, 2006
First printing, Cornell Paperbacks, 2008

*Library of Congress Cataloging-in-Publication Data
are available from the Library of Congress.*

978-0-8014-7500-9

Cornell University Press strives to use environmentally
responsible suppliers and materials to the fullest extent possible
in the publishing of its books. Such materials include vegetable-
based, low-VOC inks and acid-free papers that are recycled,
totally chlorine-free, or partly composed of nonwood fibers. For
further information, visit our website at
www.cornellpress.cornell.edu.

Paperback printing   10 9 8 7 6 5 4 3 2

Contents

About the Authors

Ernest Gellner was born in Paris in 1925 and brought up in Prague, fleeing with his family to England in 1939. He taught at the LSE from 1949, where he was Professor of Philosophy with special reference to Sociology from 1962 until 1984, when he became William Wyse Professor of Social Anthropology at the University of Cambridge. At the end of his life, in 1995, he was Director of the Centre for the Study of Nationalism, part of the Central European University, in Prague. He wrote many books, among them *Words and Things* (1959), *Thought and Change* (1964), *Saints of the Atlas* (1969), *Legitimation of Belief* (1974), *The Psychoanalytic Movement* (1985), *Plough, Sword and Book: The Structure of Human History* (1988), *Conditions of Liberty: Civil Society and its Rivals* (1994), and the posthumous *Language and Solitude: Wittgenstein, Malinowski and the Habsburg Dilemma* (1998).

John Breuilly is Professor of Nationalism and Ethnicity at the London School of Economics and Political Science. He taught at Manchester University from 1972 until 1995 and at Birmingham University from 1995 until 2004. He has held visiting Professorships at the universities of Hamburg (1987–8) and Bielefeld (1992–3) and a Research Fellowship at the Wissenschaftskolleg Berlin (2001–2). Book publications include *Austria, Prussia and Germany 1806–1871* (2002), *Nationalismus und moderner Staat. Deutschland und Europa* (1999), *The Formation of the First German Nation-State, 1800–1871* (1996), and *Nationalism and the State* (second edition, 1993).

About this Edition

So far as Gellner's text is concerned, this book is a reprint of the text of 1983 with minor typographical corrections. The Introduction by John Breuilly has been specially written for this second edition. Gellner's original list of reading suggestions has been updated and supplemented by John Breuilly. There is also a bibliography of Gellner's writings on nationalism compiled by Ian Jarvie.

Editor's Preface to the First Edition

R. I. Moore, Founding Editor

Ignorance has many forms, and all of them are dangerous. In the nineteenth and twentieth centuries our chief effort has been to free ourselves from tradition and superstition in large questions, and from the error in small ones upon which they rest, by redefining the fields of knowledge and evolving in each the distinctive method appropriate for its cultivation. The achievement has been incalculable, but not without cost. As each new subject has developed a specialist vocabulary to permit rapid and precise reference to its own common and rapidly growing stock of ideas and discoveries, and come to require a greater depth of expertise from its specialists, scholars have been cut off by their own erudition not only from mankind at large, but from the findings of workers in other fields, and even in other parts of their own. Isolation diminishes not only the usefulness but the soundness of their labours when energies are exclusively devoted to eliminating the small blemishes so embarrassingly obvious to the fellow-professional on the next patch, instead of avoiding others that may loom much larger from, as it were, a more distant vantage point. Marc Bloch observed a contradiction in the attitudes of many historians: 'when it is a question of ascertaining whether or not some human act has really taken place, they cannot be too painstaking. If they proceed to the reasons for that act, they are content with the merest appearance, ordinarily founded upon one of those maxims of common-place psychology which are neither more nor less true than their opposites.' When the historian peeps across the fence he sees his neighbours, in literature, perhaps, or sociology, just as complacent in relying on historical platitudes which are naive, simplistic or obsolete.

New Perspectives on the Past represents not a reaction against specialization, which would be a romantic absurdity, but an attempt to come to terms with it. The authors, of course, are specialists, and their thought and conclusions rest on the foundation of distinguished professional research in different periods and fields. Here they will free themselves, as far as it is possible, from the restraints of subject, region and period within which they ordinarily and necessarily work, to discuss problems simply as problems, and not as 'history' or 'politics' or 'economics'. They will write for specialists, because we are all specialists now, and for laymen, because we are all laymen.

A series with such a goal could be inaugurated by no author more apt than Ernest Gellner, and by no subject more fitting than nationalism, whose force in shaping and reshaping the modern world is so obvious, and which yet remains obdurately alien and incomprehensible to those who are not possessed by it. Gellner's lucid command of the intellectual resources of several fields – philosophy, sociology, intellectual history and social anthropology are prominent here – has produced an explanation of nationalism which could not have been devised by an expert in any single one of them, and which makes it, for the first time, historically and humanly intelligible.

Acknowledgements for the First Edition

The writing of this book has benefited enormously from the moral and material support from my wife Susan and my secretary Gay Woolven. The penultimate draft was valuably criticized by my son David. The number of people from whose ideas and information I benefited over the years, whether in agreement or disagreement, is simply too large to be listed, though the extent of my debt, conscious and other, must be enormous. But needless to say, only I may be blamed for the contentions found in this book.

Ernest Gellner

Introduction

John Breuilly

Gellner's Intellectual Concerns

Since its publication in 1983, *Nations and Nationalism* has become a key text in the literature on nationalism. The English edition has gone through nineteen reprints and sold over 160,000 copies. It has been translated into twenty-four languages, the latest being Korean. Books of readings on nationalism routinely include extracts from Gellner; critical surveys devote considerable space to Gellner.[1] There is a collection of essays on Gellner's work on nationalism.[2] Yet nationalism was only one of many interests.

Ernest Gellner (1925–95) was a distinctive as well as outstanding intellectual. Born and raised in the new state of Czechoslovakia, he came to Britain with his family in 1939.[3] After schooling and military service, including a return to Czechoslovakia at the end of the war, he settled back in Britain, completing a first degree in Philosophy, Politics and Economics at Oxford. From 1949 he was at the London School of Economics (LSE), where he became Professor of Philosophy with Special Reference to

[1] See, for example, Smith 1998, pp. 27–46; Lawrence 2005, pp. 139–47; Özkirimli 2000, pp. 127–43; Day & Thompson, 2004, pp. 43–54.

[2] Hall 1998.

[3] For details of Gellner's life and writings see John A. Hall & Ian Jarvie, 'The Life and Times of Ernest Gellner' as well as the 'Complete Bibliography of Gellner's Work' compiled by Jarvie in Hall & Jarvie 1996. The influence of his early years in Czechoslovakia is considered by Jiri Musil, 'The Prague Roots of Ernest Gellner's Thinking', in ibid., pp. 25–44. A complete bibliography, biographical details and much else can be found on a website: http://members.tripod.com/GellnerPage/. For a general study of Gellner's ideas see Michael Lessnoff, *Ernest Gellner and Modernity* (University of Wales Press, Cardiff, 2002).

Sociology in 1962. His doctoral research was in social anthropology, with fieldwork in Morocco, laying the foundations for a monograph[4] and other studies of north African and Muslim societies,[5] and reflecting on how anthropology explains social patterns and changes. Bronislaw Malinowski and the tradition of structural-functionalism in British anthropology after 1918 deeply influenced Gellner's understanding of nationalism.[6]

However, his first book was about philosophy, *Words and Things* was a biting criticism of linguistic philosophy as practised in post-1945 Oxford. Gellner situated the arguments of philosophers in thrall to Wittgenstein, that is, the later Wittgenstein of *Philosophical Investigations*, within the milieu of Oxford college life: philosophy understood anthropologically. In a posthumously published book, *Language and Solitude*, Gellner returned to those two exiles from the former Habsburg Empire, Malinowski and Wittgenstein, characteristically connecting ideas to social and political experiences.[7] Gellner asserted that philosophers must try to understand the general nature of human beings and the world, and not confine themselves to how language worked, while social scientists must acquire real knowledge about real societies, how they changed and how their modes of organization and culture shaped people.

His early anthropological and philosophical studies evinced concerns which informed Gellner's work on nationalism. As an anthropologist he was acutely aware of the radical differences between non-literate and literate, stateless and state societies, as well as between different kinds of literate state-societies (e.g., Christian and Muslim, agrarian and industrial). Such differences could not plausibly be explained in racial or genetic or environmental terms but only by reference to organization and culture. Gellner depicted fundamental historical change as transformation from one kind of organization and culture to another, rather than as a process of gradual evolution. Modes of thought were treated as functions of organization and culture. As a philosopher Gellner was deeply opposed both to fundamentalism which considered one social and intellectual

---

[4]   *Saints of the Atlas* (London: Weidenfeld and Nicolson, 1969).
[5]   For example, *Muslim Society* (Cambridge: Cambridge University Press, 1981).
[6]   See Chris Hann, 'Gellner on Malinowski: Words and Things in Central Europe', in Hall & Jarvie 1996, pp. 45–64.
[7]   *Words and Things: A Critical Account of Linguistic Philosophy and a Study in Ideology* (London: Gollancz, 1959); *Language and Solitude: Wittgenstein, Malinowski and the Habsburg Dilemma* (Cambridge: Cambridge University Press, 1998).

order as absolutely valid and to relativism which denied the possibility of objective knowledge of the world transcending social and cultural differences.[8] He argued that Enlightenment rationality, above all in the form of natural science, was not just one cognitive style amongst many but provided objective knowledge of the world, a knowledge which enabled unprecedented mastery of that world. Reason and science, however, were the product of one particular social order, that of modernity which he equated with industrialism.

These views raised fundamental questions. What was distinctive about modernity and how did it come about as a radical break from earlier kinds of social organization and culture? In his most ambitious work, *Plough, Sword, Book*, Gellner organized an analytical history around three stages of human development: hunter-gatherer, agrarian, industrial. The emphasis was on describing the different ways cognition, coercion and production related to one another in these three kinds of society rather than explaining the transitions.

Gellner's style was established early in his career. He worked in a speculative manner,[9] eschewing dense empiricism and detailed scholarship for bold sketches, whether in his prolific essays and book reviews or his broad-brush, argumentative books. A central concern was to connect ideas to societies, tending to see the latter as dominant, whether dealing with philosophers in post-imperial Oxford colleges, the celibate clerisies of medieval Europe or the nationalist intellectuals of modern Europe. These connections were set out in brilliantly illuminating and constantly fresh ways.

Gellner's treatment of ideas meant that their origin, emergence, dominance and decline had little to do with their intellectual validity. The dominant ideas of a society were banal and unreflective; false ideas could often more effectively generate social solidarity than true ones.[10] Rational non-context-dependent thought was by contrast very rare and it needed a very special set of conditions to give rise to modern scientific thought. Nationalist thought was important not because it was novel or illuminating or rational but rather because it was the product of certain social

---

[8] See his collection of essays under the title of *Relativism and the Social Sciences* (Cambridge: Cambridge University Press, 1985), especially 'Relativism and Universals', pp. 83–100.
[9] He did not do any anthropological fieldwork after that for his doctorate.
[10] See his essay 'Notes Towards a Theory of Ideology', *L'Homme*, vol. XVIII (3–4), July–December, pp. 69–82. David Gellner brought this point and reference to my attention.

conditions. To appreciate the originality of this approach we need to survey the field of nationalism studies up to around 1980.

Nationalism Studies before Gellner

Until 1918 the study of nationalism was closely linked to the formation of nation states and of a historical profession.[11] Nationalism was regarded as a component of national history rather than as a distinct subject. Academic history was organized on national lines. There was little theorization of the subject and what there was was ethical or philosophical rather than analytical or sociological. The great theorists of modern society – Marx, Durkheim, Weber – wrote little on the subject.[12] Nationality was treated as a given, whether for good or bad, though mainly for good as it was associated with the formation of constitutional states and progressive, liberal cultures in place of petty princedoms and dynastic empires.

The most sustained theoretical engagement came from the Austro-Marxists, Karl Renner and Otto Bauer. For them, nation, state and society could not be equated, and national conflicts posed a mortal threat to their socialist politics within the multinational Habsburg Empire. Whereas orthodox Marxists treated nationalism as a form of false consciousness, as class ideology, Renner and Bauer argued that it had a truth value based on the reality of national culture which they associated with language.[13] This specific difference between conventional Marxists and the Austro-Marxists reflected a broader division between those who treated

---

[11] See Stefan Berger et al. (eds), *Writing National Histories: Western Europe since 1800* (London: Routledge, 1999). Berger is co-ordinating a major research project which will produce a multi-volume set of studies on the development of professional history and national historiography in modern Europe.

[12] Not because of indifference. Marx was anti-nationalist. Durkheim was concerned with how society could hold together under the fragmentation induced by the modern division of labour. His own French republican patriotism was an answer of sorts. Weber was a passionate German nationalist and did recognize there was a puzzle as to why people believed they belonged to ethnic groups or nations and valued this 'fact'. For a clear and succinct acount of his views, see Fritz Ringer, *Max Weber: An Intellectual Biography* (Chicago: University of Chicago Press, 2004), pp. 49–55. However, all three largely equated nation with society and state and concerned themselves with the internal workings of societies.

[13] On Otto Bauer, see now the translation of his major contribution to nationalism studies: *The Question of Nationalities and Social Democracy*, transl. J. O'Donnell, ed. Ephraim Nimni (Minneapolis: University of Minnesota Press, 2000). The first German edition was published in 1908; this translation is based on the second edition of 1924. On Karl Renner and arguments about his treatment of nationalities see now Nimni 2005.

nationalism as a fictive idea about difference and those who regarded it as a sentiment expressing real difference.[14]

It was in the inter-war period that nationalism became a subject of explicit and general analysis, principally by historians. In 1931 Carlton J. Hayes published *The Historical Evolution of Nationalism*.[15] Hayes had already published *Essays on Nationalism* (1926) which dealt 'primarily with the extreme militant type of contemporary nationalism'.[16] This threatening nationalism stimulated Hayes to '. . . treat of nationalism as an "ism", as a body of doctrines, as a political philosophy'. 'Modern nationalism signifies a more or less purposeful effort to revive primitive tribalism on an enlarged and more artificial scale. The first definite doctrines to such effect were put forth in the eighteenth century'.[17]

The other major historical treatment came from Hans Kohn. He published a book on nationalism in Eastern Europe as early as 1929 but his most influential work was *The Idea of Nationalism*, published in 1944.[18] Like Hayes, Kohn treated nationalism as an idea or doctrine but focused less on specific intellectuals, instead connecting the idea to national histories. Whereas Hayes regarded nationalism negatively as irrational and aggressive, Kohn – a supporter of cultural Zionism – discerned a good as well as a bad side. This perception was embodied in his influential distinction between Western and Eastern nationalism. Western nationalism formed within national states (Britain, France, the USA). The drive to liberalize and democratize these states appealed to the nation as a community of citizens. Eastern nationalism formed within sub- or multinational states and in its drive for national independence appealed to the nation as an ethnic or language group. One can see how the distinction worked in 1944, pitting the civic nationalism of Britain and the USA against the ethnic nationalism of Germany, Italy and Japan.[19]

If the rise of fascism and the road to war stimulated these pioneering historical treatments of nationalism, the Allied victory in 1945 appeared to terminate ethnic nationalism.[20] The very title of E.H. Carr's book

---

[14] These three paragraphs draw on Lawrence 2005, ch. 2.

[15] New York: Macmillan, 1931, reprinted New York: Russell and Russell, 1968.

[16] Preface, *Historical Evolution of Nationalism*, p. v.

[17] Ibid., pp. vi, 12.

[18] Kohn 2005. This new edition has a very informative introduction by Craig Calhoun on which I draw heavily.

[19] The position of the USSR is not clear in this contrast.

[20] If the nobler word 'patriotism' then replaced 'civic/Western nationalism', nationalism as a phenomenon had ceased to exist.

Nationalism and After expressed the sense that the subject was now a matter of history.[21] Interest in nationalism diminished, although historians continued to study modern history on a national basis.

However, in such work the nation served as a framing device, not as an historical force or political value.[22] Historians turned to economic and social history or continued with conventional political and diplomatic history, all operating within the nation-state framework. Other disciplines took little interest in nationalism. Sociology equated 'society' with the membership of the nation-state. 'Nation' was thus naturalized as 'society' and attention devoted to internal relationships (class, status, power).[23] The study of colonial societies was left to anthropologists who deployed other framing devices such as tribe or clan for their practice of participant-observation within small-scale societies. In the USSR and China Marxism privileged class over nation. Those countries stimulated the formation of area studies departments in the West which studied them as 'whole societies' (i.e., nations).[24] Interest was in foreign policy (Kremlinology, Sinology), high politics and the successes and failures of socialist policies. Nationalism as conflict between states was the preserve of political science and diplomatic history, disciplines which treated states as equivalent and autonomous units operating within the field of 'international relations'.[25]

Nationalism as a distinct subject in its own right was left to the historian of political doctrines, usually seen as irrational and which had

[21]   E.H. Carr, *Nationalism and After* (London: Macmillan, 1945).

[22]   I consider this at some length for British historiography in 'Historians and the Nation', in *History and Historians in the Twentieth Century*, ed. Peter Burke (Oxford: published for the British Academy by Oxford University Press, 2002), pp. 55–87.

[23]   Billig 1995, especially ch. 2, 'Nations and Languages', considers how the idea of the nation was 'naturalized'. On sociological theory, see Day & Thompson 2004, ch. 1, 'Theorizing Nationalism: Contrasting "Classical" and "Post-Classical" Social Theory'.

[24]   There was some interest in the nationalities policy of the USSR but this was seen as separate from nationalism.

[25]   See Mayall 1990, ch. 1 for an account of different views of international relations. The classical statement of the view that international relations was about the relations between hard states each pursuing its own interest comes in Hans Morgenthau, *Politics Among Nations* (6th edn, New York: Knopf, 1985). The equation of states with nations is clear from the title; Morgenthau is emphatically dealing with states. For a recent critique of such approaches see Barry Buzan, *From International to World Society: English Social Theory and the Social Structure of Globalisation* (Cambridge: Cambridge University Press, 2004). My thanks to George Lawson for advice on this matter.

fortunately come to an end with the defeat of fascism in 1945.[26] This approach was given sharp and influential form by Elie Kedourie. The opening sentence of his book *Nationalism* summarized his argument: 'Nationalism is a doctrine invented in Europe at the beginning of the nineteenth century.'[27] What made Kedourie's book special was that he shifted attention from individual writers to intellectuals as a class of people who were able to exert great political influence under the destabilizing conditions of modernization.

However, a new concern with a different kind of nationalism was forming. If 1945 had seen the defeat of fascism, it has also fatally weakened the hold of the Western European powers over their overseas empires. In 1947 the largest single colony, India, achieved independence and Dutch control over Java (Indonesia) ceased a year later. By the mid-1950s the French were in retreat from Indochina, formal British and French rule had ceased in the Middle East, and, after the Suez crisis of 1956, Belgian, British and French colonial rule in Africa quickly unravelled, except where stubborn white settlers created obstacles. By the mid-1960s decolonization was in full flow.[28] Anti-colonial nationalism was understood in one of two ways.[29] If imperialists were prepared to leave, nationalism might be treated as a new form of civic nationalism, rather like American independence movements. If imperial states opposed demands for independence, nationalism was labelled a tool of the communist powers. Such was the view taken in the early 1950s of Korea and later, when the USA replaced France in Indochina, of Vietnam.

Kedourie shifted perspective in his introduction to and selection of writings by Asian and African nationalists.[30] Confronted with violent resistance and protest, nationalism was treated as an irrational idea based on mythical ideas of the nation as an ethnic community, but with a greater emphasis on appeals to atavistic emotions. It was a little unclear as to

---

[26] The irrational, emotional, manipulative and transitory character of nationalism meant that it was not worthy of the attention that political theorists might give to serious ideas such as conservatism, liberalism and socialism.

[27] Kedourie 1993, p. 1. I have considered Kedourie's arguments at length in 'Nationalism and the History of Ideas', in *Proceedings of the British Academy*, 105 (2000), pp. 187–223.

[28] Portugal's African empire hung on a little longer, with major consequences for domestic Portuguese politics.

[29] I leave aside the view that anti-colonial nationalism is not important because decolonization was driven by forces in the imperial centres which needed nationalists to whom they could hand over nominal power.

[30] Kedourie 1970.

which was the most important: the importation of the irrational doctrine of nationalism from the West or the revival of 'primitive' identities and emotions.[31]

To summarize, there were two major approaches to nationalism by the mid-1960s. In the first, nationalism was an aspect of national history, a sentiment associated with the nation. The sentiment could take good or bad forms. The best way to understand nationalism was through broad narrative histories of individual nations, perhaps linked to a typology such as that between Western and Eastern nationalism. In the second approach, nationalism was a modern, irrational doctrine which could acquire sufficient power so as actually to generate nationalist sentiments and even nation-states. Understanding nationalism began with the ideas and the intellectuals who expressed those ideas, and moved on to consider how they changed the world.

Gellner and Modernity

Gellner's arguments broke sharply with these conventional understandings of nationalism. He came to the subject not as a sociologist, political scientist or historian, that is from the disciplines which hitherto had dominated the study of nationalism, but with a background in philosophy and anthropology. His anthropology was informed by the view that ideas were a function of social organization. His philosophy was that one could obtain objective knowledge of society by means of empirical and rational procedures.

Gellner thought of modernity as a distinctive form of social organization and culture. He considered nationalism to be a function of modernity. He did not believe that history, with its descriptive and individualizing approach, could understand the modernity/nationalism relationship. He rejected any evolutionary approach which understood current society as shaped by earlier practices which survived into the present. Such a view conflicted with Gellner's conception of modernity as a rupture with earlier social orders which was necessarily accompanied by corresponding changes in dominant ideas.[32]

---

[31]   The latter point of view was taken up in political science with notions such as 'clientelism' and 'neo-patrimonialism'. These continue to be used to provide fatalist 'explanations' of corruption and misgovernment in African states.

[32]   See especially ch. 1, 'Time and Validity', in *Thought and Change* (London: Weidenfeld and Nicolson, 1964).

The one intellectual current which shared Gellner's assumptions about the distinctive character of modernity, the primacy of social organization over ideas, and the possibility of objective scientific knowledge was Marxism. However, Gellner rejected the Marxist views that the central feature of modernity was capitalism, that class was the principal source of identity and conflict, and that this conflict would drive capitalism towards socialism.[33]

Consequently, Gellner was at odds with all existing approaches to nationalism. Narrative history of nations failed to understand that modernity was both a rupture with earlier epochs and a unity rather than a series of unique stories. Although in agreement with his LSE colleague Kedourie, that nationalism was modern and nationalism produced nations, not the other way around, Gellner could not agree that this was due to the power of nationalism *as an idea*, or of an intelligentsia as the bearer of this idea. The *idea* of nationalism was product, not producer, of modernity.[34] Its success was not due to its intellectual power but to its function within a modern social order. Finally, Gellner rejected the Marxist notion that nationalism was a class ideology formed within capitalism.

So if nationalism was not an expression of nations, classes or intelligentsias, if its roots were not to be found in the study of nations, capitalism, classes or ideas, how was it to be understood?

First and foremost, Gellner had to identify the central feature of modernity. He then had to develop an argument which demonstrated the functionality of nationalism for modernity. Gellner sketched out his arguments in a chapter entitled 'Nationalism' in his book *Thought and Change*. He published little more on the subject until *Nations and Nationalism* eighteen years later,[35] but following that book Gellner published many essays on nationalism, the most important of which were brought together in book form in *Encounters with Nationalism*. However, the general points made in

---

[33] Some of these issues are considered in ch. 6 of *Thought and Change*, 'The Stuff of Change'.

[34] Nevertheless, it was the sharpness with which Kedourie argued this point that stimulated Gellner to develop his own views on nationalism.

[35] The most important of these publications are: 'Nationalism', *Theory and Society*, 10 (1981), pp. 753–76; 'The Individual Division of Labour and National Cultures', *Government and Society*, 117 (1982), pp. 268–78; 'Nationalism and the Two Forms of Cohesion in Complex Societies', *Proceedings of the British Academy*, 58 (1983), pp. 165–87.

those essays are repeated in his final statement on the subject: the post-humously published book *Nationalism*.[36] I will outline Gellner's major arguments from *Thought and Change* and *Nations and Nationalism*. Then I will consider the impact of *Nations and Nationalism*. Next I will look at how Gellner modified his arguments after 1983 in the light of criticisms and changing circumstances. Finally I will try to situate his work within current debates on nationalism.

Gellner and Nationalism

Chapter 7 of *Thought and Change* is a chapter in a book and one must understand its place in that book. Gellner was concerned about the rela-tionship between ideas and society, recognized that both had changed radically in modern times and sought some stable position from which to understand these changes.[37] Intead of denying the significance of social change for ideas (a position he caustically criticized as anti- or a-historical) or fetishizing change itself as the unchanging feature of human society (the evolutionist approach) or collapsing into relativism which acknowledged change and difference but lacked any secure position from which to make such acknowledgements, Gellner focused on a break in human history. This is the transition from pre-industrial (usually agrar-ian) to industrial society. He argued that this transition radically changed the human condition but was also sufficiently specific to be understood, especially as it was accompanied by the emergence of reason and science which provide us with the requisite intellectual tools.

The transition also determined what kind of knowledge could under-stand it: 'It is only in transitional situations that it is really true that men learn nothing from history: they cannot. They have to invent sociology instead' (*Thought and Change*, p. 66). Gellner explored various aspects of the transition: the difficulty of using the language of either pre-industrial or industrial society to describe the transition; the emergence of new kinds

---

[36] For example, the points about stages and time zones which he makes in the essay on E.H. Carr, 'Nationalism and the International Order', *Encounters with Nationalism*, pp. 20–33, are reiterated in chs 6 and 7 of *Nationalism*.

[37] *Words and Things* was about false preoccupations (especially the divorce of language from reality). One should study *thought* rather than *words*, reality should be understood as *change* rather than *things*, and the job of the social philosopher was to connect the two rather than keep them apart. In this way the contrast between the titles *Words and Things* and *Thought and Change* summarizes the shift by Gellner from critical to positive mode.

of knowledge and values; the defects of other ways of analysing the transition (e.g., the Marxist notion of transitions from feudalism to capitalism to socialism). Chapter 7, 'Nationalism', considers just one more aspect of the transition.

Gellner insists that nations and nationalism are not natural because they are not a permanent feature of the human condition but came into being with the transition to industrialism. Neither are they arbitrary, in the sense of being accidental or avoidable; they have a close, almost necessary, link with industrialism. Indeed, this is what makes them appear natural to the members of industrial society and it is that 'naturalness' which gives nationalism its power.

What is it about the transition to industrialism which accounts for the near universality of nations and nationalism in modern times? Gellner begins with a distinction between *structure* and *culture* drawn from anthropology. Structure refers to the distinct roles people play and the relationships between these roles. Gellner does not provide an equivalent definition of culture but contrasts the presentations people make of themselves to others (dress, dance, ritual) with the roles they perform. He argues that in pre-industrial, face-to-face societies, people are defined through structure. Everyone knows everyone else's roles and, therefore, their social positions. Structure furnishes identity; culture simply reinforces structure.

Large-scale, complex agrarian society also does not permit the development of nations and nationalism. Although there are overarching identities (usually furnished by scriptural world religions and the priestly castes who codify and police those religions), there are divisions which undermine the possibility of nations and nationalism. Polity and culture are not congruent. Polities range from city-states and small principalities to sprawling empires. The state does not seek to penetrate far into the lives of different communities. In one footnote Gellner compares the impossibility of a modern polity (Cyprus) being able to tolerate two autonomous communities with the ease with which the Ottoman Empire tolerated many more communities through its *milet* system.[38] In agrarian

---

[38] Note at foot of pp. 164–5. The argument resembles that made more recently on the distinction between indirect and direct rule. Hechter (2000) suggests that a plurality of communities can each preserve their identity under a system of indirect rule but will come to assert such identity against an 'alien' state when it seeks to impose direct rule. Gellner additionally stresses that this shift in form of rule transforms the nature of the 'communities'.

society, groups develop distinct identities, expressed through institutions such as privileged estates or castes. Privileged groups such as dynasties, the clergy and the nobility share identities which transcend political boundaries. By contrast, immobile peasant communities can identify neither with higher social groups (social division) nor other peasant communities (absence of communication). The idea of the nation as a significant group occupying a bounded territory which does or should enjoy political autonomy and with a common identity across the 'whole' society could not make headway under such conditions.

Complex, large-scale industrial society works differently from either small-scale society (usually hunter-gatherers) or large-scale and complex agrarian society. The scale of industrial society, especially in the modern city, means that people have encounters with one another, rather than enduring relationships. The occupational structure exhibits few fixed roles and positions but rather constant change. People move between many positions, migrating and changing jobs. It is impossible to identify people in terms of structure: 'a man is a man, and is not fully identified with his role' (p. 155).[39]

Identity is based instead on culture which acquires new functions in industrial society. Occupational change and mobility mean that people have to be prepared not for unique jobs and positions that will last a lifetime and furnish an identity (priest, guildsman, aristocrat, peasant, king) but rather must be equipped with the skills to move between roles in industrial society. They need to engage in 'context-free communication'. Literacy is vital, both to discharge specific roles and for context-free communication. Mass literacy must be in a standardized, written vernacular and can only be provided by mass education which only the state is capable of underwriting, if not directly supplying. The remorseless pressure towards a standard culture based on a written vernacular which is congruent with the state is what produces 'nations'. The sense that national identity is natural is one expression of this irresistible convergence of state, population and culture within industrial society.

So far the argument fits with the spread of a standard culture amongst the subjects of an increasingly interventionist state in the transition to

---

[39] Arguably the crucial point is not scale or complexity as such but occupational change and mobility. Yet this *is* a matter of scale and complexity. Crucial to Gellner's account of agrarian society is that the great bulk of the population, those who work the land, *do* live in small, face-to-face communities with a fixed and restricted division of labour.

industrialism. Nationalism appears as a unifying process, resembling Eugen Weber's account of peasants being turned into Frenchmen, or D'Azeglio's observation that, having created Italy, it was now necessary to make Italians.[40] Nationalism, however, more often (and certainly in Gellner's work) refers to conflict and separation from the existing state than to assimilation and unification. The next step in Gellner's argument is that industrialization spreads unevenly. More backward groups and regions are disadvantaged in relation to those who are further forward with the process. This will not lead to nationalism if there is cultural homogeneity between the groups (more precisely, if there is no clear incentive and opportunity to construct cultural distinctions based on such 'diacritical marks' as skin colour, language or religion). If there is such potential for differentiation, the better-placed groups have an incentive to use cultural differences to restrict competition for resources such as jobs, houses and schooling. Equally, the disadvantaged groups can use such distinctions to justify and motivate the goal of political autonomy in which one's own language will dominate the educational system, speakers of one's own language will rule and government can promote the 'national' interest. This leads to an alliance between an intelligentsia, which as the most literate class identifies itself with the national culture, and a proletariat (Gellner uses the term broadly to mean the mass of disadvantaged workers), even if such an alliance often breaks down once national independence is achieved.

That is Gellner's theory of nationalism. Nationalism is not a sentiment expressed by pre-existing nations; rather it creates nations where they did not previously exist. Gellner concedes that certain prior conditions (written vernacular, territorial state, distinctive religion) influence specific nation formations but these conditions do not amount to pre-nationalist nations. He recognizes that where nationalism has acquired power and prestige, it can give rise to derivative or imitative forms, for example, the creation of 'nation-states' in central Europe by the victor states after 1918. He notes that nationalism can serve as an instrument of industrialization. Finally, he observes that nationalism does not always accompany industrialism. The Swiss have managed without it.[41] Islam manages to serve as the functional equivalent of nationalism in a way which has not been

---

[40] Weber 1979. D'Azeglio's reputed remark was made following Italian unification in 1860.

[41] *Thought and Change*, p. 174. Or rather, they have managed with linguistic pluralism.

possible for Christianity.[42] Nevertheless, even admitting these qualifications and concessions, Gellner had outlined a remarkably powerful and coherent theory of nationalism.

This chapter in *Thought and Change* had little impact. One can suggest various reasons. It was one chapter in a book concerned with the broad question of the transition to industrial society. Gellner was an idiosyncratic thinker, working across various disciplines and occupying unfashionable positions in most of them. More important, nationalism did not attract much interest in the 1960s. Historians were engrossed by social history, labour history, history from below.[43] Social scientists were not ready for the propositions that nations counted for more than classes, nationalism more than socialism. There was a process of decolonization but this was seen as a combination of sensible disengagement by imperial powers and a civic, rather than ethnic, demand for equality and democracy by colonized societies. Such theoretical work as there was drew on American modernization theory and ideas of 'nation-building'. Within that paradigm, nation was identified with state, society and economy and the main issue was how backward economies could modernize. This fitted well with the anti-imperialist values preached by the two world powers in the name of progress towards industrial society in either a liberal or a socialist form. The equation of nation with state blocked theoretical reflection on nation and nationalism.[44]

This contrasted sharply with nationalism as applied to backward, primitive, violent, 'tribal' movements, for example, the Mau Mau in

[42] Gellner continued for the rest of his life to elaborate arguments about the special qualities of Islam which made this possible. See, for example, *Conditions of Liberty: Civil Society and its Rivals* (London: Hamish Hamilton, 1994). His arguments are criticized by Dale F. Eickelman, 'Nationalism and Islamic fundamentalism', in Hall 1998, pp. 258–71.

[43] In modern English historiography the book with the greatest impact was *The Making of the English Working Class* (London: Vintage, 1963) by E.P. Thompson.

[44] Typical texts of the time were Daniel Lerner, *The Passing of Traditional Society* (New York, 1958); Lucian Pye and Sidney Verba (eds), *Political Culture and Political Development* (Princeton, N.J.: Princeton University Press, 1965). Gellner himself draws much from such literature with his assumptions that nationalism can motivate industrialization understood as a distinct social transformation which can be deliberately pursued once observed elsewhere. See, for example, David Apter, 'Political religion in the new nations', in Geertz 1962. However, unlike Gellner, this literature did not focus on nation and nationalism as something distinct from state and citizens.

Kenya.[45] These were often seen as opposed to progressive, constitutional nationalist parties led by Western-educated intellectuals. In this way the Kohn distinction, with its strong moral implications, was applied to anti-colonial nationalism. It separated precisely what Gellner sought to connect, namely modernity and nationalism based on ethnicity and language. For all these reasons, Gellner in 1965 was a voice crying in the wilderness.

Nations and Nationalism reiterated many of the central arguments made in *Thought and Change*: how cultures homogenize under pressure of industrialization, how they need to be underpinned and validated by a powerful state, how the uneven spread of industrialization conjoined with cultural distinctions generate conflicting nationalisms. However, in a book-length treatment central ideas can be elaborated and additional arguments introduced.

Gellner defines his subject, something missing from *Thought and Change*.

> Nationalism is primarily a political principle, which holds that the political and the national unit should be congruent.
>
> Nationalism as a sentiment, or as a movement, can best be defined in terms of this principle. Nationalist *sentiment* is the feeling of anger aroused by the violation of the principle, or the feeling of satisfaction aroused by its fulfilment. A nationalist *movement* is one actuated by a sentiment of this kind. (p. 1)

Note the implicit assumption that arguments about nationalism apply equally to nationalism as political principle, sentiment and movement. I will return to problems with this assumption.

The point about the contingency of specific nationalisms is strengthened and linked to Gellner's criticism of those who stress the power of the nationalist idea. Gellner points out that there are far more potential than actual nations. It is implausible to argue that the successful cases were more real as nations or that their nationalist ideas were intrinsically

---

[45] Kedourie 1970 includes material on the Kikuyu oathing ceremonies performed for recruits to the Mau Mau. This was typical of the studies published on the Mau Mau in the 1950s and 1960s. What makes Kedourie original is that he considered the idea not so much as a primitive throwback to traditional non-Western values but as the translation of a modern, Western form of irrationalism beyond Europe.

more powerful than those of the 'failures'. There must be certain 'objective' conditions, for example an actual language on which a standard culture can be built.[46] However, there are many other factors involved in the work of selecting, constructing and establishing 'national' cultures. Nationalism validates the particular standard cultures formed in the transition to industrialism. These cultures are like breathing chambers; only in such containers can industrial man function. Nevertheless, it would be wrong to regard the particular breathing chambers as the only possible ones.

Gellner elaborates on these national cultures. At one end of the spectrum are pre-existing 'high cultures' with a written vernacular linked to a powerful state which acts to extend this culture to all strata of society. Britain, France and the USA are such cases. At the other end are groups lacking high cultures or states of their own. Nationalism constructs and transforms a 'folk culture' into a high culture (creating a standardized written vernacular, manufacturing national histories and traditions) and seeks a state of its own. Czech nationalism is such a case. In between are groups with a high-culture but divided under the rule of a number of states. These groups need only bring about political change, linking this to the existing high-culture. 'Unification nationalism' in Italy and Germany are examples.

One could take this idea further. There are high-culture groups under foreign rule such as Hungarians under the Habsburgs. There are high-culture groups fragmented under different foreign states such as the Poles under Habsburg, Hohenzollern and Romanov rule or Arabs under French and British rule. There are 'folk cultures' with states of their own; Switzerland might be so regarded. However, Gellner does not explore these possibilities.

The relationships between high and folk cultures and nationalism are considered in chapter 5, 'What is a Nation?' Gellner invents a Ruritanian nationalism formed in reaction against the empire of Megalomania. Conceptually this goes little further than *Thought and Change* but the detail is telling and amusing. For example, Gellner describes the official reverence displayed by the Socialist Republic of Ruritania for past bandits as national heroes (though accompanied by disquiet as to whether this might encourage dissent), although he also 'reports' that the lyrics of certain folk

---

[46] Though this can be in a fairly vestigial condition as the cases of Gaelic and Hebrew demonstrate.

songs, another integral part of national high culture, suggest a different popular view of bandits. This is barely a caricature of myth-making in many central European nationalist movements. However, underlying these myths is the uneven spread of industrialization and the capacity of Ruritanian intellectuals to build upon cultural difference, real even if slight, to mobilize popular support for nationalism.

This capacity for differentiation concerns chapter 6 where Gellner considers exceptions to the rule that industrialism promotes 'entropy', that is, removes barriers to individual mobility. In European overseas empires, racial difference operated as such a barrier, and nationalism was insistent that white Europeans could no longer rule, not just as imperialists but as members of the new state.[47] However, such obstacles are regarded by Gellner as exceptions to the rule of cultural homogenization. If that were not the case, it would undermine his theory.[48]

In chapter 7 Gellner devised an elaborate typology of nationalism. This typology was derived from the theory, combining binary factors about the capacity of rulers and ruled to acquire high culture, whether rulers and ruled were culturally homogenous or not and whether the transition to industrialism was at an early or a mature stage (see figure 2, p. 91.) This yielded eight types. However, nationalism only emerged in the presence of cultural difference. Furthermore, if neither ruler nor ruled could access 'modern-style' education there could be no nationalism. That left three types of nationalism, which Gellner labelled 'Habsburg', 'classical liberal Western' and 'diaspora' nationalism.

This typology was taken no further by Gellner. That is hardly surprising. The ruler/ruled distinction does not make it clear whether it refers to actual power-holders or complete cultural groups.[49] The cultural homogeneity/difference distinction can only be operated retrospectively. Provençal in southern France around 1800 was more distinct from French than Ukrainian was from Russian. Even if one accepts Gellner's argument

---

[47] However, one irritating fact for Gellner is the way in which new 'nation'-states in nineteenth-century southeast Europe, such as Greece, Bulgaria and Romania, imported foreign princes, usually cadet branches of German dynasties, to rule them. It suggests that the real issues were imperial rule and/or the domination of one cultural/ethnic group over another rather than the nationality of the head of state.

[48] Unless one sees the nationalist removal of such exceptions (through separation or assimilation) as part of the industrialization process. The problem then is that nationalism becomes both cause and effect of cultural homogenization. This raises issues about the explanatory claims of Gellner's theory of nationalism to which I will return.

[49] See above, n. 47.

that there must be *some* prior difference on which to base opposing nationalisms, it is impossible to specify in advance what will count as such a difference. The fact that an apparently very slight difference can suffice, added to Gellner's argument that there is no common culture reaching across social groups in pre-industrial societies, makes it impossible to imagine *any* prior condition of cultural homogeneity which would preclude the possibility of conflicting nationalisms. Furthermore, Gellner's insistence that nationalism be based on *cultural* division excludes civic and assimilationist forms of nationalism. French nationalism was a movement which identified a cultural difference such as Provençal speech communities as something to be destroyed through assimilation. It was also a civic movement based on republicanism.[50]

Reception and Criticism

The impact of *Nations and Nationalism*

Nations and Nationalism rapidly established itself as a major contribution to the understanding of nationalism. Why did it have a much greater impact than *Thought and Change* where the essential elements of the theory had already been outlined? It might be because it was a book, not one chapter in a book concerned with other matters.[51] However, the crucial reason was that the intellectual climate had become more favourable.

In the 1970s there were few theoretical writings on nationalism other than those operating within political science and the nation-building paradigm.[52] Otherwise the pattern continued of history of doctrines or national narratives.[53] This was paralleled in studies of individual cases. The major exception was Anthony D. Smith (a student of Gellner's at the

---

[50] Nineteenth-century French anti-republicans asserted other forms of nationalism, showing both that nationalism is internally divided and can be framed in terms of opposing political principles instead of cultural differences.

[51] More cynically, one could add that *Thought and Change* is a longer and more difficult book than *Nations and Nationalism*.

[52] That is not to say nothing of significance was published in the 1960s and 1970s. For example, Barth 1969 had a great impact on theoretical studies of nationalism. However, the focus was on ethnicity rather than nationalism, for reasons related above all to the internal politics of the USA.

[53] A distinguished version of national narrative history is Seton-Watson 1977. Kedourie remained the most important exponent of the history of ideas approach.

LSE), who published *Theories of Nationalism* in 1971 and followed this with further studies.[54]

In the early 1980s there was a marked change.[55] The major reason was the revival of nationalism itself in the Western world. The social sciences derive their questions, if not their answers, from current problems. In Britain the resurgence of Irish nationalism in Ulster from 1969 and the political successes of Scottish nationalism in the 1970s stimulated the publication of books with such titles as *The Break-up of Britain*.[56] Spain was riven by nationalist protests amongst Basques and Catalans. French Canadians in Quebec posed a serious challenge to the territorial integrity of Canada. There were similar, if politically less significant and more culturally oriented movements in France, Belgium, Wales and elsewhere. Nation-building was running out of steam in the less developed world. The global economic crisis of the mid-1970s destabilized new states and stimulated the emergence of more aggressive, anti-Western movements.[57]

The crisis introduced a sharper ideological tone into political debates, influenced in the West by the aggressive neo-liberalism associated with the election of Reagan in the USA and Thatcher in Britain. This stimulated a shift to more theoretical debate within the social sciences and a questioning of the political and ideological consensus which had dominated the postwar decades of affluence.[58]

Gellner's book represented a distinctive form of the modernist approach which set the pace in the 1980s. Nationalism was understood as modern and nations as effects rather than causes of nationalism. The key

---

[54] There are other pioneers. Walker Connor published his seminal essay 'A nation is a nation, is a state, is an ethnic group, is a . . .', in 1978 (*Ethnic and Racial Studies*, vol. 1, no. 4, pp. 378–400).

[55] Examples of book publications 1982–5: Anderson 1983; Armstrong 1982; Breuilly 1982; Giddens 1985; Hobsbawm & Ranger 1983; Hroch 1985. Hroch is a pioneer in that his book is an abridged translation of a German text of 1968. Nevertheless, the translation only appeared with the revival of interest in nationalism.

[56] Nairn 1977. Nairn also made an important contribution to theoretical debates on nationalism.

[57] Not always obviously or only nationalist. A key moment in the rise of political Islamic fundamentalism was the Iranian revolution of 1979.

[58] See the two essays by Perry Anderson, the first on the period of consensus and the second on the 'return to theory': 'Components of the National Culture' (1968) and 'A Culture in Contraflow' (1990), in Anderson, *English Questions* (London: Verso, 1992), pp. 48–104, 193–301. For a global historical treatment see Eric Hobsbawm, *Age of Extremes: The Short Twentieth Century 1914–1991* (London: Abacus, 1994), esp. ch. 9, 'The Golden Years', and ch. 14, 'The Crisis Decades'.

debates between modernists concerned the nature of modernity rather than nationalism. Anderson focused upon the rise of 'print-capitalism' which, in conjunction with the challenge to the European multi-national empires, enabled a new kind of political imagining: nationalist imagining. Mann, Tilly, Giddens and myself, in different ways, emphasized the modern state as a new kind of power container which, in its relationship with its subject-citizens and with other states, turned the people into the nation and the state into a nation-state in conflict with other nation-states.[59] Brass treated nationalist and ethnic conflicts in terms of modern elite manipulation of symbols and sentiments.[60] Writers in the Marxist tradition like Nairn turned to notions of uneven and combined development to make sense of nationalism.[61]

Although Gellner fitted into this modernist paradigm his contribution was distinctive. Other modernist approaches focused on the media and imagination (Anderson, Hobsbawm & Ranger), the modern state and mass politics (Tilly, Mann, Giddens, Breuilly, Brass) or class and economic conflict (Nairn, Hechter). Gellner with his sociological focus on the transition to industrialism and its cultural and political consequences was very different.

Gellner also advanced the most ambitious and complete theory. Many other writers explicitly conceded their partial reach. They could make some sense of the politics or the sentiments or the doctrines of nationalism but not of 'nationalism-as-a-whole'.[62] They did not place the understanding of nationalism within a universal historical framework as did Gellner. They developed their arguments on the basis of case studies, comparisons and specific historical sequences of events, whereas Gellner's

---

[59] In addition to works already cited, see Michael Mann, 'The Emergence of Modern European Nationalism', in Hall & Jarvie 1996, pp. 147–70, and Charles Tilly, 'States and Nationalism in Europe 1492–1992', in J.L. Comaroff & P.C. Stern (eds), *Perspectives on Nationalism and War* (Amsterdam: Gordon and Breach, 1995), pp. 187–204. I cite work published in the 1990s but both Mann and Tilly had already begun to work out these ideas in the 1980s, if not explicitly in terms of modern theories of nationalism.

[60] Paul Brass (ed.), *Ethnic Groups and the State* (London: Croom Helm, 1985) as well as Brass 1991.

[61] See also Hechter 1975.

[62] I argue the case for such narrow claims in 'Culture, Doctrine, Politics: Three Ways of Constructing Nationalism', in *Nationalism in Europe. Past and Present*, edited by J. Beramendi, R. Máiz & X. Núñez (Santiago de Compostela: Universidade de Santiago de Compostela, 1994), pp. 127–34. More recently Smith 1998, in his conclusion, has suggested we should be more ambitious but has put the case in terms of taking the best of what a variety of approaches have to offer.

book was highly abstract and indeed dismissive of the individualizing and descriptive historical approach. His typology was based on his theory and then applied to cases. His most detailed case study was the fiction of Ruritania!

Criticisms

Not surprisingly, therefore, Gellner's book has been heftily criticized ever since its publication: an indication of both its influence and its problems. Here I summarize the major criticisms. I then consider Gellner's responses and where this leaves his arguments about nationalism.[63]

One can identify three kinds of criticism: conceptual, empirical, explanatory. Conceptual debates centre upon the properties Gellner ascribed to industrialism and nationalism. Empirical debates relate to the correlations between industrialism and nationalism. There is the issue of functionalist as opposed to causal explanation. Finally, what does Gellner omit from his theory and how significant are such omissions?

Conceptual criticisms

The concept of industrialism includes what it means and what it entails. Gellner meant the achievement of industrial society, distinguishing between an early stage which he considered especially hard and crisis-ridden and a later stage in which industrial society reached maturity. His analysis implied that this was a determinate transition (not an open-ended process of change) which affected distinct social units in comparable ways. Finally, Gellner argued that industrialism was within the grasp of all societies once its nature was understood.[64]

Gellner used the concept in a broad and flexible way. He conceded, for example, that early stages in the development of commercial capitalism could be included, thus tracing industrialization to the early eighteenth

---

[63]   The most important sets of critiques are in Hall 1998, and part 2, 'Nations and Nationalism', in Hall & Jarvie 1996. Every survey of theories of nationalism devotes space to Gellner (see n. 1 above). I wrote a review article of Anderson's *Imagined Communities* and *Nations and Nationalism*: 'Reflections on Nationalism', *Philosophy of the Social Sciences* 15 (1985), pp. 65–73, reprinted in *Nationalism in Europe: 1815 to the Present*, ed. S.J. Woolf (London: Routledge, 1996), pp. 137–54.

[64]   Gellner thought that the first industrialization, that of Britain, took a unique and unintended form but after that it was knowable change which other societies could pursue deliberately.

century, if not earlier.[65] If this included agrarian capitalism and rural industry, one can go back further.[66] Economic historians treat industrialization as a global process, its form in one country affecting that in another, or alternatively inducing de-industrialization or under-development. How far one can deliberately industrialize is debatable. After British industrialization people were able to think in such terms but it is not clear that they were as important as those pursuing narrower goals. Arguably, only with Stalinism was there a state-led pursuit of industrialization and there are disputes about how effective and long-term that project was. The role of nationalism in such a project also raises problems of explanation.[67]

Gellner insisted that industrialization required or entailed cultural homogenization based on literacy in a standardized vernacular language conveyed by means of state-supported mass education. Gellner understood the division of labour in industrial societies along lines sketched out by Adam Smith (and, later, one might add, Karl Marx). The labour market becomes increasingly homogenous and less skilled, such that generic training plus a small amount of on-the-spot training suffices to fill jobs. Ricardo and Babbage took a different view, arguing that labour markets remained segmented, such segmentation often

[65]   In his comments on criticisms by Michael Mann in 'Reply to my Critics', in Hall & Jarvie 1996, pp. 623–86 (p. 636).

[66]   Economic historians concerned with 'proto-industrialization' have identified many pre-modern periods of such development. This might suggest that it is industrialization in a narrower sense (e.g., factory production and modern machinery concentrated on towns) that should be used to identify what is distinctively modern. From a large literature see Maxine Berg (ed.), *Manufacture in Town and Country before the Factory* (Cambridge: Cambridge University Press, 1983). More complications are caused not just by the presence of pre-modern industry but the continued significance of non-factory industry in the industrial age. See *World of Possibilities: Flexibility and Mass Production in Western Industrialization*, ed. Charles Sabel & Jonathan Zeitlin (Cambridge: Cambridge University Press, 1997).

[67]   The literature is vast and cannot be cited here. Most ambitious are attempts to understand why industrialization started in the West and the global implications of that. At the other extreme are studies of particular cases and aspects of industrialization. In between are studies of the relationship between industrialization in one place and whether it promotes or hinders industrialization in other places. Finally, literature in the 'nation-building' tradition considers the role of ideology in inducing change. Every one of these fields is marked by different approaches and lively disputes. One text I have found helpful is E.L. Jones, *The European Miracle: Environments, Economies and Geopolitics in the History of Europe and Asia* (second edn, Cambridge: Cambridge University Press, 1987).

being based on skill differences. If so, cultural standardization and social mobility need not proceed as Gellner suggests.[68] More generally, one can observe the continuation of cultural difference based on communal patterns of settlement and association in modern towns and industrial labour forces.

It is debatable how far industrialization 'requires' mass literacy in a single language. Britain was notoriously laggard in introducing compulsory mass education, long after initial industrialization had been achieved. Arguably there were other reasons such as policing and humanitarian concerns with children out of supervision as a consequence of home–work separation and bans on child labour. Furthermore, the move to mass conscript armies provoked concerns amongst elites about the mental and physical standards of soldiers. Insofar as education was about work-skills training, this was mainly due to anxiety that countries like Germany were overtaking Britain in a second-wave industrialization in which formal knowledge was more significant than earlier. By contrast, a number of pre-industrial societies such as Prussia had already advanced much further than early industrial Britain down the path of elementary education.[69]

It is also debatable whether the modern city or industrial enterprises require much in the way of a standard culture, especially when we are dealing with early or fairly crude systems of production. Indeed, such systems of production might well disrupt what education in literacy had already developed. People can function effectively with the basic elements of a lingua franca or a pidgin language, as the functioning of multi-ethnic labour forces has demonstrated.[70] London today is a city with a

---

[68] These points are made in an important critique by Nick Stargardt, 'Gellner's Nationalism: The Spirit of Modernisation?', in Hall & Jarvie 1996, pp. 171–89. For an empirical consideration of the British case, see Charles More, *Skill and the English Working Class* (London: Croom Helm, 1980) and, more generally, Craig Littler, *The Development of the Labour Process in Capitalist Societies* (London: Heinemann Educational, 1982).

[69] For a good, brief introduction to some of these issues see Michael Sanderson, *Education, Economic Change and Society in England 1780–1870* (Basingstoke: Macmillan, 1991). See also Andy Green, *Education and State Formation* (second edn, Basingstoke: Macmillan, 1992).

[70] An interesting example is that of Fanakalo, a pidgin developed on the diamond and gold fields of South Africa as early as 1870 and which is still in use in some gold mines. See Ralph Adendorff, 'Fanakalo: a pidgin in South Africa', in *Language in South Africa*, ed. Rajend Mestrie (Cambridge: Cambridge University Press, 2002), pp. 179–98. I am grateful to Mariana Kriel for advising me on this matter.

bewildering array of first languages.[71] Arguably it is only in the tertiary sector, a late and post-industrial development, that high levels of literacy in a standard language become economically important. Where Gellner perhaps is on safer ground is in maintaining that there cannot be autonomous communities in a modern industrial society. However, that may have more to do with how state authority operates in modern societies (e.g., refusing to concede communal systems of law and policing) than with job requirements.[72]

The concept of nationalism is much more precisely defined by Gellner than is industrialism. Gellner distinguishes three aspects: *principle, sentiment, movement*.[73] Nationalist sentiment is characterized in terms of attitudes towards rule by co-nationals or foreigners. That would seem to include cases which lack serious internal nationalist political conflict and movements (e.g., the French). However, Gellner's typology of nationalisms excludes such cases. His description of nationalist sentiment also seems to exclude more general identification with one's own nation, including the government of the day, against other nations and their governments.

[71] There are currently some thirty groups each with more than ten thousand members speaking distinct first languages and at least another dozen or so with more than five thousand members. Students of contemporary migration are using terms such as 'superdiversity' rather than 'multiple cultures' to describe this situation and there is a developing interest in 'transnationalism' and 'cosmopolitanism' as features of such migrants rather than 'nationalism' or 'ethnic community'. See, for example, the work of COMPAS (The Centre on Migration Policy and Society) at Oxford University, and especially of its director, Steven Vertovec. These contemporary interests are also stimulating new kinds of historical work on transnationalism and cultural transfer which also suggest we have exaggerated the degree of cultural homogenization and the dominance of national identity.

[72] In *Thought and Change,* Gellner refers to the way becoming a member of the state, a citizen, involves a general identity distinct from specific roles. However, the construction of a mass citizenry was a matter of state action, often for reasons such as military conscription or for regulation of immigration, reasons which are at best indirectly linked to industrialization. I consider some of these questions in relation to the case of Germany in 'Sovereignty, Citizenship and Nationality: Reflections on the Case of Germany', in *The Frontiers of Europe*, ed. Malcolm Anderson & Eberhard Bort (London and Washington: Pinter, 1998), pp. 36–67.

[73] One might argue that the principle serves to define the concept which then takes the two forms of sentiment and movement. However, given that Gellner also recognizes that there is a distinct 'idea' of nationalism, even if he disputes the significance of such an idea, I think one can use the term principle (meaning idea or doctrine) as a way both of defining nationalism and representing one aspect of the subject. After all, words ending in 'ism' are understood to refer to ideas.

Gellner implicitly assumes that the three aspects of nationalism accompany one another but that is not so. Sometimes nationalist movements form prior to any widespread diffusion of nationalist sentiment, something of which the nationalist elite is often acutely aware. Conversely, there can be a widespread sense of national identity (nationalist sentiment) in the absence of a nationalist movement. If one accepts this, what might best explain nationalist *movements* will not necessarily explain nationalist *sentiments*. Finally, both movements and sentiments may fall short of demanding independent statehood, thus not being nationalist in terms of the political principle as Gellner defined it.

Empirical criticisms

The broad nature of the concept of industrialism and the diverse aspects of the concept of nationalism create problems when one seeks to establish empirical connections between the two. I will leave aside the many cases where one can argue for such connections either broadly or by adopting narrower definitions of the two concepts, although these may require substantial qualifications to Gellner's basic theory. Instead I consider the problems posed by industrialization without nationalism and nationalism without industrialization.

Gellner partly counters the first of these problems by confining nationalism to instances of cultural difference, as in the typology outlined in *Nations and Nationalism*. Thus there is no nationalism during British, French or US industrialization because of the lack of such cultural difference. However, there were strong expressions of national, if not nationalist sentiments in Britain and France during the Napoleonic Wars. There was a powerful current of national(ist) sentiment which worked to assimilate streams of culturally distinct immigrants from Europe into the USA. Clearly there were no nationalist *movements* because internally no conflicting nationalist politics developed.[74] Yet one could argue that it was

---

[74] Such a movement did develop in Britain, namely Irish nationalism. There was a good deal of ethnic conflict in the USA, both between different European immigrant groups and between whites and Afro-Americans or Native Americans. What prevented these turning into nationalism was not the absence of industrialism or cultural difference but the impracticality of seeking a separate state. The exception proves the rule: the Civil War of the 1860s was arguably a case of opposing nationalisms, accompanied by Confederate arguments for cultural difference. See Eugene Genovese, *The World the Slaveholders Made* (London: Allen Lane, 1970).

precisely the power of a homogenizing culture built on mass education and the dominance of one language which enabled assimilation to prevent the emergence of conflicting nationalisms. Not only are the two aspects of nationalism – sentiments and movements – separate from each other, they can appear to be opposed. For Gellner, however, there was no nationalism in such cases.

Gellner developed strong counter-arguments for why Islam could operate as the functional equivalent of nationalism.[75] This is especially pertinent in the light of the recent prominence of Islamic fundamentalist movements which oppose the culture of the 'West' and their own states if they take a pro-Western stance. However, Islam cannot completely overshadow nationalism, as demonstrated by the rise of Arab nationalism and nationalism focused on individual states such as Egypt. Furthermore, it is arguable that Islam is not so much peculiar as the most significant of religious fundamentalisms which oppose secular modernity, including certain kinds of nationalism, although also taking up anti-modern strands in nationalism. Arguably one finds such elements in Hinduism in India, Judaism in Israel and Christianity in the USA.

There is also the problem of rapid shifts between different kinds of nationalism within the same society. How is this possible if industrialization creates an ever more homogenous culture and nationalism is based on cultural difference? The same people in East Bengal could, over a period of some forty years, shift from secular all-India nationalism in the 1930s to Muslim separatist nationalism in the 1940s to Bengali nationalism in the 1960s, with the cultural 'other' being identified as the British, the Hindus and the Urdu speakers of West Pakistan respectively. One could explain this in various ways but all take one away from Gellner's central ideas. One possibility is that cultural differences continued to provide a rich foundation for different nationalist sentiments, meaning that nationalism asserted rather than reflected cultural homogeneity. A second is that nationalist movements operated separately from everyday culture, linked instead to specific economic and political interests, a view which takes us close to a Marxist or some other instrumental approach. A third is that nationalist ideas, or at least the bearers of such ideas, the intelligentsia, could mobilize populations behind very different sets of ideas which did not in some banal way reflect their cultural situation, a position that takes one close to writers like Kedourie.

---

[75] These are brought together in ch. 13 of *Nationalism*.

The other major empirical problem is nationalism without industrialization. Gellner concedes this, especially when he argues that nationalism can function as an ideology of industrialization, as Marxism did in the Soviet Union. Nationalists, beginning with Friedrich List in early nineteenth-century Germany, proclaimed an economic nationalism designed to catch up with more advanced countries.[76]

There are two difficulties with this argument. First, not all cases of 'pre-industrial nationalism' are about industrialization. Many nationalists reject westernization (e.g., Gandhi) even if they are opposed by others in the same nationalist movement (like Nehru). Many nationalists act in ways which push their country backwards (e.g., Pol Pot's genocide of Western-educated elites in Cambodia). Pre-industrial nationalism can be about many things other than industrialization.

Leaving that complication aside, what are the implications of the argument for Gellner's basic model? Clearly there are nationalists in less developed countries who see only too clearly what they lack: decent standards of living, freedom from want and oppression, the capacity to act independently in the modern world. Quite understandably for many, ordinary people as well as elites, industrialization becomes the most pressing aim. One can hardly understand many cases of late industrialization (e.g., in Asian economies such as Japan, Singapore, Malaysia, and today India and China) without taking into account this deliberate and explicit project, often framed in nationalist terms.[77]

Yet this means that nationalism is not a function of *industrialization* but rather that nationalism, as the *idea of industrialization*, is the agent of social change. There are two quite different situations. In the first, industrialization as a 'natural' process brings about homogenization through the creation and diffusion of a high culture. Where there is uneven development combined with cultural difference, this can give rise to nationalism. Nationalism *reflects* or *expresses* the centrality of standardized culture in industrial societies. In the second situation, industrialization is an

---

[76] See Gellner's extended review of Roman Szporluk, *Communism and Nationalism: Karl Marx versus Friedrich List*, 'Nationalism and Marxism', in *Encounters with Nationalism*, pp. 1–19.

[77] Nevertheless, one should not assume that there is any direct or obvious link between the intention to industrialize and industrialization itself. What is more, a selective appropriation of modernity may enable one to avoid its more general consequences. For example, one could argue that the wealth produced by oil has enabled Saudi Arabia to avoid modernizing its culture and politics.

'artificial' process deliberately pursued by nationalists. These nationalists may have observed cultural standardization as one accompaniment of earlier industrialization, along with more strictly economic features such as raising levels of investment in manufacturing industry and providing tariff protection to infant industries. They deliberately introduce these features into their society. Nationalism *effects* or *produces* the standardization of culture (along with other industrialization features) in order to induce industrialization. Not only is this a very different kind of explanation, it is one which makes ideas and the intellectuals who are the bearer of such ideas, central to the process of change.[78] Yet Gellner had rejected a central role for ideas and intellectuals in his theory of nationalism.

Some economic historians have argued that every case of industrialization after the first one, the British one, had something of this deliberate, 'artificial' character.[79] Gellner refers to the economic theorist and publicist Friedrich List (died 1846) as the first nationalist advocate of industrialization. This could mean that the 'natural' model – industrialization produces standard national culture – only works for one case, and one which did not give rise to nationalism. Nationalism as a significant phenomenon in the last 150 years appears as the pursuit rather than a function of industrialization.

The problem of explanation

These criticisms raise questions about Gellner's mode of explanation. His dismissal of the role of ideas and his insistence that nationalists do not understand what they are doing make it clear that he is seeking to *explain* and not *interpret* nationalism.[80] Gellner can quite properly insist that this

---

[78]   This also raises another possible argument, that nationalist intellectuals pursue cultural homogenization for reasons that have nothing to do with economic projects but that such homogenization turns out to be functional for industrialization.

[79]   Alexander Gerschenkron argued for a series of 'substitutes' for the free market, starting with centralized industrial investment banks (e.g., in France and Germany) and ending with the all-powerful state under Stalin; see his *Economic Backwardness in Historical Perspective* (Cambridge, Mass.: Harvard University Press, 1976). Gerschenkron represents a powerful corrective to W.W. Rostow, *Stages of Economic Growth* (London, 1960) which, although criticized by Gellner, underpins his view of industrialization as a set of distinct stages which takes place in discrete societies. A good survey of the problems involved in the 'Gerschenkron thesis' is provided in *Patterns of European Industrialization: The Nineteenth Century*, ed. Richard Sylla & Gianni Toniolo (London: Routledge, 1991).

[80]   This is the opening point made by Stargardt, 'Gellner's Nationalism', in Hall & Jarvie 1996.

does not mean that ideas do not matter, that differences between liberal nationalist and fascist values are not deeply important; and that the passion with which nationalist sentiments are held is not vital for understanding its nature and significance. The point is rather: ideas, values and passions are *not the primary level at which explanations of nationalism work*. It is only possible for nationalist values (in whatever form, nice or nasty) and passions to come about on the basis of a deeper sociological transformation involved in the transition to industrial society. Anyone proposing an explanation in terms of some feature of modernity must argue in this way.

Nevertheless, there remains the question of *how* Gellner explains nationalism. He has frequently been accused of the sin of 'functionalism'. Gellner however sees the merits of functionalism.[81] It is essential to distinguish between a useful and useless form of functionalism. In the useless form, different institutions or practices are said to function for 'society'. The problem is that as society is nothing more than the totality of such institutions or practices, one is confronted with a circular argument. If one raises 'society' to some level above this totality, it acquires a mystical, undemonstrable quality which can 'explain' anything.[82] However, if one regards society as the sum of its parts (or functions), then the useful way functionalism works is in terms of part/part relationships, not whole (mystical)/part relationships. It *is* illuminating to show how the power supply system functions for industry and households. Just as we understand one form of the 'explanation' of a machine to be a clear account of how its different components mesh together, so there can be useful functionalist 'explanations' of society. Gellner's arguments concerning the relationship between industrial labour requirements, educational provision, the role of the state in underpinning such provision and the standardization of culture is a powerful functionalist account of this kind.

Furthermore, it is difficult to envisage a better account. No one 'designs' a society to work like this, although at the level of the individual functions there is an awareness of relationships to other parts. (Managers of power stations know who their customers are and what they need. If not, they are poor managers.) But a more general awareness

---

[81] See his essay 'Zeno of Cracow' dealing with the a-historical functionalism of Malinowski, in *Culture, Identity, and Politics* (Cambridge: Cambridge University Press, 1987), pp. 47–74. He returns to the issue in *Language and Solitude*, esp. pp. 133–5.

[82] So long as the society 'exists', everything in it can be said to function for it.

of these functional relationships only comes about when they break down. There is nothing like a power supply failure or a major strike in public transport to lay bare the manifold and complex connections between different parts of society. Intelligent modern warfare includes functionalist analysis of one's opponent in order to identify where the most crippling damage can be delivered – attacking transport networks, key manufacturing plants, communications centres or public morale. In such analyses, intentional action is no more than one element. There are a series of feedback mechanisms which constantly adjust the way one part works for another part. The concept of the free market provides such an account with prices supplying the feedback mechanism. There is nothing wrong with functionalist accounts. The explanatory challenges Gellner faces are more specific.

First, such functionalism cannot assign causal primacy to the various institutions and practices it considers. Part A functions for Part B functions for Part C functions for Part A. It does not make sense to say A causes B. If A can only function with B, how could it exist prior to B? Only if there was some pre-B equivalent of B. In which case why was B required? So it is difficult to see why Gellner should regard nationalism as a function of industrialization but not the other way round. The danger is that industrialization, rather than being treated as a part, becomes the 'whole' (as in 'industrial society') which has some kind of primacy over any part such as nationalism. If industrialism is a discrete element of a society, a functionalist account must show how it relates to other discrete elements (standardized national culture and sentiments, nationalist movements).

Second, functionalism notoriously works best for stable societies. In principle, one can provide functionalist accounts of Gellner's three major types of society: hunter-gatherer, agrarian, industrial. However, his theory of nationalism focuses on the transition from agrarian to industrial society, on industrialization rather than industrialism. Gellner makes very penetrating remarks on the inadequacy of languages that explain one or another type of society at the same time to account for the transition between the two types.[83]

A key element in such transitions, from a functionalist perspective, is *dysfunction*. That is how Gellner characterizes the early stage of industrialization. The institutions of agrarian society are dysfunctional for industrialization (e.g., an anti-scientific world view, an attachment to rigid

---

[83] *Thought and Change*, ch. 3, 'Metamorphosis'.

social distinctions, an antipathy to mass literacy). They must be trans-formed or replaced. One can argue about how to account for particular changes. (I have already mentioned different explanations of the rise of mass educational institutions.) But *none* of these explanations can take a functionalist form. As Gellner recognizes, transitions are times of funda-mental conflict, when incompatible practices oppose one another, when people project competing visions of an uncertain future. Only after some sorting process (revolution, reform, warfare) can something settled emerge. In such transitions therefore, functionalist sociology will not serve. That is not to say one must abandon sociology for history (precisely reversing Gellner), but that the sociology deployed must be historical, attentive to the particular dynamics of transition to industrial society.[84]

Omissions

Finally, there are the omissions in Gellner's theory and their significance. A general problem is that the abstract and sociological form of his model makes it difficult to relate to actual cases. However, even in terms of the abstract model, there is no serious treatment of the state and politics as a particular level of society. More generally there is the problem of agency or action, whether political, cultural or economic.

Gellner's treatment of the state and politics is cursory, even dismissive. He writes, for example, of the politics of unification nationalism as an easy sequel to the prior achievement of a standard high culture.

> All that needed to be corrected was that inequality of power and the absence of a political roof over a culture (and over an economy), and institutions which would be identified with it and committed to its maintenance. The Risorgimento and the unification of Germany corrected these imbalances.[85]

'Corrected', 'imbalances', 'all that was needed' – the wars of 1864, 1866 and 1870–1 sound like fine-tuning adjustments.

---

[84] Gellner is positive about such kinds of sociology, for example, Marxism when it works to uncover mechanisms of change such as class conflict, or Max Weber when he seeks to connect Protestant values to the development of capitalism. Yet Gellner's approach in many ways is in the tradition of the third member of the holy trinity of 'founders of sociology', Emile Durkheim, who was much better at describing how a particular kind of society worked in terms of its division of labour (or functions) than accounting for social change.
[85] See, p. 96 below.

Or consider Gellner describing the emergence of a nationalist politics and the attainment of independence in his fictional Ruritania:

> The manner in which, when the international political situation came to favour it, Ruritania eventually attained independence, is now part of the historical record and need not be repeated here.[86]

These specific judgements are consistent with Gellner's general statement that: 'Nationalism as such is fated to prevail, but not any one particular nationalism.'[87] If nationalism 'as such' and the nation-state 'as such' are inevitable, the particular ways these come about are of little interest. There are several problems with this indifference to the actual historical record.

First, how can we know that there would have been Italian or German nation-states if, say, Austria had defeated France in 1859 or France had defeated Prussia in 1870–1? Or if the international situation had not 'come to favour' Ruritania? Second, the indifference to the particular path taken paradoxically produces accounts similar to those of nationalist historians who consider that the existence of a nation (in Gellner's terms of a high culture which can present itself as national) is the principal explanation for the success of nationalism. Although Gellner stresses the contingency of the particular nationalism, his fatalism about nationalism 'as such' in practice translates into a fatalism about the actual, successful cases of nationalism.

If nationalism did prevail universally, one might nevertheless concede that any other outcomes would also have been nationalist. A victorious Confederacy would have led to two national states instead of the USA. The Italian South might have formed its own state. (Certainly, contrary to Gellner's remarks about the nature of Italian high culture, there was no significant shared culture between north and south.) However, in ethnic or linguistic terms (which are mainly the terms in which Gellner understands nationalism), the nation-state is *not* a universal form. Indeed, strictly speaking, it could be regarded as a minority form compared with the multinational state.[88] There are many multi-national states in these terms, even if in many cases common bonds of citizenship and political loyalty produce a single 'nationality' understood in a different way. For example, even following the collapse of the Soviet Union, the Russian Federation remains

---

[86] See, p. 59 below.
[87] See, p. 45 below.
[88] See, for example, Walker Connor, 'Homelands in a World of States', in Guibernau & Hutchinson 2001, pp. 53–73.

multi-national. The new concerns with multiculturalism express the recognition that cultural nationality and statehood do not go together.

This suggests that one must consider the political aspect of nationalism as significant in its own right. If not all cases of industrialization plus cultural nationality produce nationalism and nation-states, and if nationalism and nation-states can be produced in the absence of industrialization and cultural nationality, we must recognize that the modern state is not necessarily national or nationalist. Even if one remains within the abstract framework of a structural sociological theory of modernity, it is necessary to look at the modern state as a special institution or set of institutions which shapes organization and thinking and even identity in new ways. It cannot just be considered as some quasi-automatic consequence of economic and cultural change.

More general is the problem of agency. For example, at the level of culture Gellner's focus is on standardization, especially of language in the form of a written vernacular. If one adds assimilation to separation, this covers a great deal. Nevertheless, these cultural processes are not specified; they appear to flow from industrialization. A full account, however, must specify the forms of cultural *action* involved. Benedict Anderson, for example, has made us aware of the particular ways mass print media can work to alter people's images of themselves. In the late twentieth century one has to add other media such as radio, film and television to the account, each with their specific dynamics and modes of action. Once one accepts that intellectuals and their ideas can shape social change, for example, by helping in the quest for industrialism, it becomes necessary to analyse the specific networks and intellectual fields within which such intellectuals are formed and operate. The point can be generalized. Schools and armies, churches and voluntary associations not only bring people together in novel ways and seek to imprint particular messages, but these forms of association shape the way individuals feel and think.

Precisely the same point can be made about the other levels of social action, political and economic. The ways in which nationalist politicians form parties and mobilize support matters a great deal not just for the specific form taken by nation-states but even whether such states are established. Industrialization is much less the result of a deliberate pursuit of 'industrialization as a whole' and more the work of particular entrepreneurs or state-sponsored activities.

These points do not necessarily undermine Gellner's theory. Rather, they suggest the problems that need to be addressed if it is to work more satisfactorily.

Gellner's Responses

Gellner responded to criticisms in various ways.

First, he systematized his universal analytical history by providing his most complete account of how the three different kinds of society functioned and just what would prove functional or dysfunctional for the next stage.[89] This strengthened his case for the need for a sociological theory which operated at a deeper level than historical accounts.

Second, and moving in the opposite direction, he introduced specific historical arguments. Some of these were first formulated in essays or reviews written in the early 1990s. In a lecture on the historian E.H. Carr, Gellner outlined a chronology of nationalism along with a set of 'time-zones'.[90] These ideas were elaborated in chapters 6 and 7 of *Nationalism*. The four chronological stages derived fairly directly from Carr's own work *Nationalism and After* (1945): Europe after the 1815 peace; the rise of 'irredentism', starting with the Greek independence movement; the 'Versailles/Wilson' era which constructed many new nation-states; the era of ethnic cleansing in the later 1930s and through the 1940s. In *Nationalism* Gellner added a fifth stage, 'Attenuation', where he predicted, in hopeful tone, that growing affluence would induce a diminution in nationalist passions. This set of stages is not related to Gellner's sociological types outlined in *Nations and Nationalism*, is Eurocentric and presents many problems. Why, for example, no consideration of the 'nationalism' of the Napoleonic era which arguably laid foundations for the subsequent period? Why single out 'irredentism' for the whole of the nineteenth century when one is confronted with many other kinds of nationalism, arguably of greater significance? The Versailles peace settlement generalized the nation-state form across much of Europe but there is a problematic relationship between nationalism (as sentiment or movement) and such state formation, as Gellner had earlier recognized.[91] The 'ethnic cleansing' stage is not related to important debates on fascism and genocide. Above all, the stages are purely descriptive.

---

[89] In *Plough, Sword, Book* (1988).

[90] 'Nationalism and the International Order', in *Encounters with Nationalism*, pp. 20–33. The essay was originally published in 1992.

[91] *Thought and Change*, p. 175: 'The easy Czech achievement of a national state in 1918 was not so much the fruit of an alliance of intellectuals and proletarians (rural and urban), but rather of intellectuals alone plus Western foreign policy.'

More interesting and valuable is the idea of 'time-zones', which combines chronology and geography but is based on structural principles. The first time-zone is nineteenth-century Western Europe where nations were constructed on the basis of pre-existing states (Britain, France, Spain, etc.). High cultures and polities matched up before the era of industrialization and nationalism. The second time-zone, parts of central Europe in the later nineteenth century, were cases where high cultures coexisted with political fragmentation. The challenge of nationalism was confined to unifying those fragments. The third time-zone was the central Europe of the multi-national empires where there were subordinate cultural groups ('folk cultures') without states of their own. Nationalism had to construct its own high cultures and states against the imperial centre. This was achieved after the First World War in the former Habsburg and Ottoman empires. However, it was not achieved in Russia, which was transformed from a dynastic into a new kind of empire, the USSR. The level of state control and suppression of nationalism were much more ruthless and effective here than in any dynastic empire. Only with the collapse of the USSR in 1989–90 did the nationalist principle manage to assert itself in this region. That was the fourth time-zone.

This historical classification combines Gellner's high/folk-culture distinction with different kinds of nationalist movements. One could in principle relate it to his arguments about industrialization. It shows that a useful typology cannot be purely chronological and descriptive (too many different types of nationalism coexist at the same time) but has to be based on structural principles. Indeed, the 'zone' is really a label for structural differences based on the high/folk-culture distinction combined with whether the polity, at the start of the nationalist era, was sub-national (unification nationalism), national (state-based nationalism) or multi-national (separatist nationalism). A classification of this sort, based purely on the state/nationalism principle, was developed some time ago by Theodor Schieder.[92] I utilized a similar distinction in *Nationalism and the State* to make distinctions between reform, separatist and unification

---

[92] Theodor Schieder, 'Typologie und Erscheinungsform des Nationalstaats in Europa', in *Nationalismus und Nationalstaat* (Göttingen: Vandenhoeck & Ruprecht, 1991), pp. 65–86. This is one of a set of essays brought together and edited by Otto Dann and Hans-Ulrich Wehler. The essay was originally published in 1966 and many of its central ideas go back at least a decade or so before then. It is a great pity that Schieder's pioneering work on nationalism has not appeared in English.

nationalism.[93] Gellner makes this a richer and more powerful framework with his high/folk-culture distinction and also by separating the Russia/USSR case from that of the Ottoman and Habsburg empires. Once one recognizes that it is these political and cultural criteria which provide the typology that roughly maps onto 'time-zones', in principle one could cope with complications in the European case and extend the typology to non-European cases.[94]

Gellner also made concessions relating to his argument that nations are modern, nationalist inventions.[95] There were pre-modern lineages which appear to be national. There were pre-modern cases of cultural chauvinism (e.g., in the ancient Greek city-states), even if this did not suffice to produce political unity. Gellner admits that ancient Israel provides us with an example of a pre-modern nation. The Hussites expressed a Czech national consciousness.[96] Centralizing states in the early modern era promoted a sense of national identity. The Protestantism of the Reformation era displayed national characteristics.[97] However, in a characteristically combative and vivid way, he disarmed the threat many of these concessions posed to his modernism with the analogy of navels.[98] It may be that

---

[93]   However, I sought to free it from specific geographical references and generalize it beyond Europe. Whereas Gellner combined it with his high/folk-culture distinction, I combined it with a broad chronological distinction between the pre-nationalist and nationalist eras.

[94]   Complications in the European case include 'high-culture' groups in multi-national empires (Poles, Magyars) and 'folk culture' groups in national states (Flemings in Belgium). China or Japan would seem to represent 'high-culture' zones beyond Europe; the segmented societies of sub-Saharan Africa examples of 'folk culture'. Pan-Arabism and Pan-Africanism seem to be examples of unification nationalism. There are many separatist cases, most unsuccessful. I would suggest that classical anti-colonial nationalism be regarded as an example of 'national state' or reform nationalism because the territory of the colonial state is not questioned, simply the issue of who controls it.

[95]   See ch. 3 of *Nationalism*.

[96]   Though Gellner explored a very different view of Hussitism in a review of a history of the Czechs: 'Reborn from Below: The Forgotten Beginnings of the Czech National Revival', in *Encounters with Nationalism*, pp. 130–44.

[97]   Such arguments for England, for example, have been presented forcefully in Hastings 1997. I think Gellner conceded too much. I argue the case against pre-modern nations and nationalism in some detail in 'Changes in the Political Uses of the Nation: Continuity or Discontinuity?', in Scales & Zimmer 2005, pp. 67–101, and 'Dating the Nation: How Old is an Old Nation?', in Ichijo & Uzelac 2005, pp. 17–41.

[98]   This idea was originally expressed in a debate with Anthony D. Smith held shortly before Gellner's death, a version of which was published in *Nations and Nationalism*, 10 (1996). Gellner was responding to Smith's arguments about the importance of an 'ethnic past' to modern nationalism.

some nations can appeal to a persuasive pre-modern history (just as navels show that children were born of a mother). However, it is not necessary (there are modern nations without such a past to which they can appeal) and it is the appeal rather than its truth or falsity which matters.

> Some nations have navels, some achieve navels, some have navels thrust upon them. Those possessed of genuine ones are probably in a minority, but it matters little. It is the need for navels engendered by modernity that matters. (*Nationalism*, p. 101)

The point about wholly modern nations without navels actually goes further than earlier arguments where Gellner had insisted that nationalism must have some 'diacritical' marks on which to assert itself as peculiar. It now becomes possible to include cases of 'civic' or 'assimilationist' nationalism in the account.

This attention to history was not just a matter of responding to critics. In the late 1980s and early 1990s the intellectual climate changed yet again with the crisis and collapse of the USSR and Yugoslavia. Suddenly, 'nationalism' returned to Europe, and in a more virulent form than it had taken in Western Europe in the 1970s. The events also had a personal impact on Gellner. He retired from his chair at Cambridge in 1993. He was already working at the newly established Central European University (CEU) where he directed the Centre for the Study of Nationalism. The CEU was (and is) funded by George Soros. At that time its headquarters was in Prague. (This has since moved to Budapest.) The CEU was deliberately conceived as an expression of liberal Western values of science and the open society.[99] Gellner, with his philosophical indebtedness to Karl Popper and his debunking of both nationalism and Marxism, along with his Czech roots, was an ideal choice. History, in particular recent central European history, understandably loomed large in his writings in the 1990s.

Gellner and Current Debates on Nationalism

These changes have also brought about an explosion of interest in nationalism. If in the early 1980s one could point to a few general and

---

[99] Soros had studied philosophy with Karl Popper. Within the CEU is an Open Society organization. The CEU is registered as a US university, and only now (2005) is it going through the process of gaining recognition from its host state, Hungary. Arguably its first stage of being a missionary outpost of the West in an unreformed, post-communist eastern Europe is coming to an end. Gellner's involvement in the CEU was in that first stage.

theoretical works on nationalism, in the 1990s the flow of publications turned into a flood which continues to the present. Every year sees readers and surveys in the subject being published.[100] There are a number of specialist journals and scholarly associations concerned with the subject.[101] There are web pages and graduate programmes in the field.[102] If one adds such related topics as ethnic conflict and its regulation and issues to do with multiculturalism, there are numerous policy institutes and much coverage of such matters in the daily press. Many different disciplines are involved: history, political science and theory, sociology, cultural studies, anthropology, psychology, geography, literary criticism, art history and more.

This resurgence of interests has led to many innovations. The notion of the nation as a social construct has been deepened with such ideas as the nation as an 'event' or a 'category' rather than a social group.[103] An emphasis upon the fluid and multiple nature of identities has underpinned postmodern approaches to nationalism. This had led to arguments about 'imagining', 'inventing' or 'narrating' nations which do not, as in the work of Anderson, Hobsbawm and Ranger and Gellner himself, relate these processes to some underlying reality such as 'print-capitalism' or 'industrialism' or the 'state' but treat them as self-fashioning.[104] At the

---

[100] For example, so far in 2005 (and I write only in August 2005) an incomplete and arbitrary list of general books includes the following: Lawrence 2005; Spencer & Wollman 2005; Özkirimli 2005. I exclude collections of essays. The last few years have also seen a number of encyclopedias or handbooks of nationalism and I know of a number which are forthcoming.

[101] For example, *Nations and Nationalism* and *Studies in Ethnicity and Nationalism*, both published by the Association for the Study of Ethnicity and Nationalism; *Ethnic and Racial Studies*; *Nationalism and Ethnic Politics*; *Ethnopolitics*.

[102] For example, *The Nationalism Project* (http://www.nationalismproject.org/). There are graduate programmes specializing in nationalism at the London School of Economics, Edinburgh University and the Central European University, Budapest, the latter a continuation of a programme started by Gellner in Prague.

[103] See, for example, Brubaker 1996. Brubaker deploys these arguments in a critique of Gellner in 'Myths and Misconceptions in the Study of Nationalism', in Hall 1998, pp. 272–306.

[104] Exemplary is Bhabha 1990. This self-fashioning is implied in the use of the present participle to describe the process. In place of 'imagined' communities we have, for example, Geoffrey Cubitt (ed), *Imagining Nations* (Manchester: Manchester University Press, 1998) and Maria Todorova, *Imagining the Balkans* (New York: Oxford University Press, 1997). There is a series with the title *Inventing the Nation* (general editor Keith Robbins; published by Edward Arnold, London) with volumes already published on India and Pakistan, Russia, Italy, China, Ireland and Germany and further studies of France and the USA in preparation.

other extreme, there have been vigorous assertions about the primordial character of nations (whether rooted in socio-biological or cultural universals). Others have insisted on the definite existence of nations and nationalism in periods well before the eighteenth century, or at least about the significance of pre-modern ethnicity and ethnic pasts for an understanding of modern nations and nationalism.[105]

Feminism has had a marked impact on studies of nationalism, especially given the gendered character of nationalist movements, ideologies and imagery. So far as I know, no one has sought to relate the gendered nature of nationalism to the gendered nature of industrialization (on which there is a rich literature) to see how it might extend rather than undermine Gellner's central argument. It would be a challenging and interesting task.[106]

The distinction between statehood and state nationality/citizenship on the one hand and ethnicity or cultural nationality on the other hand has also generated much new work. First, there is a concern with understanding ethnicity as distinct from nationality.[107] The resurgence of ethnic cleansing has led to monographic and comparative studies, and attempts to relate it to earlier movements such as fascism and the Nazi genocide. This in turn breaks down the pre/post-1945 barrier which has characterized most work on nationalism except that in the individualizing, narrative, tradition.[108] It also has led to a specific concern with the impact of war on the development of nationalism.[109]

At a policy level, there is a concern with the management of conflicts between ethnic groups within a single state. This has led to much work on constitutions and other design features of states where conflict has been violent and severe.[110] There has been a great deal of interest in multiculturalism, though this takes different forms according to whether the 'problem' is the treatment of disadvantaged 'indigenous' peoples (e.g., in

---

[105] The literature is too abundant to cite. Smith 1998 provides a judicious survey and critique. There are also good critical accounts in Day & Thompson 2004, especially chs 4, 5 and 7; and Özkirimli 2000, chs 2 and 5.

[106] See Özkirimli 2000, ch. 6; Day & Thompson 2005, ch. 6; Nira Yuval-Davis, 'Nationalism, Feminism and Gender Relations', in Guibernau & Hutchinson 2001, pp. 120–41.

[107] See the *Ethnicity* reader (Hutchinson & Smith 1996).

[108] See, for example, Michael Mann, *The Dark Side of Democracy: Explaining Ethnic Cleansing* (Cambridge: Cambridge University Press, 2005).

[109] The work of Charles Tilly is of central importance. See, for example, *Coercion, Capital and European States, AD990–1990* (Cambridge, Mass.: Basil Blackwell 1990).

[110] See, for example, McGarry & O'Leary 1993.

Canada, the USA and Australia), relations between well-established groups in different regions of a country (e.g., Tamils and Sinhalese in Sri Lanka, French and English speakers in Canada), between well-established groups without such territorial distribution (e.g., Catholics and Protestants in Ulster) or the treatment of recent groups of immigrants (e.g., in many Western European countries). In all these cases there is a separation of state citizenship from cultural nationality or ethnic identity in ways which pose challenges to Gellner's basic approach. That is also reflected in historical studies of nationalism as a cultural rather than a political movement.[111]

Policy concerns such as these also highlight the need to examine the normative aspects of nationalism, whether as a separate issue from historical or sociological approaches (posing 'ought' rather than 'is' questions) or needing to be integrated with those approaches.[112] Debates over multiculturalism, for example, raise arguments for and against granting particular groups explicit and distinct rights within the state.[113]

In the light of all these new concerns and approaches, Anthony Smith concluded that 'classical modernism', with which he associated Gellner, had reached its zenith in the early 1980s.[114] It also raises the issue of whether the broadly defined field of nationalism has become so differentiated and fragmented that it has rendered obsolete any attempt to devise a theory of 'nationalism as a whole'.

In the light of these considerations, how can one justify a new edition of *Nations and Nationalism*? Even if the terms of debate have changed and widened from those of the 1980s, it is clear in the readers and surveys of the subject that Gellner remains one of a handful of writers whose work is regarded as central for an understanding of nationalism. Gellner is also the most cogent critic of approaches which dissolve the subject into discourse and subjectivity and surrender any firm ground from which to understand nationalism. It is as much Gellner's rationalist philosophy

---

[111] For a good introduction see John Hutchinson, 'Nations and Culture', in Guibernau & Hutchinson 2001, pp. 74–96.

[112] See, for example, Özkirimli 2005, especially chapters 4 and 5. This chapter in turn draws upon a large amount of recent literature, especially by political theorists.

[113] See Bhiku Parekh, *Rethinking Multiculturalism: Cultural Diversity and Political Theory* (London: Macmillan, 2000) as well as the contributions to Nimni 2005.

[114] Smith 1998, esp. ch. 9, 'Beyond Modernism?' See also many of the essays in Scales & Zimmer 2005 and Ichijo & Uzelac 2005.

which matters in his approach to nationalism as his specifically sociological explanations.[115]

Furthermore, Gellner's work still represents the single most important attempt to provide a theory of nationalism as a whole. It is one grounded in an overall vision of human history and an insistence on the uniqueness of the modern world. This is presented in the form of a sociological model based on three major stages in human history and the relationships between cognition, production and coercion in each of those stages, culminating in a functionalist analysis of the relationship between economy, culture and state in the third of those stages, that is in the age of industrialism. It is there that nationalism is to be located and understood. By comparison, other efforts at locating and theorizing nationalism appear parochial.

In all these ways he remains a distinct and significant voice.

One might argue that his theory is *too* ambitious; that key concepts such as industrialism and nationalism must be differentiated and examined separately; that historical complexity is better served by comparative and interpretative approaches which silently relinquish the project of a 'theory of nationalism as a whole', let alone locating this within a universal history. Indeed, many of the criticisms made in this introduction point in that direction. However, only by reading Gellner can we appreciate just what we would be surrendering if we take this path. More fruitfully, one could explore whether such differentiating and historicizing of nationalism can be combined with Gellner's positivist, sociological, abstract modelling approach. Gellner's own deployment of the idea of time-zones in his last book on nationalism provides a suggestive example of how that path might be pursued. It is precisely because the study of nationalism appears to be fragmenting into many specialized fields that we need help from Ernest Gellner. A new edition of *Nations and Nationalism* can serve to remind us of his uniquely powerful, multi-disciplinary and generalizing approach to one of the most difficult yet significant challenges confronting contemporary social scientists: understanding nationalism.

I would like to acknowledge the help of my colleague John Hutchinson, who read through and commented on a draft of this Introduction.

---

[115]   A good example of Gellner's polemical application of his rationalist values is his strong criticisms of the work of Edward Said. See, for example, 'The Mightier Pen: The Double Standards of Inside-Out Colonialism', in *Encounters with Nationalism*, pp. 159–69.

Tuzenbach: In years to come, you say, life on earth will be marvellous, beautiful. That's true. But to take part in that now, even from afar, one must prepare, one must work . . .

Yes, one must work. Perhaps you think – this German is getting over-excited. But on my word of honour, I'm Russian. I cannot even speak German. My father is Orthodox . . .

Anton Chekhov, Three Sisters

Politika u nás byla však spíše méně smělejší formou kultury.
(Our politics however was a rather less daring form of culture.)

J. Sládeček, Osmašedesátý ('68), Index, Köln, 1980, and
previously circulated in samizdat in Prague.

Our nationality is like our relations to women: too implicated in our moral nature to be changed honourably, and too accidental to be worth changing.

George Santayana

Definitions

Nationalism is primarily a political principle, which holds that the political and the national unit should be congruent.

Nationalism as a sentiment, or as a movement, can best be defined in terms of this principle. Nationalist *sentiment* is the feeling of anger aroused by the violation of the principle, or the feeling of satisfaction aroused by its fulfilment. A nationalist *movement* is one actuated by a sentiment of this kind.

There is a variety of ways in which the nationalist principle can be violated. The political boundary of a given state can fail to include all the members of the appropriate nation; or it can include them all but also include some foreigners; or it can fail in both these ways at once, not incorporating all the nationals and yet also including some non-nationals. Or again, a nation may live, unmixed with foreigners, in a multiplicity of states, so that no single state can claim to be *the* national one.

But there is one particular form of the violation of the nationalist principle to which nationalist sentiment is quite particularly sensitive: if the rulers of the political unit belong to a nation other than that of the majority of the ruled, this, for nationalists, constitutes a quite outstandingly intolerable breach of political propriety. This can occur either through the incorporation of the national territory in a larger empire, or by the local domination of an alien group.

In brief, nationalism is a theory of political legitimacy, which requires that ethnic boundaries should not cut across political ones, and, in particular, that ethnic boundaries within a given state – a contingency already formally excluded by the principle in its general formulation – should not separate the power-holders from the rest.

The nationalist principle can be asserted in an ethical, 'universalistic' spirit. There could be, and on occasion there have been, nationalists-in-the-abstract, unbiased in favour of any special nationality of their own, and generously preaching the doctrine for all nations alike: let all nations have their own political roofs, and let all of them also refrain from including non-nationals under it. There is no formal contradiction in asserting such non-egoistic nationalism. As a doctrine it can be supported by some good arguments, such as the desirability of preserving cultural diversity, of a pluralistic international political system, and of the diminution of internal strains within states.

In fact, however, nationalism has often not been so sweetly reasonable, nor so rationally symmetrical. It may be that, as Immanuel Kant believed, partiality, the tendency to make exceptions on one's own behalf or one's own case, is *the* central human weakness from which all others flow; and that it infects national sentiment as it does all else, engendering what the Italians under Mussolini called the *sacro egoismo* of nationalism. It may also be that the political effectiveness of national sentiment would be much impaired if nationalists had as fine a sensibility to the wrongs committed by their nation as they have to those committed against it.

But over and above these considerations there are others, tied to the specific nature of the world we happen to live in, which militate against any impartial, general, sweetly reasonable nationalism. To put it in the simplest possible terms: there is a very large number of potential nations on earth. Our planet also contains room for a certain number of independent or autonomous political units. On any reasonable calculation, the former number (of potential nations) is probably much, *much* larger than that of possible viable states. If this argument or calculation is correct, not all nationalisms can be satisfied, at any rate at the same time. The satisfaction of some spells the frustration of others. This argument is further and immeasurably strengthened by the fact that very many of the potential nations of this world live, or until recently have lived, not in compact territorial units but intermixed with each other in complex patterns. It follows that a territorial political unit can only become ethnically homogeneous, in such cases, if it either kills, or expels, or assimilates all non-nationals. Their unwillingness to suffer such fates may make the peaceful implementation of the nationalist principle difficult.

These definitions must, of course, like most definitions, be applied with common sense. The nationalist principle, as defined, is not violated by the presence of *small* numbers of resident foreigners, or even by the presence of the occasional foreigner in, say, a national ruling family. Just how many resident foreigners or foreign members of the ruling class there must be before the principle is effectively violated cannot be stated with precision. There is no sacred percentage figure, below which the foreigner can be benignly tolerated, and above which he becomes offensive and his safety and life are at peril. No doubt the figure will vary with circumstances. The impossibility of providing a generally applicable and precise figure, however, does not undermine the usefulness of the definition.

State and Nation

Our definition of nationalism was parasitic on two as yet undefined terms: state and nation.

Discussion of the state may begin with Max Weber's celebrated definition of it, as that agency within society which possesses the monopoly of legitimate violence. The idea behind this is simple and seductive: in well-ordered societies, such as most of us live in or aspire to live in, private or sectional violence is illegitimate. Conflict as such is not illegitimate, but it cannot rightfully be resolved by private or sectional violence. Violence may be applied only by the central political authority, and those to whom it delegates this right. Among the various sanctions of the maintenance of order, the ultimate one – force – may be applied only by one special, clearly identified, and well centralized, disciplined agency within society. That agency or group of agencies *is* the state.

The idea enshrined in this definition corresponds fairly well with the moral intuitions of many, probably most, members of modern societies. Nevertheless, it is not entirely satisfactory. There are 'states' – or, at any rate, institutions which we would normally be inclined to call by that name – which do not monopolize legitimate violence within the territory which they more or less effectively control. A feudal state does not necessarily object to private wars between its fief-holders, provided they also fulfil their obligations to their overlord; or again, a state counting tribal populations among its subjects does not necessarily object to the institution of the feud, as long as those who indulge in it refrain from endangering neutrals on the public highway or in the market. The Iraqi state, under British tutelage after the First World War, tolerated tribal raids, provided the raiders dutifully reported at the nearest police station before and after the expedition, leaving an orderly bureaucratic record of slain and booty. In brief, there are states which lack either the will or the means to enforce their monopoly of legitimate violence, and which nonetheless remain, in many respects, recognizable 'states'.

Weber's underlying principle does, however, seem valid *now*, however strangely ethnocentric it may be as a general definition, with its tacit assumption of the well-centralized Western state. The state constitutes one highly distinctive and important elaboration of the social division of labour. Where there is no division of labour, one cannot even begin to speak of the state. But not any or every specialism makes a state: the state is the specialization and concentration of order maintenance. The 'state' is that institution or set of institutions specifically concerned with the enforcement of order (whatever else they may also be concerned with). The state exists where specialized order-enforcing agencies, such as police forces and courts, have separated out from the rest of social life. They *are* the state.

Not all societies are state-endowed. It immediately follows that the problem of nationalism does not arise for stateless societies. If there is no state, one obviously cannot ask whether or not its boundaries are congruent with the limits of nations. If there are no rulers, there being no state, one cannot ask whether they are of the same nation as the ruled. When neither state nor rulers exist, one cannot resent their failure to conform to the requirements of the principle of nationalism. One may perhaps deplore statelessness, but that is another matter. Nationalists have generally fulminated against the distribution of political power and the nature of political boundaries, but they have seldom if ever had occasion to deplore the absence of power and of boundaries altogether. The circumstances in which nationalism has generally arisen have not normally been those in which the state itself, as such, was lacking, or when its reality was in any serious doubt. The state was only too conspicuously present. It was its boundaries and/or the distribution of power, and possibly of other advantages, within it which were resented.

This in itself is highly significant. Not only is our definition of nationalism parasitic on a prior and assumed definition of the state: it also seems to be the case that nationalism emerges only in milieux in which the existence of the state is already very much taken for granted. The existence of politically centralized units, and of a moral-political climate in which such centralized units are taken for granted and are treated as normative, is a necessary though by no means a sufficient condition of nationalism.

By way of anticipation, some general historical observations should be made about the state. Mankind has passed through three fundamental stages in its history: the pre-agrarian, the agrarian, and the industrial.

Hunting and gathering bands were and are too small to allow the kind of political division of labour which constitutes the state; and so, for them, the question of the state, of a stable specialized order-enforcing institution, does not really arise. By contrast, most, but by no means all, agrarian societies have been state-endowed. Some of these states have been strong and some weak, some have been despotic and others law-abiding. They differ a very great deal in their form. The agrarian phase of human history is the period during which, so to speak, the very existence of the state is an option. Moreover, the form of the state is highly variable. During the hunting-gathering stage, the option was not available.

By contrast, in the post-agrarian, industrial age there is, once again, no option; but now the *presence*, not the absence of the state is inescapable. Paraphrasing Hegel, once none had the state, then some had it, and finally all have it. The form it takes, of course, still remains variable. There are some traditions of social thought – anarchism, Marxism – which hold that even, or especially, in an industrial order the state is dispensable, at least under favourable conditions or under conditions due to be realized in the fullness of time. There are obvious and powerful reasons for doubting this: industrial societies are enormously large, and depend for the standard of living to which they have become accustomed (or to which they ardently wish to become accustomed) on an unbelievably intricate general division of labour and co-operation. Some of this co-operation might under favourable conditions be spontaneous and need no central sanctions. The idea that all of it could perpetually work in this way, that it could exist without any enforcement and control, puts an intolerable strain on one's credulity.

So the problem of nationalism does not arise when there is no state. It does not follow that the problem of nationalism arises for each and every state. On the contrary, it arises only for *some* states. It remains to be seen which ones do face this problem.

The Nation

The definition of the nation presents difficulties graver than those attendant on the definition of the state. Although modern man tends to take the centralized state (and, more specifically, the centralized national state) for granted, nevertheless he is capable, with relatively little effort, of seeing its contingency, and of imagining a social situation in which the state is absent. He is quite adept at visualizing the 'state of nature'. An anthropologist can explain to him that the tribe is not necessarily a state writ small, and that forms of tribal organization exist which can be described as stateless. By contrast, the idea of a man without a nation seems to impose a far greater strain on the modern imagination. Chamisso, an *emigré* Frenchman in Germany during the Napoleonic period, wrote a powerful proto-Kafkaesque novel about a man who lost his shadow: though no doubt part of the effectiveness of this novel hinges on the intended ambiguity of the parable, it is difficult not to suspect that, for the author, the Man without a Shadow was the Man without a Nation. When his followers and acquaintances detect his aberrant shadowlessness they shun the otherwise well-endowed Peter Schlemiehl. A man without a nation defies the recognized categories and provokes revulsion.

Chamisso's perception – if indeed this is what he intended to convey – was valid enough, but valid only for one kind of human condition, and not for the human condition as such anywhere at any time. A man must have a nationality as he must have a nose and two ears; a deficiency in any of these particulars is not inconceivable and does from time to time occur, but only as a result of some disaster, and it is itself a disaster of a kind. All this seems obvious, though, alas, it is not true. But that it should have come to *seem* so very obviously true is indeed an aspect, or perhaps the very core, of the problem of nationalism. Having a nation is not an inherent attribute of humanity, but it has now come to appear as such.

In fact, nations, like states, are a contingency, and not a universal necessity. Neither nations nor states exist at all times and in all circumstances. Moreover, nations and states are not the *same* contingency. Nationalism holds that they were destined for each other; that either without the other is incomplete, and constitutes a tragedy. But before they could become intended for each other, each of them had to emerge, and their emergence was independent and contingent. The state has certainly emerged without the help of the nation. Some nations have certainly emerged without the blessings of their own state. It is more debatable whether the normative idea of the nation, in its modern sense, did not presuppose the prior existence of the state.

What then is this contingent, but in our age seemingly universal and normative, idea of the nation? Discussion of two very makeshift, temporary definitions will help to pinpoint this elusive concept.

1   Two men are of the same nation if and only if they share the same culture, where culture in turn means a system of ideas and signs and associations and ways of behaving and communicating.

2   Two men are of the same nation if and only if they *recognize* each other as belonging to the same nation. In other words, *nations maketh man*; nations are the artefacts of men's convictions and loyalties and solidarities. A mere category of persons (say, occupants of a given territory, or speakers of a given language, for example) becomes a nation if and when the members of the category firmly recognize certain mutual rights and duties to each other in virtue of their shared membership of it. It is their recognition of each other as fellows of this kind which turns them into a nation, and not the other shared attributes, whatever they might be, which separate that category from non-members.

Each of these provisional definitions, the cultural and the voluntaristic, has some merit. Each of them singles out an element which is of real importance in the understanding of nationalism. But neither is adequate. Definitions of culture, presupposed by the first definition, in the anthropological rather than the normative sense, are notoriously difficult and unsatisfactory. It is probably best to approach this problem by using this term without attempting too much in the way of formal definition, and looking at what culture *does*.

2

Culture in Agrarian Society

One development which takes place during the agrarian epoch of human history is comparable in importance with the emergence of the state itself: the emergence of literacy and of a specialized clerical class or estate, a clerisy. Not all agrarian societies attain literacy: paraphrasing Hegel once again, we may say that at first none could read; then some could read; and eventually all can read. That, at any rate, seems to be the way in which literacy fits in with the three great ages of man. In the middle or agrarian age literacy appertains to some only. Some societies have it; and within the societies that do have it, it is always some, and never all, who can actually read.

The written word seems to enter history with the accountant and the tax collector: the earliest uses of the written sign seem often to be occasioned by the keeping of records. Once developed, however, the written word acquires other uses, legal, contractual, administrative. God himself eventually puts his covenant with humanity and his rules for the comportment of his creation in writing. Theology, legislation, litigation, administration, therapy: all engender a class of literate specialists, in alliance or more often in competition with freelance illiterate thaumaturges. In agrarian societies literacy brings forth a major chasm between the great and the little traditions (or cults). The doctrines and forms of organization of the clerisy of the great and literate cultures are highly variable, and the depth of the chasm between the great and little traditions may vary a great deal. So does the relationship of the clerisy to the state, and its own internal organization: it may be centralized or it may be loose, it may be hereditary or on the contrary constitute an open guild, and so forth.

Literacy, the establishment of a reasonably permanent and standardized script, means in effect the possibility of cultural and cognitive storage and centralization. The cognitive centralization and codification effected by a clerisy, and the political centralization which *is* the state, need not go hand in hand. Often they are rivals; sometimes one may capture the other; but more often, the Red and the Black, the specialists of violence and of faith, are indeed independently operating rivals, and their territories are often not co-extensive.

Power and Culture in the Agro-literate Polity

These two crucial and idiosyncratic forms of the division of labour – the centralizations of power and of culture/cognition – have profound and special implications for the typical social structure of the agro-literate polity. Their implications are best considered jointly, and they can be schematized as shown in figure 1.

In the characteristic agro-literate polity, the ruling class forms a small minority of the population, rigidly separate from the great majority of direct agricultural producers, or peasants. Generally speaking, its ideology exaggerates rather than underplays the inequality of classes and the degree of separation of the ruling stratum. This can in turn be sub-divided into a number of more specialized layers: warriors, priests, clerics, administrators, burghers. Some of these layers (for example, Christian clergy) may be non-hereditary and be re-selected in each generation, though recruitment may be closely predetermined by the other hereditary strata. The most important point, however, is this: both for the ruling stratum as a whole, and for the various sub-strata within it, there is great stress on cultural differentiation rather than on homogeneity. The more differentiated in style of all kinds the various strata are, the less friction and ambiguity there will be between them. The whole system favours horizontal lines of cultural cleavage, and it may invent and reinforce them when they are absent. Genetic and cultural differences are attributed to what were in fact merely strata differentiated by function, so as to fortify the differentiation, and endow it with authority and permanence. For instance, in early nineteenth-century Tunisia, the ruling stratum considered itself to be Turkish, though quite unable to speak that language, and in fact of very mixed ancestry and reinforced by recruits from below.

Below the horizontally stratified minority at the top, there is another world, that of the laterally separated petty communities of the lay

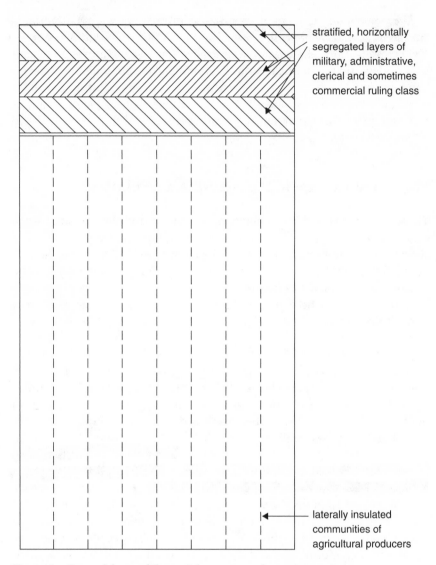

stratified, horizontally
segregated layers of
military, administrative,
clerical and sometimes
commercial ruling class

laterally insulated
communities of
agricultural producers

Figure 1   General form of the social structure of agrarian societies

members of the society. Here, once again, cultural differentiation is very
marked, though the reasons are quite different. Small peasant communities generally live inward-turned lives, tied to the locality by economic
need if not by political prescription. Even if the population of a given area
starts from the same linguistic base-line – which very often is not the case

– a kind of culture drift soon engenders dialectal and other differences. No one, or almost no one, has an interest in promoting cultural homogeneity at this social level. The state is interested in extracting taxes, maintaining the peace, and not much else, and has no interest in promoting lateral communication between its subject communities.

The clerisy may, it is true, have a measure of interest in imposing certain shared cultural norms. Some clerisies are contemptuous of and indifferent towards folk practices, while others, in the interest of monopolizing access to the sacred, to salvation, therapy and so forth, combat and actively denigrate folk culture and the freelance folk shamans who proliferate within it. But, within the general conditions prevailing in agroliterate polities, they can never really be successful. Such societies simply do not possess the means for making literacy near-universal and incorporating the broad masses of the population in a high culture, thus implementing the ideals of the clerisy. The most the clerisy can achieve is to ensure that its ideal is internalized as a valid but impracticable norm, to be respected or even revered, perhaps even aspired to in periodic outbursts of enthusiasm, but to be honoured more in the breach than in the observance in normal times.

But perhaps the central, most important fact about agro-literate society is this: almost everything in it militates against the definition of political units in terms of cultural boundaries.

In other words, had nationalism been invented in such a period its prospects of general acceptance would have been slender indeed. One might put it this way: of the two potential partners, culture and power, destined for each other according to nationalist theory, *neither* has much inclination for the other in the conditions prevailing in the agrarian age. Let us take each of them in turn.

Culture

Among the higher strata of agro-literate society it is clearly advantageous to stress, sharpen and accentuate the diacritical, differential, and monopolizable traits of the privileged groups. The tendency of liturgical languages to become distinct from the vernacular is very strong: it is as if literacy alone did not create enough of a barrier between cleric and layman, as if the chasm between them had to be deepened, by making the language not merely recorded in an inaccessible script, but also incomprehensible when articulated.

The establishment of horizontal cultural cleavages is not only attractive, in that it furthers the interests of the privileged and the power-holders; it is also feasible, and indeed easy. Thanks to the relative stability of agro-literate societies, sharp separations of the population into estates or castes or millets can be established and maintained without creating intolerable frictions. On the contrary, by externalizing, making absolute and underwriting inequalities, it fortifies them and makes them palatable, by endowing them with the aura of inevitability, permanence and naturalness. That which is inscribed into the nature of things and is perennial, is consequently not personally, individually offensive, nor psychically intolerable.

By contrast, in an inherently mobile and unstable society the maintenance of these social dams, separating unequal levels, is intolerably difficult. The powerful currents of mobility are ever undermining them. Contrary to what Marxism has led people to expect, it is pre-industrial society which is addicted to horizontal differentiation within societies, whereas industrial society strengthens the boundaries between nations rather than those between classes.

The same tends to be true, in a different form, lower down on the social scale. Even there, preoccupation with horizontal, often subtle but locally important differentiations can be intense. But even if the local group is internally more or less homogeneous, it is most unlikely to link its own idiosyncratic culture to any kind of political principle, to think in terms of a political legitimacy defined in a way which refers to the local culture. For a variety of obvious reasons, such a style of thinking is, in these conditions, most unnatural, and would indeed seem absurd to those concerned, were it explained to them. Local culture is almost invisible. The self-enclosed community tends to communicate in terms whose meaning can only be identified *in context*, in contrast to the relatively context-free scholasticism of the scribes. But the village patois (or shorthand or 'restricted code') has no normative or political pretensions; quite the reverse. The most it can do is identify the village of origin or anyone who opens his mouth at the local market.

In brief, cultures proliferate in this world, but its conditions do not *generally* encourage what might be called cultural imperialisms, the efforts of one culture or another to dominate and expand to fill out a political unit. Culture tends to be branded either horizontally (by social caste), or vertically, to define very small local communities. The factors determining political boundaries are totally distinct from those determining cultural limits. Clerisies sometimes endeavour to extend the zone of a culture, or rather, of the faith they codified for it; and states sometimes indulge in crusades, faith-endorsed aggression. But these are not the normal, pervasive conditions of agrarian society.

It is important to add that cultures in such a world proliferate in a very complex way: in many cases, it is far from clear how a given individual is to be assigned to his 'cultural background'. A Himalayan peasant, for instance, may be involved with priests and monks and shamans of several religions in different contexts at different times of the year; his caste, clan and language may link him to diverse units. The speakers of a given tribal language may, for instance, not be treated as members of it, if they happen to be of the wrong occupational caste. Life-style, occupation, language, ritual practice, may fail to be congruent. A family's economic and political survival may hinge, precisely, on the adroit manipulation and maintenance of these ambiguities, on keeping options and connections open. Its members may not have the slightest interest in, or taste for, an unambiguous, categorical self-characterization such as is nowadays associated with a putative nation, aspiring to internal homogeneity and external autonomy. In a traditional milieu an ideal of a single overriding and cultural identity makes little sense. Nepalese hill peasants often have links with a variety of religious rituals, and think in terms of caste, clan, or village (but not of nation) according to circumstance. It hardly matters whether homogeneity is preached or not. It can find little resonance.

The State in Agrarian Society

In these circumstances there is little incentive or opportunity for cultures to aspire to the kind of monochrome homogeneity and political pervasiveness and domination for which later, with the coming of the age of nationalism, they eventually strive. But how does the matter look from the viewpoint of the state, or, more generally, of the political unit?

Political units of the agrarian age vary enormously in size and kind. Roughly speaking, however, one can divide them into two species, or perhaps poles: local self-governing communities, and large empires. On the one hand, there are the city states, tribal segments, peasant communes and so forth, running their own affairs, with a fairly high political participation ratio (to adapt S. Andreski's useful phrase), and with only moderate inequality; and on the other, large territories controlled by a concentration of force at one point. A very characteristic political form is, of course, one which fuses these two principles; a central dominant authority co-exists with semi-autonomous local units.

The question which concerns us is whether, in our world, containing these types of unit, there are forces making for that fusion of culture and polity which is the essence of nationalism. The answer must be No. The local communities depend for their functioning on a good measure of face-to-face contact, and they cannot expand in size radically without transforming themselves out of all recognition. Hence these participatory communities seldom exhaust the culture of which they are part; they may have their local accent and customs, but these tend to be but variants of a wider inter-communicating culture containing many other similar communities. City states, for instance, seldom have a language of their own. No doubt the ancient Greeks were reasonably typical in this respect. While they possessed a vigorous awareness of their own shared culture and the contrast between it and that of all barbarians (with, incidentally, a rather low degree of horizontal cultural differentiation between Hellenes), this sense of unity had little *political* expression, even in aspiration, let alone in achievement. But when a pan-Hellenic polity was established under Macedonian leadership, it very rapidly grew into an empire transcending by far the bounds of Hellenism. In ancient Greece, chauvinistic though the Greeks were in their own way, there appears to have been no slogan equivalent to *Ein Reich, Ein Volk, Ein Fuehrer*.

The Varieties of Agrarian Rulers

The agro-literate polity is a kind of society which has been in existence some five millennia or so and which, despite the variety of its forms, shares certain basic features. The great majority of its citizens are agricultural producers, living in inward-turned communities, and they are dominated by a minority whose chief distinguishing attributes are the management of violence, the maintenance of order, and the control of the official wisdom of the society, which is eventually enshrined in script. This warrior-and-scribe ruling class can be fitted into a rough typology, in terms of the following set of oppositions:

1 Centralized   Uncentralized
2 Gelded   Stallions
3 Closed   Open
4 Fused   Specialized

1   Both a clerisy and a military class can be either centralized or decentralized. The medieval Catholic Church is a splendid example of an effectively centralized clerisy which can dominate the moral climate of a civilization. The *ulama* of Islam achieved as much, but with an almost total absence of any centralized organization or internal hierarchy, and they were theoretically an open class. The Brahmins were both a clerisy and a closed kin group; the Chinese bureaucracy doubled up as scribes and administrators.

2   From the viewpoint of the central state, the major danger, as Plato recognized so long ago, is the acquisition, or retention, by its military or clerical office-holders of links with particular kin groups, whose interests are then liable to sway the officers from the stern path of duty, and whose support is, at the same time, liable to endow them on occasion with too much power.

The strategies adopted for countering this pervasive danger vary in detail, but can be generically characterized as *gelding*. The idea is to break the kin link by depriving the budding warrior/bureaucrat/cleric either of ancestry, or of posterity, or of both. The techniques used included the use of eunuchs, physically incapable of possessing posterity; of priests whose privileged position was conditional on celibacy, thereby preventing them from avowing posterity; of foreigners, whose kin links could be assumed to be safely distant; or of members of otherwise disfranchised or excluded groups, who would be helpless if separated from the employing state. Another technique was the employment of 'slaves', men who, though in fact privileged and powerful, nevertheless, being 'owned' by the state, technically had no other legitimate links, and whose property and position could revert to the state at any time, without even the fiction of a right to due process, and thus without creating any rights on the parts of some local or kin group of the destituted official.

Literal eunuchs were frequently employed.[1] Celibate priests were, of course, prominent in Christendom. Slave military bureaucracies were conspicuous in Islamic polities after the decline of the Kaliphate. Foreigners were often prominent in palace elite guards and in the financial secretariats of the empires.

However, gelding was not universal. The Chinese bureaucracy was recruited from the 'gentry'; and the European feudal class rapidly

---

[1]   Keith Hopkins, *Conquerors and Slaves* (Cambridge: Cambridge University Press, 1978), ch. 4.

succeeded in superimposing the principle of heredity on to that of the allocation of land for service. In contrast with gelding, elites whose members are formally allowed to reproduce themselves socially, and retain their positions for their offspring, may be called *stallions*.

3   There are advantages in clerisies, bureaucracies and military classes being *open*, and in their being *closed*. European clergy and Chinese bureaucrats were technically open (as were Muslim *ulama*), though they were recruited predominantly from a restricted stratum. In Hinduism, priests and warrior-rulers are both closed and distinct, and their mutual (theoretical) impenetrability may be essential to the working of the system. They are both closed and non-fused, distinct. In Islam (excluding Mamluk and Janissary periods) neither clerisy nor the military are gelded.

4   Finally, the ruling class may either *fuse* the military and clerical (and possibly other) functions, or carefully segregate them into *specialized* groups. Hinduism formally separated them. European feudalism fused them on occasion, in the military orders.

It would be intriguing to follow in concrete historical detail the various possible combinations resulting from choosing from among these alternatives. For our present purpose, however, what matters is something that all the variants tend to have in common. The power-holders are caught in a kind of field of tension between local communities which are sub-national in scale, and a horizontal estate or caste which is more than national. They are loyal to a stratum which is much more interested in differentiating itself from those below than in diffusing its own culture to them, and which quite often extends its own limits beyond the bounds of the local polity, and is trans-political and in competition with the state. Only seldom (as in the case of the Chinese bureaucracy) is it co-extensive with a state (and in that case, it did display a certain kind of nationalism).

The only stratum which can in any sense be said to have a cultural policy is the clerisy. Sometimes, as in the case of the Brahmins, its policy is in effect to create a complementarity and mutual interdependence between itself and the other orders. It seeks to strengthen its own position by making itself indispensable, and the complementary roles it ascribes to itself and to the laity, far from requiring its own universalization, formally preclude it. Notwithstanding the fact that it claims monopolistic authority over ritual propriety, it does not wish to see itself emulated. It has little wish for the sincerest form of flattery, imitation, though it does provoke it.

Elsewhere, as in Islam, the clerisy from time to time takes its own missionary duties, to be practised among the habitually relapsing weaker brethren within the faith, with becoming seriousness. There is here no rule enjoining that some must pray, some fight, and some work, and that these estates should not presume to meddle with each other's realm. As far as the actual prescriptions of the faith go, everyone is allowed to do all three of these things, if his aptitudes and energy allow. (This latent egalitarianism is very important for the successful adaptation of Islam to the modern world.) Thus there is no formal or theological obstacle to a clerical missionary cultural policy *à outrance*. In practice there is still a problem: if everyone really systematically indulged in legal-theological studies, who would look after the sheep, goats and camels? In certain parts of the Sahara there are entire tribes designated, by inter-tribal compact, as People of the Book. In practice, however, this only means that religious personnel are habitually drawn from among their number. It does not mean that all of them actually become religious specialists. Most of them continue to work and fight. The only communities in which a really very significant proportion of adult males indulged in the study of the Law were some Jewish ones in Eastern Europe. But that was a special and extreme case, and in any case these communities were themselves sub-communities in a wider and more complex society.

So for very deep, powerful and insuperable reasons, clerisies in agro-literate societies cannot properly dominate and absorb the entire society. Sometimes their own rules prohibit it, and sometimes external obstacles make it impossible; but the latter would in any case constitute a sufficient and effective impediment, even if the rules were always favourable to this aspiration.

In the agrarian order, to try to impose on all levels of society a universalized clerisy and a homogenized culture with centrally imposed norms, fortified by writing, would be an idle dream. Even if such a programme is contained in some theological doctrines, it cannot be, and is not, implemented. It simply cannot be done. The resources are lacking.

But what happens if the clerisy one day *is* universalized, becomes co-extensive with the entire society, not by its own efforts, not by some heroic or miraculous internal *jihad*, but by a much more effective, deeply rooted social force, by a total transformation of the whole nature of the division of labour and of productive and cognitive processes? The answer to this question, and the specification of the nature of that transformation, will turn out to be crucial for the understanding of nationalism.

Note also that in the agrarian order only some elite strata in some societies were systematically gelded, by one or another of the specific techniques described above. Even when it is done, it is difficult, as Plato foresaw, to enforce the gelding indefinitely. The guardians, be they Mamluks or Janissaries, bureaucrats or prebend-holders, become corrupted, acquire interests and links and continuity, or are seduced by the pursuit of honour and wealth and the lure of self-perpetuation. Agrarian man seems to be made of a corruptible metal.

His successor, industrial man, seems to be made of purer, though not totally pure, metal. What happens when a social order is accidentally brought about in which the clerisy does become, at long last, universal, when literacy is not a specialism but a pre-condition of all other specialisms, and when virtually all occupations cease to be hereditary? What happens when gelding at the same time also becomes near-universal and very effective, when every man Jack amongst us is a Mamluk *de Robe*, putting the obligations to his calling above the claims of kinship? In an age of universalized clerisy and Mamluk-dom, the relationship of culture and polity changes radically. A high culture pervades the whole of society, defines it, and needs to be sustained by the polity. *That* is the secret of nationalism.

3

Industrial Society

The origins of industrial society continue to be an object of scholarly dispute. It seems to me very probable that this will continue to be so for ever. An enormously complex transformation occurred in a very large, diversified and intricate society, and the event was *unique*: no imitative industrialization can be treated as an event *of the same kind* as the original industrialization, simply in virtue of the fact that all the others were indeed imitative, were performed in the light of the now established knowledge that the thing could be done, and had certain blatant and conspicuous advantages (though the emulated ideal was, of course, interpreted in all kinds of quite diverse ways). So we can never repeat the original event, which was perpetrated by men who knew not what they did, an unawareness which was of the very essence of the event. We cannot do it, for quite a number of cogent reasons: the sheer fact of repetition makes it different from the original occasion; we cannot in any case reproduce all the circumstances of early modern Western Europe; and experiments on such a scale, for the sake of establishing a theoretical point, are morally hardly conceivable. In any case, to sort out the causal threads of so complex a process, we should need not one, but very many re-runs, and these will never be available to us.

But while we cannot really establish the aetiology of industrialism, we can hope to make some progress in putting forward models of the generic working of industrial society. In fact, the real merit and importance of Max Weber's celebrated essay (*The Protestant Ethic and the Spirit of Capitalism*) seems to me to lie far less in his fascinating but speculative and inconclusive hypothesis about the genesis of the capitalist spirit, than in his reflections about what constitute the general distinguishing features of the new social order. In fact, although the (entirely salutary) shift of concern from the origins of capitalism to that of the origins of industrialism only occurred after Weber, and as a consequence of the emergence of non-capitalist industrial societies, nevertheless this reformulation of the crucial question is already implicit in Weber's preoccupation with bureaucracy, alongside his concern with the entrepreneurial spirit. If a centralized bureaucracy exemplifies the new *Geist* just as much as does the rational businessman, then clearly we are concerned with industrialism, rather than with capitalism as such.

In the Weberian, and I think in any plausible account of the new spirit, the notion of *rationality* must be central and important. Weber himself was not particularly deft in giving coherent and adequate definitions, particularly so in this case, though it is perfectly possible to distil from the contexts of his use of this notion of rationality what he meant by it, and that this underlying notion is indeed crucial for this topic. As it happens, this notion is explored, with unparalleled philosophic depth, by the two greatest philosophers of the eighteenth century, David Hume and Immanuel Kant, both of whom, under the fond delusion that they were analysing the human mind as such, *an sich*, anywhere, any time, were in fact giving very profound accounts of the general logic of the new spirit whose emergence characterized their age. What these two thinkers shared was at least as important as what separated them.

Two elements are conspicuously present in Weber's notion of rationality. One is coherence or consistency, the like treatment of like cases, regularity, what might be called the very soul or honour of a good bureaucrat. The other is efficiency, the cool rational selection of the best available means to given, clearly formulated and isolated ends; in other words, the spirit of the ideal entrepreneur. Orderliness and efficiency may indeed be seen as the bureaucratic and the entrepreneurial elements in an overall spirit of rationality.

I do not myself believe that these two elements are really independent of each other. The notion of means-ends efficiency implies that the agent will always choose the self-same solution to a given problem, irrespective of 'irrelevant' considerations; and consequently it carries the bureaucratic requirement of symmetry of treatment as an immediate corollary. The imperative of symmetry does not quite so immediately imply the corollary of efficiency (and indeed, as an empirical fact, bureaucrats, even or especially perfectly honest and conscientious ones, are not always particularly efficient, as Weber himself noted); nevertheless, any sustained and non-superficial implementation of the requirement of orderliness will imply the use of a general and neutral idiom for the specification both of ends and of fact, of the environment in which the ends are to be pursued. Such a language, by its clear specification of ends and means, will in the end only permit the characterization of actions in a way which ensures that clearly identified ends are attained by means selected for their optimal effectiveness, and for nothing else.

What underlies the two elements of the rational spirit of which Weber was clearly aware (orderliness and efficiency) is something deeper, well explored by Hume and Kant under the blithe impression that they were investigating the human mind in general: namely, a common measure of fact, a universal conceptual currency, so to speak, for the general characterization of things; and the *esprit d'analyse*, forcefully preached and characterized already by Descartes. Each of these elements is presupposed by rationality, in the sense in which it concerns us, as the secret of the modern spirit. By the common or single conceptual currency I mean that all facts are located within a single continuous logical space, that statements reporting them can be conjoined and generally related to each other, and so that in principle one single language describes the world and is internally unitary; or on the negative side, that there are no special, privileged, insulated facts or realms, protected from contamination or contradiction by others, and living in insulated independent logical spaces of their own. Just this was, of course, the most striking trait of pre-modern, pre-rational visions: the co-existence within them of multiple, not properly united, but hierarchically related sub-worlds, and the existence of special privileged facts, sacralized and exempt from ordinary treatment.

In a traditional social order, the languages of the hunt, of harvesting, of various rituals, of the council room, of the kitchen or harem, all form autonomous systems: to conjoin statements drawn from these various disparate fields, to probe for inconsistencies between them, to try to unify them all, this would be a social solecism or worse, probably blasphemy or impiety, and the very endeavour would be unintelligible. By contrast, in our society it is assumed that all referential uses of language ultimately refer to one coherent world, and can be reduced to a unitary idiom; and that it is legitimate to relate them to each other. 'Only connect' is an intelligible and acceptable ideal. Modern philosophies of knowledge are frequently our expression and codification of this idea and aspiration, which in turn is not a philosophical whim, but has profound social roots.

Equalization and homogenization of facts is incomplete unless accompanied by what may be called the separation of all separables, the *esprit d'analyse*, the breaking up of all complexes into their constituent parts (even if it can only be done in thought), and the refusal to countenance conceptual package deals. It is precisely by binding things together that traditional visions perpetuate themselves and the prejudgements contained within them; and it is by insisting on prising things apart that we have liberated ourselves from them. These package-deals, and the discontinuous conceptual spaces, are the equivalents, in the sphere of ideas, of the stable social groupings and structures at the level of men. Likewise, the unified and standardized, as it were metric world of facts, as conceived in the philosophies of Hume or Kant, is the analogue of the anonymous and equal collectivities of men in a mass society. In the present argument, we are concerned with men and their groupings, rather than with ideas; but the unification of their ideas in continuous and unitary systems is connected with their re-grouping in internally fluid, culturally continuous communities.

Industrial society is the only society ever to live by and rely on sustained and perpetual growth, on an expected and continuous improvement. Not surprisingly, it was the first society to invent the concept and ideal of progress, of continuous improvement. Its favoured mode of social control is universal Danegeld, buying off social aggression with material enhancement; its greatest weakness is its inability to survive any temporary reduction of the social bribery fund, and to weather the loss of legitimacy which befalls it if the cornucopia becomes temporarily jammed and the flow falters. Many societies in the past have on occasion discovered innovations and improved their lot, and sometimes it may even have been true that improvements came not as single spies but in battalions. But the improvement was never perpetual, nor expected to be so. Something special must have happened to have engendered so unusual and remarkable an expectation.

And indeed, something unusual, something unique, had happened. The conception of the world as homogeneous, subject to systematic, indiscriminate laws, and as open to interminable exploration, offered endless possibilities of new combinations of means with no firm prior expectations and limits: no possibilities would be barred, and in the end nothing but evidence would decide how things were, and how they could be combined to secure desired effects. This was a totally new vision. The old worlds were, on the one hand, each of them, a cosmos: purposive, hierarchal, 'meaningful'; and on the other hand, not quite unified, consisting of subworlds each with its own idiom and logic, not subsumable under a single overall orderliness. The new world was on the one hand morally inert, and on the other, unitary.

Hume's philosophy is one of the most important codifications of this vision. Its best-known part is his treatment of causation, which indeed follows from the overall vision and its central insights. What it amounts to in the end is this: in the very nature of things, nothing is inherently connected with anything else. The actual connections of this world can only be established by first separating in thought everything that can be thought separately – so that we can isolate the pure elements, so to speak – and then seeing what, as a matter of experience, happens to be actually conjoined to what.

Is the world like that? *Ours* is. This is the pre-condition, the price of a world of endless discovery. Inquiry must not be bound by the natural affinities and liaisons of things, built into this or that vision and style of life. And, of course, Hume's account of causation is not merely an admirable summary of the background picture facing the untrammelled, eternal inquirer: it is also an account of the comportment of his economic counterpart, the modern entrepreneur. Not for the merchant or manufacturer of the age of reason the fusion of labour, technique, material and mould, prescribed by custom, tied to a social order and rhythm; his progress and the advancement of the economy of which he is a part hinges, once again, on his untrammelled selection of whatever means, in the light of the evidence and of nothing else, serves some clear aim such as the maximization of profit. (His predecessor or indeed his surviving feudal contemporary would have been hard put to it to single out a solitary, isolable criterion of success. Profit for them would have been merged in a number of inseparable other considerations, such as the maintenance of their positions in the community. Adam Smith saw only too clearly the difference between a Glasgow burgher and, say, Cameron of Lochiel. Hume's theory of causation ratifies the perceptions of the former.)

This vision of a society which has become dependent on both cognitive and economic growth (the two being, of course, linked to each other) concerns us here, because we are primarily interested in the consequences of an ever-growing, ever-progressing society. But the consequences of such perpetual growth have striking parallels with the vision which was its condition.

The Society of Perpetual Growth

If cognitive growth presupposes that no element is indissolubly linked *a priori* to any other, and that everything is open to rethinking, then economic and productive growth requires exactly the same of human activities and hence of human roles. Roles become optional and instrumental. The old stability of the social role structure is simply incompatible with growth and innovation. Innovation means doing new things, the boundaries of which cannot be the same as those of the activities they replace. No doubt most societies can cope with an occasional re-drawing of job specifications and guild boundaries, just as a football team can experimentally switch from one formation to another, and yet maintain continuity. One change does not make progress. But what happens when such changes themselves are constant and continuous, when the persistence of occupational change itself becomes the one permanent feature of a social order?

When this question is answered, the main part of the problem of nationalism is thereby solved. Nationalism is rooted in a *certain kind* of division of labour, one which is complex and persistently, cumulatively changing.

High productivity, as Adam Smith insisted so much, requires a complex and refined division of labour. Perpetually growing productivity requires that this division be not merely complex, but also perpetually, and often rapidly, changing. This rapid and continuous change both of the economic role system itself and of the occupancy of places within it, has certain immediate and profoundly important consequences. Men located within it cannot generally rest in the same niches all their lives; and they can only seldom rest in them, so to speak, over generations. Positions are seldom (for this and other reasons) transmitted from father to son. Adam Smith noted the precariousness of bourgeois fortunes, though he erroneously attributed stability of social station to pastoralists, mistaking their genealogical myths for reality.

The immediate consequence of this new kind of mobility is a certain kind of egalitarianism. Modern society is not mobile because it is egalitarian; it is egalitarian because it is mobile. Moreover, it has to be mobile whether it wishes to be so or not, because this is required by the satisfaction of its terrible and overwhelming thirst for economic growth.

A society which is destined to a permanent game of musical chairs cannot erect deep barriers of rank, of caste or estate, between the various sets of chairs which it possesses. That would hamper the mobility, and, given the mobility, would indeed lead to intolerable tensions. Men can tolerate terrible inequalities, if they are stable and hallowed by custom. But in a hectically mobile society, custom has no time to hallow anything. A rolling stone gathers no aura, and a mobile population does not allow any aura to attach to its stratification. Stratification and inequality do exist, and sometimes in extreme form; nevertheless they have a muted and discreet quality, attenuated by a kind of gradualness of the distinctions of wealth and standing, a lack of social distance and a convergence of life-styles, a kind of statistical or probabilistic quality of the differences (as opposed to the rigid, absolutized, chasm-like differences typical of agrarian society), and by the illusion or reality of social mobility.

That illusion is essential, and it cannot persist without at least a measure of reality. Just how much reality there is in this appearance of upward and downward mobility varies and is subject to learned dispute, but there can be no reasonable doubt that it does have a good deal of reality: when the system of roles itself is changing so much, the occupants of positions within it cannot be, as some leftwing sociologists claim, tied to a rigid stratificational system. Compared with agrarian society, this society is mobile and egalitarian.

But there is more than all this to the egalitarianism and mobility engendered by the distinctively industrial, growth-oriented economy. There are some additional subtler traits of the new division of labour, which can perhaps best be approached by considering the difference between the division of labour in an industrial society and that of a particularly complex, well-developed agrarian one. The *obvious* difference between the two is that one is more stable and the other is more mobile. In fact, one of them generally wills itself to be stable, and the other wills itself to be mobile; and one of them pretends to be more stable than social reality permits, while the other often claims more mobility, in the interest of pretending to satisfy its egalitarian ideal, than its real constraints actually permit. Nevertheless, though both systems tend to exaggerate their own central features, they do indeed markedly possess the trait they claim as their own when contrasted with each other: one is rigid, the other mobile. But if that is the obvious contrast, what are the subtler features which accompany it?

Compare in detail the division of labour in a highly advanced agrarian society with that of an average industrial one. Every kind of function, for instance now has at least one kind of specialist associated with it. Car mechanics are becoming specialized in terms of the make of car they service. The industrial society will have a larger population, and probably, by most natural ways of counting, a larger number of different jobs. In *that* sense, the division of labour has been pushed much further within it.

But by some criteria, it may well be that a fully developed agrarian society actually has the more complex division of labour. The specialisms within it are more distant from each other than are the possibly more numerous specialisms of an industrial society, which tend to have what can only be described as a mutual affinity of style. Some of the specialisms of a mature agrarian society will be extreme: they will be the fruits of life-long, very prolonged and totally dedicated training, which may have commenced in early youth and required an almost complete renunciation of other concerns. The achievements of craft and art production in these societies are extremely labour- and skill-intensive, and often reach levels of intricacy and perfection never remotely equalled by anything later attained by industrial societies, whose domestic arts and decorations, gastronomy, tools and adornments are notoriously shoddy.

Notwithstanding their aridity and sterility, the scholastic and ritual complexity mastered by the schoolmen of a developed agrarian society is often such as to strain the very limits of the human mind. In brief, although the peasants, who form the great majority of an agrarian society, are more or less mutually interchangeable when it comes to the performance of the social tasks which are normally assigned to them, the important minority of specialists within such societies are outstandingly complementary to each other; each one of them, or each group of them, is dependent on the others and, when sticking to its last, its specialism, quite incapable of self-sufficiency.

It is curious that, by contrast, in industrial society, notwithstanding its larger number of specialisms, the distance between specialists is far less great. Their mysteries are far closer to mutual intelligibility, their manuals have idioms which overlap to a much greater extent, and re-training, though sometimes difficult, is not generally an awesome task.

So quite apart from the presence of mobility in the one case and stability in the other, there is a subtle but profound and important qualitative difference in the division of labour itself. Durkheim was in error when he in effect classed advanced pre-industrial civilizations and industrial society together under the single heading of 'organic solidarity', and when he failed to introduce properly this further distinction within the wider category of organic solidarity or of complementary division of labour. The difference is this: the major part of training in industrial society is *generic* training, not specifically connected with the highly specialized professional activity of the person in question, and *preceding* it. Industrial society may by most criteria be the most highly specialized society ever; but its educational system is unquestionably the *least* specialized, the most universally standardized, that has ever existed. The same kind of training or education is given to all or most children and adolescents up to an astonishingly late age. Specialized schools have prestige only at the end of the educational process, if they constitute a kind of completion of a prolonged previous unspecialized education; specialized schools intended for a younger, earlier intake have negative prestige.

Is this a paradox, or perhaps one of those illogical survivals from an earlier age? Those who notice the 'gentlemanly' or leisure-class elements in higher education have sometimes supposed so. But, although some of the frills and affectations attached to higher education may indeed be irrelevancies and survivals, the central fact – the pervasiveness and importance of generic, unspecialized training – is conjoined to highly specialized industrial society not as a paradox, but as something altogether fitting and necessary. The kind of specialization found in industrial society rests precisely on a common foundation of unspecialized and standardized training.

A modern army subjects its recruits first to a shared generic training, in the course of which they are meant to acquire and internalize the basic idiom, ritual and skills common to the army as a whole; and only subsequently are the recruits given more specialized training. It is assumed or hoped that every properly trained recruit can be re-trained from one specialism to another without too much loss of time, with the exception of a relatively small number of very highly trained specialists. A modern society is, in this respect, like a modern army, only more so. It provides a very prolonged and fairly thorough training for all its recruits, insisting on certain shared qualifications: literacy, numeracy, basic work habits and social skills, familiarity with basic technical and social skills. For the large majority of the population the distinctive skills involved in working life are superimposed on the basic training, either on the job or as part of a much less prolonged supplementary training; and the assumption is that anyone who has completed the generic training common to the entire population can be re-trained for most other jobs without too much difficulty. Generally speaking, the additional skills required consist of a few techniques that can be learned fairly quickly, plus 'experience', a kind of familiarity with a milieu, its personnel and its manner of operation. This may take a little time to acquire, and it sometimes reinforced by a little protective mystique, but seldom really amounts to very much. There is also a minority of genuine specialists, people whose effective occupancy of their posts really depends on very prolonged additional training, and who are not easily or at all replaceable by anyone not sharing their own particular educational background and talent.

The ideal of universal literacy and the right to education is a well-known part of the pantheon of modern values. It is spoken of with respect by statesmen and politicians, and enshrined in declarations of rights, constitutions, party programmes and so forth. So far, nothing unusual. The same is true of representative and accountable government, free elections, an independent judiciary, freedom of speech and assembly, and so on. Many or most of these admirable values are often and systematically ignored in many parts of the world, without anyone batting an eyelid. Very often, it is safe to consider these phrases as simple verbiage. Most constitutions guaranteeing free speech and elections are as informative about the societies they allegedly define as a man saying 'Good morning' is about the weather. All this is well known. What is so very curious, and highly significant, about the principle of universal and centrally guaranteed education, is that it is an ideal more honoured in the observance than in the breach. In this it is virtually unique among modern ideals; and this calls for an explanation. Professor Ronald Dore has powerfully criticized this tendency,[1] particularly among developing societies, of overrating formal 'paper' qualifications, and no doubt it has harmful side effects. But I wonder whether he fully appreciates the deep roots of what he castigates as the Diploma Disease. We live in a world in which we can no longer respect the informal, intimate transmission of skills, for the social structures within which such transmission could occur are dissolving. Hence the only kind of knowledge we can respect is that authenticated by reasonably impartial centres of learning, which issue certificates on the basis of honest, impartially administered examinations. Hence we are doomed to suffer the Diploma Disease.

All this suggests that the kind of education described – universal, standardized, and generic – *really* plays some essential part in the effective working of a modern society, and is not merely part of its verbiage or self-advertisement. This is in fact so. To understand what that role is, we must, to borrow a phrase from Marx (though not perhaps in the sense in which he used it), consider not merely the mode of production of modern society, but above all its mode of *reproduction*.

---

[1] Ronald Dore, *The Diploma Disease* (London: Allen and Unwin, 1976). For an approach to the social implications of literacy at an earlier stage, see Jack Goody (ed.), *Literacy in Traditional Societies* (Cambridge: Cambridge University Press, 1968).

Social Genetics

The reproduction of social individuals and groups can be carried out either on the one-to-one or on-the-job principle, or by what may be called the centralized method. There are, of course, many mixed and intermediate ways of doing this job, but their consideration can best be postponed until after the discussion of these two extreme, as it were polar, possibilities.

The one-to-one, on-the-job method is practised when a family, kin unit, village, tribal segment or similar fairly small unit takes the individual infants born into it, and by allowing and obliging them to share in the communal life, plus a few more specific methods such as training, exercises, precepts, *rites de passage* and so forth, eventually turns these infants into adults reasonably similar to those of the preceding generation; and in this manner the society and its culture perpetuate themselves.

The centralized method of reproduction is one in which the local method is significantly complemented (or in extreme cases, wholly replaced) by an educational or training agency which is distinct from the local community, and which takes over the preparation of the young human beings in question, and eventually hands them back to the wider society to fulfil their roles in it, when the process of training is completed. An extreme version of this system developed a high degree of perfection and effectiveness in the Ottoman empire, when under the *devshirme* and Janissary systems, young boys, either secured as a tax obligation from conquered populations, or purchased as slaves, were systematically trained for war and administration and, ideally, wholly weaned and separated from their families and communities of origin. A less total version of this system was and in part still is practised by the British upper class, with its reliance on boarding schools from an early age. Variants of this system can on occasion be found even in relatively simple, preliterate agrarian societies.

Societies consisting of sub-communities can be divided into those in which the sub-communities can, if necessary, reproduce themselves without help from the rest of society, and those in which mutual complementarity and interdependence are such that they cannot do this. Generally speaking, the segments and rural communities of agrarian society *can* reproduce themselves independently. The anthropological concept of a segmentary society contains precisely this idea: the 'segment' is simply a smaller variant of the larger society of which it is a part, and can do on a smaller scale everything done by the larger unit.

Furthermore, one must distinguish between economic and educational self-sufficiency, in the sense of capacity for self-reproduction. The ruling strata of an agrarian society are, of course, dependent on a surplus drawn from the rest of society, but they may nevertheless be educationally quite self-sufficient. Various other kinds of non-self-sufficiency can also be engendered by social rules, such as those which make communities dependent on external ritual specialists, or on the supply of brides from outside. Here we are concerned with educational, not economic capacity for group self-reproduction. There are numerous complex, mixed and intermediate forms of group reproduction. When feudal lords send their sons as half-trainees, half-hostages to the local court, when masters accept apprentices who are not their sons, and so forth, we are obviously in the presence of such mixed systems.

Generally speaking, the situation in agrarian society seems to be this: the great majority of the population belongs to self-reproducing units, such as in effect educate their young on the job, in their stride, as part and parcel of the general business of living, without relying much or at all on any kind of educational specialist. A minority of the population receives specialized training. The society will contain one or more strata of full-time educators, who both reproduce themselves by taking on apprentices, and perform part-time services for the rest of the community: ritual, therapeutic, admonitory, secretarial, and so on. It may be useful to distinguish between one-to-one, intra-community training, and call it acculturation, and specialized *exo-training* (on the analogy of exogamy), which calls for skills outside the community, and call that education proper.

A very important stratum in literate agrarian society are the clerks, those who can read and transmit literacy, and who thus form one of the classes of specialists in that society. They may or may not form a guild or be incorporated in an organization. As, generally speaking, writing soon transcends its purely technical use in record-keeping, and acquires moral and theological significance, the clerks or clerics are almost invariably far more than mere grapho-technicians. It is not just writing, but what is written that counts, and, in agrarian society, the ratio of the sacred to the profane, within the realm of the written, tends to be heavily weighted in favour of the first. So the writers and readers are specialists and yet more than specialists; they are both part of a society, and claim to be the voice of the whole of it. Their specialism *says* something, something special, more so perhaps than that of the woodcarvers and other designers, and much more than that of the tinkers.

Specialists are often feared and despised in this kind of society. The clerics may be viewed ambivalently, but in the main their standing is rather high. They are both specialists and a part of society among others, and yet also, as stated, claim to be the voice of the totality. They are in an inherently paradoxical situation. Logicians possess, in their armoury of allegedly deep and significant puzzles, the Problem of the Barber: in a village, all men can be divided into those who shave themselves, and those who are shaved by the barber. But what of the barber himself? Is he a self-shaver, or one of the barber-shaved? In this form, let us leave it to the logicians. But the clerics are somewhat in the barber's situation. They reproduce their own guild by training entrants, but they also give a bit of training or provide services for the rest of society. Do they or do they not shave themselves? The tension and its problems (and they are not just logical) are with them, and they are not easily resolved.

In the end, modern society resolves this conundrum by turning *everyone* into a cleric, by turning this potentially universal class into an effectively universal one, by ensuring that everyone without exception is taught by it, that exo-education becomes the universal norm, and that no-one culturally speaking, shaves himself. Modern society is one in which no sub-community, below the size of one capable of sustaining an independent educational system, can any longer reproduce itself. The reproduction of fully socialized individuals itself becomes part of the division of labour, and is no longer performed by sub-communities for themselves.

That is what developed modern societies are like. But why *must* this be so? What fate impels them in this direction? Why, to repeat the earlier question, is this one ideal, that of universal literacy and education, taken with this most unusual, untypical seriousness?

Part of the answer has already been given, in connection with the stress on occupational mobility, on an unstable, rapidly changing division of labour. A society whose entire political system, and indeed whose cosmology and moral order, is based in the last analysis on economic growth, on the universal incremental Danegeld and the hope of a perpetual augmentation of satisfactions, whose legitimacy hinges on its capacity to sustain and satisfy this expectation, is thereby committed to the need for innovation and hence to a changing occupational structure. From this it follows that certainly between generations, and very often within single life-spans, men must be ready for reallocation to new tasks. Hence, in part, the importance of the generic training, and the fact that the little bit extra of training, such as is attached to most jobs, doesn't amount to too much, and is moreover contained in manuals intelligible to all possessors of the society's generic training. (While the little bit extra seldom amounts to much, the shared and truly essential generic core is supplied at a rather high level, not perhaps when compared with the intellectual *peaks* of agrarian society, but certainly when placed alongside its erstwhile customary average.)

But it is not only mobility and re-training which engender this imperative. It is also the *content* of most professional activities. Work, in industrial society, does not mean moving matter. The paradigm of work is no longer ploughing, reaping, thrashing. Work, in the main, is no longer the manipulation of things, but of meanings. It generally involves exchanging communications with other people, or manipulating the controls of a machine. The proportion of people at the coal face of nature, directly applying human physical force to natural objects, is constantly diminishing. Most jobs, if not actually involving work 'with people', involve the control of buttons or switches or leavers which need to be *understood*, and are explicable, once again, in some standard idiom intelligible to all comers.

For the first time in human history, explicit and reasonably precise communication becomes generally, pervasively used and important. In the closed local communities of the agrarian or tribal worlds, when it came to communication, context, tone, gesture, personality and situation were everything. Communication, such as it was, took place without the benefit of precise formulation, for which the locals had neither taste nor aptitude. Explicitness and the niceties of precise, rule-bound formulation were left to lawyers, theologians or ritual specialists, and were parts of their mysteries. Among intimates of a close community, explicitness would have been pedantic and offensive, and is scarcely imaginable or intelligible.

Human language must have been used for countless generations in such intimate, closed, context-bound communities, whereas it has only been used by schoolmen and jurists, and all kinds of context-evading conceptual puritans, for a very small number of generations. It is a very puzzling fact that an institution, namely human language, should have this potential for being used as an 'elaborate code', in Basil Bernstein's phrase, as a formal and fairly context-free instrument, given that it had evolved in a milieu which in no way called for this development, and did not selectively favour it if it manifested itself. This puzzle is on a par with problems such as that posed by the existence of skills (for example, mathematical ability) which throughout most of the period of the existence of humanity had no survival value, and thus could not have been in any direct way produced by natural selection. The existence of language suitable for such formal, context-liberated use is such a puzzle; but it is also, clearly, a fact. This potentiality, whatever its origin and explanation, happened to be there. Eventually a kind of society emerged – and it is now becoming global – in which this potentiality really comes into its own, and within which it becomes indispensable and dominant.

To sum up this argument: a society has emerged based on a high-powered technology and the expectancy of sustained growth, which requires both a mobile division of labour, and sustained, frequent and precise communication between strangers involving a sharing of explicit meaning, transmitted in a standard idiom and in writing when required. For a number of converging reasons, this society must be thoroughly exo-educational: each individual is trained by specialists, not just by his own local group, if indeed he has one. Its segments and units – and this society is in any case large, fluid, and in comparison with traditional, agrarian societies very short of internal structures – simply do not possess the capacity or the resources to reproduce their own personnel. The level of literacy and technical competence, in a standardized medium, a common conceptual currency, which is required of members of this society if they are to be properly employable and enjoy full and effective moral citizenship, is so high that it simply *cannot* be provided by the kin or local units, such as they are. It can only be provided by something resembling a modern 'national' educational system, a pyramid at whose base there are primary schools, staffed by teachers trained at secondary schools, staffed by university-trained teachers, led by the products of advanced graduate schools. Such a pyramid provides the criterion for the minimum size for a viable political unit. No unit too small to accommodate the pyramid can function properly. Units cannot be *smaller* than this. Constraints also operate which prevent them being too large, in various circumstances; but that is another issue.

The fact that sub-units of society are no longer capable of self-reproduction, that centralized exo-education is the obligatory norm, that such education complements (though it does not wholly replace) local-ized acculturation, is of the very first importance for the political soc-iology of the modern world; and its implications have, strangely enough, been seldom understood or appreciated or even examined. At the base of the modern social order stands not the executioner but the professor. Not the guillotine, but the (aptly named) *doctorat d'état* is the main tool and symbol of state power. The monopoly of legitimate education is now more important, more central than is the monopoly of legitimate violence. When this is understood, then the imperative of nationalism, its roots, not in human nature as such, but in a certain kind of now pervasive social order, can also be understood.

Contrary to popular and even scholarly belief, nationalism does not have any very deep roots in the human psyche. The human psyche can be assumed to have persisted unchanged through the many many millennia of the existence of the human race, and not to have become either better or worse during the relatively brief and very recent age of nationalism. One may not invoke a *general* substrate to explain a *specific* phenomenon. The substrate generates many surface possibilities. Nationalism, the organization of human groups into large, centrally educated, culturally homogeneous units, is but one of these, and a very rare one at that. What is crucial for its genuine explanation is to identify its specific roots. It is these specific roots which alone can properly explain it. In this way, specific factors are superimposed on to a shared universal human substrate.

The roots of nationalism in the distinctive structural requirements of industrial society are very deep indeed. This movement is the fruit neither of ideological aberration, nor of emotional excess. Although those who participate in it generally, indeed almost without exception, fail to understand what it is that they do, the movement is nonetheless the external manifestation of a deep adjustment in the relationship between polity and culture which is quite unavoidable.

The Age of Universal High Culture

Let us recapitulate the general and central features of industrial society. Universal literacy and a high level of numerical, technical and general sophistication are among its functional prerequisites. Its members are and must be mobile, and ready to shift from one activity to another, and must possess that generic training which enables them to follow the manuals and instructions of a new activity or occupation. In the course of their work they must constantly communicate with a large number of other men, with whom they frequently have no previous association, and with whom communication must consequently be explicit, rather than relying on context. They must also be able to communicate by means of written, impersonal, context-free, to-whom-it-may-concern type messages. Hence these communications must be in the same shared and standardized linguistic medium and script. The educational system which guarantees this social achievement becomes large and is indispensable, but at the same time it no longer possesses monopoly of access to the written word: its clientele is co-extensive with the society at large, and the replaceability of individuals within the system by others applies to the educational machine at least as much as to any other segment of society, and perhaps more so. Some very great teachers and researchers may perhaps be unique and irreplaceable, but the average professor and schoolmaster can be replaced from outside the teaching profession with the greatest of ease and often with little, if any, loss.

What are the implications of all this for the society and for its members? The employability, dignity, security and self-respect of individuals, typically, and for the majority of men now hinges on their *education*; and the limits of the culture within which they were educated are also the limits of the world within which they can, morally and professionally, breathe. A man's education is by far his most precious investment, and in effect confers his identity on him. Modern man is not loyal to a monarch or a land or a faith, whatever he may say, but to a culture. And he is, generally speaking, gelded. The Mamluk condition has become universal. No important links bind him to a kin group; nor do they stand between him and a wide, anonymous community of culture.

The obverse of the fact that a school-transmitted culture, not a folk-transmitted one, alone confers his usability and dignity and self-respect on industrial man, is the fact that nothing else can do it for him to any comparable extent. It would be idle to pretend that ancestry, wealth or connections are unimportant in modern society, and that they are not on occasion even sources of pride to their beneficiaries; all the same, advantages secured in these ways are often explained away and are viewed at best ambivalently. It is interesting to ask whether the pervasive work ethic has helped to produce this state of affairs, or whether, on the contrary, it is a reflection of it. Drones and rentiers persist, of course, but they are not very conspicuous, and this in itself is highly significant. It is an important fact that such privilege and idleness as survive are now discreet, tending to prefer obscurity to display, and needing to be uncovered by eager researchers bent on unmasking the inequality which lurks underneath the surface.

It was not so in the past, when idle privilege was proud and brazen, as it persists in being in some surviving agrarian societies, or in societies which continue to uphold the ethos of pre-industrial life. Curiously enough, the notion of conspicuous waste was coined by a work-oriented member of a work-addicted society, Thorsten Veblen, scandalized by what he saw as the survivals from a pre-industrial, predatory age. The egalitarian, work- and career-oriented surface of industrial society is as significant as its inegalitarian hidden depths. Life, after all, is lived largely on the surface, even if important decisions are on occasion made deep down.

The teacher class is now in a sense more important – it is indispensable – and in another sense much less so, having lost its monopoly of access to the cultural wisdom enshrined in scripture. In a society in which everyone is gelded by identification with his professional post and his training, and hardly anyone derives much or any security and support from whatever kin links he may have, the teaching clerics no longer possess any privileged access to administrative posts. When everyone has become a Mamluk, no special mamluk class predominates in the bureaucracy. At long last the bureaucracy can recruit from the population at large, without needing to fear the arrival of dozens of cousins as unwanted attachments of each single new entrant.

Exo-socialization, education proper, is now the virtually universal norm. Men acquire the skills and sensibilities which make them acceptable to their fellows, which fit them to assume places in society, and which make them 'what they are', by being handed over by their kin groups (normally nowadays, of course, their nuclear family) to an educational machine which alone is capable of providing the wide range of training required for the generic cultural base. This educational infrastructure is large, indispensable and expensive. Its maintenance seems to be quite beyond the financial powers of even the biggest and richest organizations within society, such as the big industrial corporations. These often provide their personnel with housing, sports and leisure clubs, and so forth; they do not, except marginally and in special circumstances, provide schooling. (The may subsidize school bills, but that is another matter.) The organization man works and plays with his organization, but his children still go to state or independent schools.

So, on the one hand, this educational infrastructure is too large and costly for any organization other than the biggest one of all, the state. But at the same time, though only the state can sustain so large a burden, only the state is also strong enough to control so important and crucial a function. Culture is no longer merely the adornment, confirmation and legitimation of a social order which was also sustained by harsher and coercive constraints; culture is now the necessary shared medium, the life-blood or perhaps rather the minimal shared atmosphere, within which alone the members of the society can breathe and survive and produce. For a given society, it must be one in which they can *all* breathe and speak and produce; so it must be the *same* culture. Moreover, it must now be a great or high (literate, training-sustained) culture, and it can no longer be a diversified, locality-tied, illiterate little culture or tradition.

But some organism must ensure that this literate and unified culture is indeed being effectively produced, that the educational product is not shoddy and sub-standard. Only the state can do this, and, even in countries in which important parts of the educational machine are in private hands or those of religious organizations, the state does take over quality control in this most important of industries, the manufacture of viable and usable human beings. That shadow-state dating back to the time when European states were not merely fragmented but socially weak – the centralized Church – did put up a fight for the control of education, but it was in the end in-effectual, unless the Church fought on behalf of an inclusive high culture and thereby indirectly on behalf of a new nationalist state.

Time was when education was a cottage industry, when men could be made by a village or clan. That time has now gone, and gone forever. (In education, small can now be beautiful only if it is covertly parasitic on the big.) Exo-socialization, the production and reproduction of men outside the local intimate unit, is now the norm, and must be so. The imperative of exo-socialization is the main clue to why state and culture *must* now be linked, whereas in the past their connection was thin, fortuitous, varied, loose, and often minimal. Now it is unavoidable. That is what nationalism is about, and why we live in an age of nationalism.

4

The Transition to an Age of Nationalism

The most important steps in the argument have now been made. Mankind is irreversibly committed to industrial society, and therefore to a society whose productive system is based on cumulative science and technology. This alone can sustain anything like the present and anticipated number of inhabitants of the planet, and give them a prospect of the kind of standard of living which man now takes for granted, or aspires to take for granted. Agrarian society is no longer an option, for its restoration would simply condemn the great majority of mankind to death by starvation, not to mention dire and unacceptable poverty for the minority of survivors. Hence there is no point in discussing, for any practical purpose, the charms and the horrors of the cultural and political accompaniments of the agrarian age: they are simply not available. We do not properly understand the range of options available to industrial society, and perhaps we never shall; but we understand some of its essential concomitants. The kind of cultural homogeneity demanded by nationalism is one of them, and we had better make our peace with it. It is not the case, as Elie Kedourie claims,[1] that nationalism imposes homogeneity; it is rather that a homogeneity imposed by objective, inescapable imperative eventually appears on the surface in the form of nationalism.

Most of mankind enters the industrial age from the agrarian stage. (The tiny minority which enters it directly from the pre-agrarian condition does not affect the argument, and the same points apply to it.) The social organization of agrarian society, however, is not at all favourable to the

[1] Kedourie 1960.

nationalist principle, to the convergence of political and cultural units, and to the homogeneity and school-transmitted nature of culture within each political unit. On the contrary, as in medieval Europe, it generates political units which are either smaller or much larger than cultural boundaries would indicate; only very occasionally, by accident, it produced a dynastic state which corresponded, more or less, with a language and a culture, as eventually happened on Europe's Atlantic seabord. (The fit was never very close. Culture in agrarian society is much more pluralistic than its empires, and generally much broader than its small participatory social units.)

All this being so, the age of transition to industrialism was bound, according to our model, also to be an age of nationalism, a period of turbulent readjustment, in which either political boundaries, or cultural ones, or both, were being modified, so as to satisfy the new nationalist imperative which now, for the first time, was making itself felt. Because rulers do not surrender territory gladly (and every change of a political boundary must make someone a loser), because changing one's culture is very frequently a most painful experience, and moreover, because there were rival cultures struggling to capture the souls of men, just as there were rival centres of political authority striving to suborn men and capture territory: given all this, it immediately follows from our model that this period of transition was bound to be violent and conflict-ridden. Actual historical facts fully confirm these expectations.

Nevertheless, it would not be correct to proceed by simply working out the implications of the implementation of the nationalist imperative for agrarian society. Industrial society did not arrive on the scene by divine fiat. It was itself the fruit of developments within one particular agrarian society, and these developments were not devoid of their own turbulence. When it then conquered the rest of the world, neither this global colonization, nor the abandonment of empire by those who had been carried forward on the wave of industrial supremacy but eventually lost their monopoly of it, were peaceful developments. All this means that in actual history the effects of nationalism tend to be conflated with the other consequences of industrialism. Though nationalism is indeed an effect of industrial social organization, it is not the *only* effect of the imposition of this new social form, and hence it is necessary to disentangle it from those other developments.

The problem is illustrated by the fascinating relationship between the Reformation and nationalism. The stress of the Reformation on literacy and scripturalism, its onslaught on a monopolistic priesthood (or, as

Weber clearly saw, its universalization rather than abolition of priesthood), its individualism and links with mobile urban populations, all make it a kind of harbinger of social features and attitudes which, according to our model, produce the nationalist age. The role of Protestantism in helping to bring about the industrial world is an enormous, complex and contentious topic; and there is not much point in doing more than cursorily alluding to it here. But in parts of the globe in which both industrialism and nationalism came later and under external impact, the full relationship of Protestant-type attitudes and nationalism is yet to be properly explored.

This relationship is perhaps the most conspicuous in Islam. The cultural history of the Arab world and of many other Muslim lands during the past hundred years is largely the story of the advance and victory of Reformism, a kind of Islamic Protestantism with a heavy stress on scripturalism and above all a sustained hostility to spiritual brokerage, to the local middlemen between man and God (and, in practice, between diverse groups of men), who had become so very prominent in pre-modern Islam. The history of this movement and that of modern Arab (and other) nationalisms can hardly be separated from each other. Islam always had an inbuilt proclivity or potential for this kind of 'reformed' version of the faith, and had been seduced away from it, presumably, by the social need of autonomous rural groups for the incarnated, personalized location of sanctity which is invaluable for local mediation purposes. Under modern conditions its capacity to be a more abstract faith, presiding over an anonymous community of equal believers, could reassert itself.

But even religions which might be thought to have had little inherent potential for such 'protestant' interpretation, could nonetheless be turned in that direction during the age when the drives to industrialism and to nationalism were making their impact. Formally speaking, one would not expect Shintoism to have any marked resemblance to, say, English nonconformity. Nevertheless, during the Japanese modernization drive, it was the sober, orderly, as it were Quaker elements in it (which evidently can be found or imposed anywhere if one tries hard enough) which were stressed to the detriment of any ecstatic elements and any undue private familiarity with the sacred.[2] Had ancient Greece survived into the modern age, Dionysiac cults might have assumed a more sober garb as Hellas lurched forward along the path of development.

---

[2] Personal communication from Ronald Dore.

Apart from the links between the Protestant and nationalist ethos, there are the direct consequences of industrialization itself. The general and pervasive consequences of an established industrial order have already been discussed, in connection with our general model linking the industrial division of labour with the implementation of the nationalist principle. But certain specific consequences of early industrialization which do not generally persist later nevertheless have a significant role to play. Early industrialism means population explosion, rapid urbanization, labour migration, and also the economic and political penetration of previously more or less inward-turned communities, by a global economy and a centralizing polity. It means that the at least relatively stable and insulated Babel system of traditional agrarian communities, each inward-turned, kept separate by geography sideways, and by an enormous social distance upwards, is replaced by quite a new kind of Babel, with new cultural boundaries that are not stable but in constant and dramatic movement, and which are seldom hallowed by any kind of custom.

There is also a link between nationalism and the processes of colonialism, imperialism and de-colonization. The emergence of industrial society in Western Europe had as its consequence the virtual conquest of the entire world by European powers, and sometimes by European settler populations. In effect the whole of Africa, America, Oceania, and very large parts of Asia came under European domination; and the parts of Asia which escaped this fate were often under strong indirect influence. This global conquest was, as conquests go, rather unusual. Normally, political empire is the reward of a military orientation and dedication. It is perpetrated by societies strongly committed to warfare, either because, let us say, their tribal form of life includes an automatic military training, or because they possess a leading stratum committed to it, or for some such similar reason. Moreover, the activity of conquest is arduous and takes up a large part of the energy of the conquering group.

None of this was true of the European conquest of the world. It was eventually carried out and completed by nations increasingly oriented towards industry and trade, not by a militaristic machine, nor by a swarm of temporarily cohesive tribesmen. It was achieved without any total preoccupation with the process on the part of the conqueror nations. The point made about the English, that they acquired their Empire in a state of absence of mind, can to some extent be generalized. (The English also, most laudably, lost the Empire with a similar lack of attention.) When Europe was conquering and dominating the world, it had, on the whole, other, more pressing and internal things to occupy its attention. It did not even pay the conquered nations the compliment of being specially interested in the conquest. A few untypical periods of self-conscious and vainglorious imperialism apart, and disregarding the early conquest of Latin America, which was inspired by good old-fashioned noncommercial rapacity, that was how it was. The conquest had not been planned, and was the fruit of economic and technological superiority, and not of a military orientation.

With the diffusion of this technological and economic might, the balance of power changed, and between about 1905 and 1960 the pluralistic European empire was lost or voluntarily abandoned. Once again, the specific circumstances of all this cannot be ignored; even if the core or essence of nationalism flows from the general, abstractly formulable premisses which were initially laid out, nevertheless the specific forms of nationalist phenomena are obviously affected by these circumstances.

A Note on the Weakness of Nationalism

It is customary to comment on the strength of nationalism. This is an important mistake, though readily understandable since, whenever nationalism has taken root, it has tended to prevail with ease over other modern ideologies.

Nevertheless, the clue to the understanding of nationalism is its weakness at least as much as its strength. It was the dog who failed to bark who provided the vital clue for Sherlock Holmes. The numbers of potential nationalisms which failed to bark is far, far larger than those which did, though *they* have captured all our attention.

We have already insisted on the dormant nature of this allegedly powerful monster during the pre-industrial age. But even within the age of nationalism, there is a further important sense in which nationalism remains astonishingly feeble. Nationalism has been defined, in effect, as the striving to make culture and polity congruent, to endow a culture with its own political roof, and not more than one roof at that. Culture, an elusive concept, was deliberately left undefined. But an at least provisionally acceptable criterion of culture might be language, as at least a sufficient, if not a necessary touchstone of it. Allow for a moment a difference of language to entail a difference of culture (though not necessarily the reverse).

If this is granted, at least temporarily, certain consequences follow. I have heard the number of languages on earth estimated at around 8,000.

The figure can no doubt be increased by counting dialects separately. If we allow the 'precedent' argument, this becomes legitimate: if a kind of differential which in some places defines a nationalism is allowed to engender a 'potential nationalism' wherever else a similar difference is found, then the number of potential nationalisms increases sharply. For instance, diverse Slavonic, Teutonic and Romance languages are in fact often no further apart than are the mere dialects within what are elsewhere conventionally seen as unitary languages. Slav languages, for instance, are probably closer to each other than are the various forms of colloquial Arabic, allegedly a single language.

The 'precedent' argument can also generate potential nationalisms by analogies invoking factors other than language. For instance, Scottish nationalism indisputably exists. (It may indeed be held to contradict my model.) It ignores language (which would condemn some Scots to Irish nationalism, and the rest to English nationalism), invoking instead a shared historical experience. Yet if such additional links be allowed to count (as long as they don't contradict the requirement of my model, that they can serve as a base for an *eventually* homogeneous, internally mobile culture/polity with one educational machine servicing that culture under the surveillance of that polity), then the number of potential nationalisms goes up even higher.

However, let us be content with the figure of 8,000, once given to me by a linguist as a rough number of languages based on what was no doubt rather an arbitrary estimate of language alone. The number of states in the world at present is some figure of the order of 200. To this figure one may add all the irredentist nationalisms, which have not yet attained their state (and perhaps never will), but which are struggling in that direction and thus have a legitimate claim to be counted among actual, and not merely potential, nationalisms. On the other hand, one must also subtract all those states which have come into being without the benefit of the blessing of nationalist endorsement, and which do not satisfy the nationalist criteria of political legitimacy, and indeed defy them; for instance, all the diverse mini-states dotted about the globe as survivals of a pre-nationalist age, and sometimes brought forth as concessions to geographical accident or political compromise. Once all these had been subtracted, the resulting figure would again, presumably, not be too far above 200. But let us, for the sake of charity, pretend that we have four times that number of reasonably effective nationalisms on earth, in other words, 800 of them. I believe this to be considerably larger than the facts would justify, but let it pass.

This rough calculation still gives us only *one* effective nationalism for *ten* potential ones! And this surprising ratio, depressing presumably for any enthusiastic pan-nationalist, if such a person exists, could be made much larger if the 'precedent' argument were applied to the full to determine the number of potential nationalisms, and if the criteria of entry into the class of effective nationalisms were made at all stringent.

What is one to conclude from this? That for every single nationalism which has so far raised its ugly head, nine others are still waiting in the wings? That all the bomb-throwing, martyrdoms, exchange of populations, and worse, which have so far beset humanity, are still to be repeated tenfold?

I think not. For every effective nationalism, there are *n* potential ones, groups defined either by shared culture inherited from the agrarian world or by some other link (on the 'precedent' principle) which *could* give hope of establishing a homogeneous industrial community, but which nevertheless do not bother to struggle, which fail to activate their potential nationalism, which do not even try.

So it seems that the urge to make mutual cultural substitutability the basis of the state is not so powerful after all. The members of *some* groups do indeed feel it, but members of most groups, with analogous claims, evidently do not.

To explain this, we must return to the accusation made against nationalism: that it insists on imposing homogeneity on the populations unfortunate enough to fall under the sway of authorities possessed by the nationalist ideology. The assumption underlying this accusation is that traditional, ideologically uninfected authorities, such as the Ottoman Turks, had kept the peace and extracted taxes, but otherwise tolerated, and been indeed profoundly indifferent to, the diversity of faiths and cultures which they governed. By contrast, their gunman successors seem incapable of resting in peace till they have imposed the nationalist principle of *cuius regio, eius lingua*. They do not want merely a fiscal surplus and obedience. They thirst after the cultural and linguistic souls of their subjects.

This accusation must be stood on its head. It is not the case that nationalism imposes homogeneity out of a wilful cultural *Machtbedürfniss*; it is the objective need for homogeneity which is reflected in nationalism. If it is the case that a modern industrial state can only function with a mobile, literate, culturally standardized, interchangeable population, as we have argued, then the illiterate, half-starved populations sucked from their erstwhile rural cultural ghettoes into the melting pots of shanty-towns yearn for incorporation into some one of those cultural pools which already has, or looks as if it might acquire, a state of its own, with the subsequent promise of full cultural citizenship, access to primary schools, employment, and all. Often, these alienated, uprooted, wandering populations may vacillate between diverse options, and they may often come to a provisional rest at one or another temporary and transitional cultural resting place.

But there are some options which they will refrain from trying to take up. They will hesitate about trying to enter cultural pools within which they know themselves to be spurned; or rather, within which they expect to *continue* to be spurned. Poor newcomers are, of course, almost always spurned. The question is whether they will continue to be slighted, and whether the same fate will await their children. This will depend on whether the newly arrived and hence least privileged stratum possesses traits which its members and their offspring cannot shed, and which will continue to identify them: genetically transmitted or deeply engrained religious-cultural habits are impossible or difficult to drop.

The alienated victims of early industrialism are unlikely to be tempted by cultural pools that are very small – a language spoken by a couple of villages offers few prospects – or very diffused or lacking in any literary traditions or personnel capable of carrying skills, and so on. They require cultural pools which are large, and/or have a good historic base, or intellectual personnel well equipped to propagate the culture in question. It is impossible to pick out any single qualification, or set of qualifications, which will either guarantee the success as a nationalist catalyst of the culture endowed with it (or them), or which on the contrary will ensure its failure. Size, historicity, reasonably compact territory, a capable and energetic intellectual class: all these will obviously help; but no single one is necessary, and it is doubtful whether any firm predictive generalization can be established in these terms. That the principle of nationalism will be operative can be predicted; just which groupings will emerge as its carriers can be only loosely indicated, for it depends on too many historic contingencies.

Nationalism as such is fated to prevail, but not any one particular nationalism. We know that reasonably homogeneous cultures, each of them with its own political roof, its own political servicing, are becoming the norm, widely implemented but for few exceptions; but we cannot predict just which cultures, with which political roofs, will be blessed by success. On the contrary, the simple calculations made above, concerning the number of cultures or potential nationalisms and concerning the room available for proper national states, clearly shows that most potential nationalisms must either fail, or, more commonly, will refrain from even trying to find political expression.

This is precisely what we do find. Most cultures or potential national groups enter the age of nationalism without even the feeblest effort to benefit from it themselves. The number of groups which in terms of the 'precedent' argument could try to become nations, which could define themselves by the kind of criterion which in some other place does in fact define some real and effective nation, is legion. Yet most of them go meekly to their doom, to see their culture (though not themselves as individuals) slowly disappear, dissolving into the wider culture of some new national state. Most cultures are led to the dustheap of history by industrial civilization without offering any resistance. The linguistic distinctiveness of the Scottish Highlands within Scotland is, of course, incomparably greater than the cultural distinctiveness of Scotland within the UK; but there is no Highland nationalism. Much the same is true of Moroccan Berbers. Dialectal and cultural differences within Germany or Italy are as great as those between recognized Teutonic or Romance languages. Southern Russians differ culturally from Northern Russians, but, unlike Ukrainians, do not translate this into a sense of nationhood.

Does this show that nationalism is, after all, unimportant? Or even that it is an ideological artefact, an invention of febrile thinkers which has mysteriously captured some mysteriously susceptible nations? Not at all. To reach such a conclusion would, ironically, come close to a tacit, oblique acceptance of the nationalist ideologue's most misguided claim: namely, that the 'nations' are there, in the very nature of things, only waiting to be 'awakened' (a favourite nationalist expression and image) from their regrettable slumber, by the nationalist 'awakener'. One would be inferring from the failure of most potential nations ever to 'wake up', from the lack of deep stirrings waiting for reveille, that nationalism was not important after all. Such an inference concedes the social ontology of 'nations', only admitting, with some surprise perhaps, that some of them lack the vigour and vitality needed if they are to fulfil the destiny which history intended for them.

But nationalism is *not* the awakening of an old, latent, dormant force, though that is how it does indeed present itself. It is in reality the consequence of a new form of social organization, based on deeply internalized, education-dependent high cultures, each protected by its own state. It uses some of the pre-existent cultures, generally transforming them in the process, but it cannot possibly use them all. There are too many of them. A viable higher culture-sustaining modern state cannot fall below a certain minimal size (unless in effect parasitic on its neighbours); and there is only room for a limited number of such states on this earth.

The high ratio of determined slumberers, who will not rise and shine and who refuse to be woken, enables us to turn the tables on nationalism-as-seen-by-itself. Nationalism sees itself as a natural and universal ordering of the political life of mankind, only obscured by that long, persistent and mysterious somnolence. As Hegel expressed this vision: 'Nations may have had a long history before they finally reach their destination – that of forming themselves into states.'[3] Hegel immediately goes on to suggest that this pre-state period is really 'pre-historical' (*sic*): so it would seem that on this view the real history of a nation only begins when it acquires its own state. If we invoke the sleeping-beauty nations, neither possessing a state nor feeling the lack of it, against the nationalist doctrine, we tacitly accept its social metaphysic, which sees nations as the bricks of which mankind is made up. Critics of nationalism who denounce the political movement but tacitly accept the existence of nations, do not go far enough. Nations as a natural, God-given way of classifying men, as an inherent though long-delayed political destiny, are a myth; nationalism, which sometimes takes pre-existing cultures and turns them into nations, sometimes invents them, and often obliterates pre-existing cultures: *that* is a reality, for better or worse, and in general an inescapable one. Those who are its historic agents know not what they do, but that is another matter.

But we must not accept the myth. Nations are not inscribed into the nature of things, they do not constitute a political version of the doctrine of natural kinds. Nor were national states the manifest ultimate destiny of ethnic or cultural groups. What do exist are cultures, often subtly grouped, shading into each other, overlapping, intertwined; and there exist, usually but not always, political units of all shapes and sizes. In the past the two did not generally converge. There were good reasons for their failing to do so in many cases. Their rulers established their identity by differentiating themselves downwards, and the ruled micro-communities differentiated themselves laterally from their neighbours grouped in similar units.

But nationalism is not the awakening and assertion of these mythical, supposedly natural and given units. It is, on the contrary, the

---

[3] G.W.F. Hegel, *Lectures on the Philosophy of World History*, transl. H.B. Nisbet (Cambridge: Cambridge University Press, 1975), p. 134.

crystallization of new units, suitable for the conditions now prevailing, though admittedly using as their raw material the cultural, historical and other inheritances from the pre-nationalist world. This force – the drive towards new units constructed on the principles corresponding to the new division of labour – is indeed very strong, though it is not the only force in the modern world, nor altogether irresistible. In most cases it prevails, and above all, it determines the *norm* for the legitimacy of political units in the modern world: most of them must satisfy the imperatives of nationalism, as described. It sets the accepted standard, even if it does not prevail totally and universally, and some deviant cases do succeed in defying the norm.

The ambiguity of the question – is nationalism strong or not? – arises from this: nationalism sees and presents itself as the affirmation of each and every 'nationality'; and these alleged entities are supposed just to be there, like Mount Everest, since long ago, antedating the age of nationalism. So, ironically, in its own terms nationalism is astonishingly weak. Most of the potential nations, the latent differentiable communities which could claim to be nations by criteria analogous to those which somewhere else have succeeded, fail altogether even to raise their claim, let alone press it effectively and make it good. If, on the other hand, one interprets nationalism in the manner which I hold to be correct, and which indeed contradicts and offends its own self-image, then the conclusion must be that it is a very strong force, though not perhaps a unique or irresistible one.

Wild and Garden Cultures

One way of approaching the central issue is this. Cultures, like plants, can be divided into savage and cultivated varieties. The savage kinds are produced and reproduce themselves spontaneously, as parts of the life of men. No community is without some shared system of communication and norms, and the wild systems of this kind (in other words, cultures) reproduce themselves from generation to generation without conscious design, supervision, surveillance or special nutrition.

Cultivated or garden cultures are different, though they have developed from the wild varieties. They possess a complexity and richness, most usually sustained by literacy and by specialized personnel, and would perish if deprived of their distinctive nourishment in the form of specialized institutions of learning with reasonably numerous, full-time and dedicated personnel. During the agrarian epoch of human history the high cultures or great traditions became prominent, important, and in one sense, but one sense only, dominant. Though they could not altogether impose themselves on the totality, or even the majority of the population, nevertheless they generally succeeded in imposing themselves on it as authoritative, even if (or because) they were inaccessible and mysterious. They sometimes strengthened, and sometimes competed with, the centralized state. They could also deputize for that state, when it weakened or disintegrated during times of troubles or a dark age. A church or a ritual system could stand in for the shadow of a past or ghost empire. But the high cultures did not generally define the limits of a political unit, and there are good reasons why, in the agrarian age, they should not have been able to do so.

In the industrial age all this changes. The high cultures come to dominate in quite a new sense. The old doctrines associated with them mostly lose their authority, but the literate idioms and styles of communication they carried become far more effectively authoritative and normative, and, above all, they come to be pervasive and universal in society. In other words, virtually everyone becomes literate, and communicates in an elaborate code, in explicit, fairly 'grammatical' (regularized) sentences, not in context-bound grunts and nods.

But the high culture, newly universalized in the population, now badly needs political support and underpinning. In the agrarian age, it sometimes had this and benefited from it, but at other times it could dispense with political protection, and that was indeed one of its strengths. In a dark age when anarchy prevailed and the king's peace was no longer kept, Christian or Buddhist monasteries, dervish *zawiyas* and Brahmin communities could survive and in some measure keep alive the high culture without benefit of protection by the sword.

Now that the task of the high culture is so much greater and so much more onerous, it cannot dispense with a political infrastructure. As a character in *No Orchids for Miss Blandish* observed, every girl ought to have a husband, preferably her own; and every high culture now wants a state, and preferably its own. Not every wild culture can become a high culture, and those without serious prospects of becoming one tend to bow out without a struggle; they do not engender a nationalism. Those which think they do have a chance – or, if anthropomorphic talk about cultures is to be avoided, those whose human carriers credit them with good prospects – fight it out among themselves for available populations and for the available state-space. This is one kind of nationalist or ethnic conflict. Where existing political boundaries, and those of old or crystallizing high cultures with political aspirations, fail to be in harmony, another kind of conflict so highly characteristic of the age of nationalism breaks out.

Another analogy, in addition to the above botanical one, is available to describe the new situation. Agrarian man can be compared with a natural species which can survive in the natural environment. Industrial man can be compared with an artificially produced or bred species which can no longer breathe effectively in the nature-given atmosphere, but can only function effectively and survive in a new, specially blended and artificially sustained air or medium. Hence he lives in specially bounded and constructed units, a kind of giant aquarium or breathing chamber. But these chambers need to be erected and serviced. The maintenance of the life-giving and life-preserving air or liquid within each of these giant receptacles is not automatic. It requires a specialized plant. The name for this plant is a national educational and communications system. Its only effective keeper and protector is the state.

It would not in principle be impossible to have a single such cultural/educational goldfish bowl for the entire globe, sustained by a single political authority and a single educational system. In the long run this may yet come to pass. But in the meantime, and for very good reasons yet to be discussed, the global norm is a set of discontinuous breathing chambers or aquaria, each with its own proprietary, not properly interchangeable, medium or atmosphere. They do share some general traits. The formula for the medium of the fully developed industrial goldfish bowls is fairly similar in type, though it is rich in relatively superficial, but deliberately stressed, brand-differentiating characteristics.

There are some good and obvious reasons for this new pluralism, which will be explored further. The industrial age inherited both the political units and the cultures, high and low, of the preceding age. There was no reason why they should all suddenly fuse into a single one, and there were good reasons why they should *not*: industrialism, in other words the type of production or of the division of labour which makes these homogeneous breathing tanks imperative, did not arrive simultaneously in all parts of the world, nor in the same manner. The differential timing of its arrival divided humanity into rival groups very effectively. These differences in arrival-time of industrialism in various communities became acute if they could utilize some cultural, genetic or similar differentiae, left behind by the agrarian world. The dating of 'development' constitutes a crucial political diacritical mark, if it can seize upon some cultural difference inherited from the agrarian age, and use it as its token.

The process of industrialization took place in successive phases and in different conditions, and engendered various new rivalries, with new gains and losses to be made and avoided. Internationalism was often predicted by the prophets and commentators of the industrial age, both on the left and on the right, but the very opposite came to pass: the age of nationalism.

5

What is a Nation?

We are now at last in a position to attempt some kind of plausible answer to this question. Initially there were two especially promising candidates for the construction of a theory of nationality: will and culture. Obviously, each of them is important and relevant; but, just as obviously, neither is remotely adequate. It is instructive to consider why this is so.

No doubt will or consent constitutes an important factor in the formation of most groups, large and small. Mankind has always been organized in groups, of all kinds of shapes and sizes, sometimes sharply defined and sometimes loose, sometimes neatly nested and sometimes overlapping or intertwined. The variety of these possibilities, and of the principles on which the groups were recruited and maintained, is endless. But two generic agents or catalysts of group formation and maintenance are obviously crucial: will, voluntary adherence and identification, loyalty, solidarity, on the one hand; and fear, coercion, compulsion, on the other. These two possibilities constitute extreme poles along a kind of spectrum. A few communities may be based exclusively or very predominantly on one or the other, but they must be rare. Most persisting groups are based on a mixture of loyalty and identification (on *willed* adherence), and of extraneous incentives, positive or negative, on hopes and fears.

If we define nations as groups which *will* themselves to persist as communities,[1] the definition-net that we have cast into the sea will bring forth far too rich a catch. The haul which we shall have trawled in will indeed

[1] Ernest Renan, 'Qu'est-ce qu'une Nation', republished in *Ernest Renan et l'Allemagne*, Textes receuillis et commentés par Emile Bure (New York: Brentano's), 1945.

include the communities we may easily recognize as effective and cohesive nations: these genuine nations do in effect will themselves to be such, and their life may indeed constitute a kind of continuous, informal, ever self-reaffirming plebiscite. But (unfortunately for this definition) the same also applies to many other clubs, conspiracies, gangs, teams, parties, not to mention the many numerous communities and associations of the pre-industrial age which were not recruited and defined according to the nationalist principle and which defy it. Will, consent, identification, were not ever absent from the human scene, even though they were (and continue to be) also accompanied by calculation, fear and interest. (It is an interesting and moot question whether sheer inertia, the persistence of aggregates and combinations, is to be counted as tacit consent or as something else.)

The tacit self-identification has operated on behalf of all kinds of groupings, larger or smaller than nations, or cutting across them, or defined horizontally or in other ways. In brief, even if will were the basis of a nation (to paraphrase an idealist definition of the state), it is also the basis of so much else, that we cannot possibly define the nation in this manner. It is only because, in the modern, nationalist age, national units are the *preferred*, favoured objects of identification and willed adherence, that the definition seems tempting, because those other kinds of group are now so easily forgotten. Those who take the tacit assumptions of nationalism for granted erroneously also credit them to humanity at large, in any age. But a definition tied to the assumptions and conditions of one age (and even then constituting an exaggeration), cannot usefully be used to help to explain the *emergence* of that age.

Any definition of nations in terms of shared culture is another net which brings in far too rich a catch. Human history is and continues to be well endowed with cultural differentiations. Cultural boundaries are sometimes sharp and sometimes fuzzy; the patterns are sometimes bold and simple and sometimes tortuous and complex. For all the reasons we have stressed so much, this richness of differentiation does not, and indeed cannot, normally or generally converge either with the boundaries of political units (the jurisdictions of effective authorities) or with the boundaries of units blessed by the democratic sacraments of consent and will. The agrarian world simply could not be so neat. The industrial world tends to become so, or at least to approximate to such simplicity; but that is another matter, and there are now special factors making it so.

The establishment of pervasive high cultures (standardized, literacy- and education-based systems of communication), a process rapidly gathering pace throughout the world, has made it seem, to anyone too deeply immersed in our contemporary assumptions, that nationality may be definable in terms of shared culture. Nowadays people can live only in units defined by a shared culture, and internally mobile and fluid. Genuine cultural pluralism ceases to be viable under current conditions. But a little bit of historical awareness or sociological sophistication should dispel the illusion that this was always so. Culturally plural societies often worked well in the past: so well, in fact, that cultural plurality was sometimes invented where it was previously lacking.

If, for such cogent reasons, these two apparently promising paths towards the definition of nationality are barred, is there another way?

The great, but valid, paradox is this: nations can be defined only in terms of the age of nationalism, rather than, as you might expect, the other way round. It is not the case that the 'age of nationalism' is a mere summation of the awakening and political self-assertion of this, that, or the other nation. Rather, when general social conditions make for standardized, homogeneous, centrally sustained high cultures, pervading entire populations and not just elite minorities, a situation arises in which well-defined educationally sanctioned and unified cultures constitute very nearly the only kind of unit with which men willingly and often ardently identify. The cultures now seem to be the natural repositories of political legitimacy. Only *then* does it come to appear that any defiance of their boundaries by political units constitutes a scandal.

Under these conditions, though under these conditions *only*, nations can indeed be defined in terms both of will and of culture, and indeed in terms of the convergence of them both with political units. In these conditions, men will to be politically united with all those, and only those, who share their culture. Polities then will to extend their boundaries to the limits of their cultures, and to protect and impose their culture with the boundaries of their power. The fusion of will, culture and polity becomes the norm, and one not easily or frequently defied. (Once, it had been almost universally defied, with impunity, and had indeed passed unnoticed and undiscussed.) These conditions do not define the human situation as such, but merely its industrial variant.

It is nationalism which engenders nations, and not the other way round. Admittedly, nationalism uses the pre-existing, historically inherited proliferation of cultures or cultural wealth, though it uses them very selectively, and it most often transforms them radically. Dead languages can be revived, traditions invented, quite fictitious pristine purities restored. But this culturally creative, fanciful, positively inventive aspect of nationalist ardour ought not to allow anyone to conclude, erroneously, that nationalism is a contingent, artificial, ideological invention, which might not have happened, if only those damned busybody interfering European thinkers, not content to leave well alone, had not concocted it and fatefully injected it into the bloodstream of otherwise viable political communities. The cultural shreds and patches used by nationalism are often arbitrary historical inventions. Any old shred and patch would have served as well. But in no way does it follow that the principle of nationalism itself, as opposed to the avatars it happens to pick up for its incarnations, is itself in the least contingent and accidental.

Nothing could be further from the truth than such a supposition. Nationalism is not what it seems, and above all it is not what it seems to itself. The cultures it claims to defend and revive are often its own inventions, or are modified out of all recognition. Nonetheless the nationalist principle as such, as distinct from each of its specific forms, and from the individually distinctive nonsense which it may preach, has very very deep roots in our shared current condition, is not at all contingent, and will not easily be denied.

Durkheim taught that in religious worship society adores its own camouflaged image. In a nationalist age, societies worship themselves brazenly and openly, spurning the camouflage. At Nuremberg, Nazi Germany did not worship itself by pretending to worship God or even Wotan; it overtly worshipped itself. In milder but just as significant form, enlightened modernist theologians do not believe, or even take much interest in, the doctrines of their faith which had meant so much to their predecessors. They treat them with a kind of comic auto-functionalism, as valid simply and only as the conceptual and ritual tools by means of which a social tradition affirms its values, continuity and solidarity, and they systematically obscure and play down the difference between such a tacitly reductionist 'faith', and the real thing which had preceded it and had played such a crucial part in earlier European history, a part which could never have been played by the unrecognizably diluted, watered-down current versions.

But the fact that social self-worship, whether virulent and violent or gentle and evasive, is now an openly avowed collective self-worship, rather than a means of covertly revering society through the image of God, as Durkheim insisted, does not mean that the current style is any more veridical than that of a Durkheimiam age. The community may no longer be seen through the prism of the divine, but nationalism has its own amnesias and selections which, even when they may be severely secular, can be profoundly distorting and deceptive.

The basic deception and self-deception practised by nationalism is this: nationalism is, essentially, the general imposition of a high culture on society, where previously low cultures had taken up the lives of the majority, and in some cases of the totality, of the population. It means that generalized diffusion of a school-mediated, academy-supervised idiom, codified for the requirements of reasonably precise bureaucratic and technological communication. It is the establishment of an anonymous, impersonal society, with mutually substitutable atomized individuals, held together above all by a shared culture of this kind, in place of a previous complex structure of local groups, sustained by folk cultures reproduced locally and idiosyncratically by the micro-groups themselves. That is what *really* happens.

But this is the very opposite of what nationalism affirms and what nationalists fervently believe. Nationalism usually conquers in the name of a putative folk culture. Its symbolism is drawn from the healthy, pristine, vigorous life of the peasants, of the *Volk*, the *narod*. There is a certain element of truth in the nationalist self-presentation when the *narod* or *Volk* is ruled by officials of another, an alien high culture, whose oppression must be resisted first by a cultural revival and reaffirmation, and eventually by a war of national liberation. If the nationalism prospers it eliminates the alien high culture, but it does not then replace it by the old local low culture; it revives, or invents, a local high (literate, specialist-transmitted) culture of its own, though admittedly one which will have some links with the earlier local folk styles and dialects. But it was the great ladies at the Budapest Opera who really went to town in peasant dresses, or dresses claimed to be such. At the present time in the Soviet Union the consumers of 'ethnic' gramophone records are not the remaining ethnic rural population, but the newly urbanized, apartment-dwelling, educated and multi-lingual population,[2] who like to express their real or imagined sentiments and roots, and who will no doubt indulge in as much nationalist behaviour as the political situation may allow.

So a sociological self-deception, a vision of reality through a prism of illusion, still persists, but it is not the same as that which was analysed by Durkheim. Society no longer worships itself through religious symbols; a modern, streamlined, on-wheels high culture celebrates itself in

[2] Bromley 1975.

song and dance, which it borrows (stylizing it in the process) from a folk culture which it fondly believes itself to be perpetuating, defending and reaffirming.

The Course of True Nationalism Never did Run Smooth

A characteristic scenario of the evolution of a nationalism – and we shall have cause to return to this kind of scenario – ran something like this. The Ruritanians were a peasant population speaking a group of related and more or less mutually intelligible dialects, and inhabiting a series of discontinuous but not very much separated pockets within the lands of the Empire of Megalomania. The Ruritanian language, or rather the dialects which could be held to compose it, was not really spoken by anyone other than these peasants. The aristocracy and officialdom spoke the language of the Megalomanian court, which happened to belong to a language group different from the one of which the Ruritanian dialects were an offshoot.

Most, but not all, Ruritanian peasants belonged to a church whose liturgy was taken from another linguistic group again, and many of the priests, especially higher up in the hierarchy, spoke a language which was a modern vernacular version of the liturgical language of this creed, and which was also very far removed from Ruritanian. The petty traders of the small towns serving the Ruritanian countryside were drawn from a different ethnic group and religion still, and one heartily detested by the Ruritanian peasantry.

In the past the Ruritanian peasants had had many griefs, movingly and beautifully recorded in their lament-songs (painstakingly collected by village schoolmasters late in the nineteenth century, and made well known to the international musical public by the compositions of the great Ruritanian national composer L.). The pitiful oppression of the Ruritanian peasantry provoked, in the eighteenth century, the guerrilla resistance led by the famous Ruritanian social bandit K., whose deeds are said still to persist in the local folk memory, not to mention several novels and two films, one of them produced by the national artist Z., under highest auspices, soon after the promulgation of the Popular Socialist Republic of Ruritania.

Honesty compels one to admit that the social bandit was captured by his own compatriots, and that the tribunal which condemned him to a painful death had as its president another compatriot. Furthermore, shortly after Ruritania first attained independence, a circular passed between its Ministries of the Interior, Justice and Education, considering whether it might not now be more politic to celebrate the village defence units which had opposed the social bandit and his gangs, rather than the said social bandit himself, in the interest of not encouraging opposition to the police.

A careful analysis of the folk songs so painstakingly collected in the nineteenth century, and now incorporated in the repertoire of the Ruritanian youth, camping and sports movement, does not disclose much evidence of any serious discontent on the part of the peasantry with their linguistic and cultural situation, however grieved they were by other, more earthy matters. On the contrary, such awareness as there is of linguistic pluralism within the lyrics of the songs is ironic, jocular and good-humoured, and consists in part of bilingual puns, sometimes in questionable taste. It must also be admitted that one of the most moving of these songs – I often sang it by the camp fire at the holiday camp to which I was sent during the summer vacations – celebrates the fate of a shepherd boy, grazing three bullocks on the seigneurial clover (*sic*) near the woods, who was surprised by a group of social bandits, requiring him to surrender his overcoat. Combining reckless folly with lack of political awareness, the shepherd boy refused and was killed. I do not know whether this song has been suitably rewritten since Ruritania went socialist. Anyway, to return to my main theme: though the songs do often contain complaints about the condition of the peasantry, they do not raise the issue of cultural nationalism.

That was yet to come, and presumably post-dates the composition of the said songs. In the nineteenth century a population explosion occurred at the same time as certain other areas of the Empire of Megalomania – but not Ruritania – rapidly industrialized. The Ruritanian peasants were drawn to seek work in the industrially more developed areas, and some secured it, on the dreadful terms prevailing at the time. As backward rustics speaking an obscure and seldom written or taught language, they had a particularly rough deal in the towns to whose slums they had moved. At the same time, some Ruritanian lads destined for the church, and educated in both the court and the liturgical languages, became influenced by the new liberal ideas in the course of their secondary schooling, and shifted to a secular training at the university, ending not as priests but as journalists, teachers and professors. They received encouragement from a few foreign, non-Ruritanian ethnographers, musicologists and historians who had come to explore Ruritania. The continuing labour migration, increasingly widespread elementary education and conscription provided these Ruritanian awakeners with a growing audience.

Of course, it was perfectly possible for the Ruritanians, if they wished to do so (and many did), to assimilate into the dominant language of Megalomania. No genetically transmitted trait, no deep religious custom, differentiated an educated Ruritanian from a similar Megalomanian. In fact, many did assimilate, often without bothering to change their names, and the telephone directory of the old capital of Megalomania (now the Federal Republic of Megalomania) is quite full of Ruritanian names, though often rather comically spelt in the Megalomanian manner, and adapted to Megalomanian phonetic expectations. The point is that after a rather harsh and painful start in the first generation, the life chances of the offspring of the Ruritanian labour migrant were not unduly bad, and probably at least as good (given his willingness to work hard) as those of his non-Ruritanian Megalomanian fellow-citizens. So these offspring shared in the eventual growing prosperity and general embourgeoisement of the region. Hence, as far as individual life chances went, there was perhaps no need for a virulent Ruritanian nationalism.

Nonetheless something of the kind did occur. It would, I think, be quite wrong to attribute conscious calculation to the participants in the movement. Subjectively, one must suppose that they had the motives and feelings which are so vigorously expressed in the literature of the national revival. They deplored the squalor and neglect of their home valleys, while yet also seeing the rustic virtues still to be found in them; they deplored the discrimination to which their co-nationals were subject, and the alienation from their native culture to which they were doomed in the proletarian suburbs of the industrial towns. They preached against these ills, and had the hearing of at least many of their fellows. The manner in which, when the international political situation came to favour it, Ruritania eventually attained independence, is now part of the historical record and need not be repeated here.

There is, one must repeat, no need to assume any conscious long-term calculation of interest on anyone's part. The nationalist intellectuals were full of warm and generous ardour on behalf of the co-nationals. When they donned folk costume and trekked over the hills, composing poems in the forest clearings, they did not also dream of one day becoming powerful bureaucrats, ambassadors and ministers. Likewise, the peasants and workers whom they succeeded in reaching felt resentment at their condition, but had no reveries about plans of industrial development which one day would bring a steel mill (quite useless, as it then turned out) to the very heart of the Ruritanian valleys, thus totally ruining quite a sizeable area of surrounding arable land and pasture. It would be genuinely wrong to try to reduce these sentiments to calculations of material advantage or of social mobility. The present theory is sometimes travestied as a reduction of national sentiment to calculation of prospects of social promotion. But this is a misrepresentation. In the old days it made no sense to ask whether the peasants loved their own culture: they took it for granted, like the air they breathed, and were not conscious of either. But when labour migration and bureaucratic employment became prominent features within their social horizon, they soon learned the difference between dealing with a co-national, one understanding and sympathizing with their culture, and someone hostile to it. This very concrete experience taught them to be aware of their culture, and to love it (or, indeed, to wish to be rid of it) without any conscious calculation of advantages and prospects of social mobility. In stable self-contained communities culture is often quite invisible, but when mobility and context-free communication come to be of the essence of social life, the culture in which one has been *taught* to communicate becomes the core of one's identity.

So *had* there been such calculation (which there was not) it would, in quite a number of cases (though by no means in all), have been a very sound one. In fact, given the at least relative paucity of Ruritanian intellectuals, those Ruritanians who did have higher qualifications secured much better posts in independent Ruritania than most of them could even have hoped for in Greater Megalomania, where they had to compete with scholastically more developed ethnic groups. As for the peasants and workers, they did not benefit immediately; but the drawing of a political boundary around the newly defined ethnic Ruritania did mean the eventual fostering and protection of industries in the area, and in the end drastically diminished the need for labour migration from it.

What all this amounts to is this: during the early period of industrialization, entrants into the new order who are drawn from cultural and linguistic groups that are distant from those of the more advanced centre, suffer considerable disadvantages which are even greater than those of other economically weak new proletarians who have the advantage of sharing the culture of the political and economic rulers. But the cultural/linguistic distance and capacity to differentiate themselves from others, which is such a handicap for individuals, can be and often is eventually a positive advantage for entire collectivities, or potential collectivities, of these victims of the newly emergent world. It enables them to conceive and express their resentments and discontents in intelligible terms. Ruritanians had previously thought and felt in terms of family unit and village, at most in terms of a valley, and perhaps on occasion in terms of religion. But now, swept into the melting pot of an early industrial development, they had no valley and no village: and sometimes no family. But there *were* other impoverished and exploited individuals, and a lot of them spoke dialects recognizably similar, while most of the better-off spoke something quite alien; and so the new concept of the Ruritanian nation was born of this contrast, with some encouragement from those journalists and teachers. And it was not an illusion: the attainment of some of the objects of the nascent Ruritanian national movement did indeed bring relief of the ills which had helped to engender it. The relief would perhaps have come anyway; but in this national form, it also brought forth a new high culture and its guardian state.

This is one of the two important principles of fission which determine the emergence of new units, when the industrial world with its insulated cultural breathing tanks comes into being. It could be called the principle of barriers to communication, barriers based on previous, pre-industrial cultures; and it operates with special force during the early period of industrialization. The other principle, just as important, could be called that of inhibitors of social entropy; and it deserves separate treatment.

6

Social Entropy and Equality
in Industrial Society

The transition from agrarian to industrial society has a kind of entropy quality, a shift from pattern to systematic randomness. Agrarian society, with its relatively stable specializations, its persisting regional, kin, professional and rank groupings, has a clearly marked social structure. Its elements are ordered, and not distributed at random. Its sub-cultures underscore and fortify these structural differentiations, and they do not by setting up or accentuating cultural difference within it in any way hamper the functioning of the society at large. Quite the contrary. Far from finding such cultural differentiations offensive, the society holds their expression and recognition to be most fitting and appropriate. Respect for them is the very essence of etiquette.

Industrial society is different. Its territorial and work units are *ad hoc*: membership is fluid, has a great turnover, and does not generally engage or commit the loyalty and identity of members. In brief, the old structures are dissipated and largely replaced by an internally random and fluid totality, within which there is not much (certainly when compared with the preceding agrarian society) by way of genuine sub-structures. There is very little in the way of any effective, binding organization at any level between the individual and the total community. This total and ultimate political community thereby acquires a wholly new and very considerable importance, being linked (as it seldom was in the past) both to the state and to the cultural boundary. The *nation* is now supremely important, thanks both to the erosion of sub-groupings and the vastly increased importance of a shared, literary-dependent culture. The state, inevitably, is charged with the maintenance and supervision of an enormous social infrastructure (the cost of which characteristically comes close to one half of the total income of the society). The educational system becomes a very crucial part of it, and the maintenance of the cultural/ linguistic medium now becomes the central role of education. The citizens can only breathe conceptually and operate within that medium, which is co-extensive with the territory of the state and its educational and cultural apparatus, and which needs to be protected, sustained and cherished.

The role of culture is no longer to underscore and make visible and authoritative the structural differentiations within society (even if some of them persist, and even if, as may happen, a few new ones emerge); on the contrary, when on occasion cultural differences do tie in with and reinforce status differences, this is held to be somewhat shameful for the society in question, and an index of partial failure of its educational system. The task with which that system is entrusted is to turn out worthy, loyal and competent members of the total society whose occupancy of posts within it will not be hampered by factional loyalties to sub-groups within the total community; and if some part of the educational system, by default or from surreptitious design, actually produces internal cultural differences and thereby permits or encourages discrimination, this is counted as something of a scandal.

Obstacles to Entropy

All this is only a reformulation of our general theory of the bases of nationalism, of the new role of culture in mobile, educated, anonymous societies. But an important point is brought out by stressing the need for this random-seeming, entropic mobility and distribution of individuals in this kind of society. Within it, though sub-communities are partly eroded, and their moral authority is much weakened, nevertheless people continue to differ in all kinds of ways. People can be categorized as tall and short, as fat and thin, dark and light, and in many other ways. Clearly, there is simply no limit to the number of ways in which people can be classified. Most of the possible classifications will be of no interest whatever. But some of them become socially and politically very important. They are those which I am tempted to call entropy-resistant. A classification is entropy-resistant if it is based on an attribute which has a marked tendency *not* to become, even with the passage of time since the initial establishment of an industrial society, evenly dispersed throughout the entire society. In such an entropy-resistant case, those individuals who are characterized by the trait in question will tend to be concentrated in one part or another of the total society.

Suppose a society contains a certain number of individuals who are, by an accident of heredity, pigmentationally blue; and suppose that, despite the passage of a number of generations since the initial establishment of the new economy, and the official promulgation and enforcement of a policy of *la carrière ouverte aux talents*, most blues stubbornly persist in occupying places either at the top, or at the bottom, of the society in question: in other words, the blues tend to capture either too many, or too few of the advantages available in this society. That would make blueness a social-entropy-resistant trait, in the sense intended.

Note, by the way, that it is always possible to invent traits which, at any given moment, may seem entropy-resistant. It is always possible to invent a concept which will apply only to this or that class of people. But the entropy-resistance of a concept, in this sense, will normally be of interest only if it is a reasonably natural notion, one already in use in the society in question, rather than artificially invented for the present purpose. Then, if it is unevenly distributed in the wider society, trouble may well ensue.

The rest of this argument can now easily be anticipated: entropy-resistant traits constitute a very serious problem for industrial society. Almost the reverse was true of agrarian society. Far from deploring entropy-resistant traits, that kind of society habitually invented them, whenever it found itself insufficiently supplied with this commodity by nature. It liked to suppose that certain categories of men were natural rulers, and that others were natural slaves, and sanctions were deployed – punitive, ideological – to persuade men to conform with these expectations and indeed to internalize them. The society invented dubious human attributes or origins whose main purpose was, precisely, to be entropy-resistant. The religious elite in Muslim tribal lands is often defined and legitimated in terms of descent from the Prophet; status among central Asian tribes is often expressed in terms of descent from Genghis Khan's clan; European aristocracies frequently believe themselves to be descended from a distinct conquering ethnic group.

Entropy-resistance creates fissures, sometimes veritable chasms, in the industrial societies in which it occurs. How does this fissure-proneness differ from that engendered merely by cultural differences and communication problems which take place in early industrial society, and which were discussed in the preceding section?

The two phenomena do have a certain affinity and overlap. But the differences are also important. The differential access to the language/

culture of the more advanced political and economic centre, which hampers natives of more peripheral cultures and impels them and their leaders towards a cultural and eventually political nationalism, is, of course, also an entropy-resistance of a kind. The migrant labourers who do not even speak a dialectal variant of the main state language used by bureaucrats and entrepreneurs, will, for that very reason, be far more likely initially to remain at the bottom of the social hierarchy, and hence incidentally be less able to correct and compensate the disadvantages which haunt them, either for themselves or for their children. On the other hand, when their language (or rather, a standardized and streamlined version of one of its dialects) becomes the educational, bureaucratic and commercial language of a newly independent nationalist state, these particular disadvantages will disappear, and their cultural characteristics will cease to be entropy-resistant.

But it is important to note that in our hypothetical case they could *also* have escaped their handicap by assimilating to the old dominant language and culture; and in fact, many men did take this path. There is no reason to suppose that those who have trodden it are less numerous than those who took the nationalist option. Indeed, many must have taken both paths, successively or simultaneously.[1] For instance, many have become irredentist nationalists on behalf of a culture which was not that of their genuine origins, assimilating first, and then taking up political cudgels to ensure full high culture status, and its own political state roof, for their new culture.

But what differentiates this kind of case, crucially important though it is, from other kinds of entropy-resistance, is this: if all that is really at stake is a communication gap (but crucially linked to general status and economic disadvantage), then this can be remedied by either of the two methods discussed: a successful nationalism, or assimilation; or an overlap of both. But there are forms of entropy-resistance whose fissiparous social consequences cannot be remedied by correcting the communication disadvantage alone. The second option, of assimilation through education, is barred. There is more than a communication barrier involved. If the first option (successful irredentism, in effect) also happens to be closed by the balance of political power, the situation is grave, and will continue to fester.

Failure to communicate, such as arises between entrants from an alien culture into an industrializing area, is one form of entropy-inhibition

[1]   F. Colonna, *Instituteurs Algériens, 1883–1939* (Paris: Presses de la Fondation nationale des sciences politiques, 1975).

(though one which can often easily be overcome in a generation or so); but the obverse does not hold, and not all entropy-inhibitions are due to a mere failure to communicate. Those which are not due to a mere communication failure, and are remediable neither by assimilation into the dominant pool, nor by the creation of a new independent pool using the native medium of the entrants, are correspondingly more tragic. They constitute a problem whose solution is not yet in sight, and which may well be one of the gravest issues that industrial society has to face.

Let us return to our hypothetical case of a pigmentationally blue sub-population within the wider society, and let us suppose that for one reason or another this population is concentrated near the bottom of the social scale. Industrial societies are quite inegalitarian in providing their citizens with a wide variety of social positions, some very much more advantageous than others; but they are also egalitarian in that this system of posts forms a kind of continuum (there are no radical discontinuities along it), and that there is a widespread belief, possibly exaggerated but not wholly devoid of truth, that it is possible to move up and down, and that rigid barriers in the system are illegitimate. Compared at any rate with most agrarian societies, industrial society is astonishingly egalitarian, and there is, in developed industrial society, a marked convergence of life-styles and a great diminution of social distance. But in our hypothetical case of a blue-coloured population, which is concentrated at the bottom, the conjunction of easy identifiability (blue is a conspicuous colour) with the non-random, counter-entropic distribution of this category of people (the blues) has some very unfortunate consequences.

It is safe to assume that *populations* frequently differ in some measure in their innate talents. The supposition that all talents are distributed with absolute equality is about as probable as a land which is totally flat. It is equally obvious that when it comes to the deployment of talents, social factors are far more important than innate endowment. (Some of the populations most closely associated with the achievements of humanity in recent centuries were backward savages not so many generations earlier, though it is unlikely that their genetic equipment could have changed much in the brief period which elapsed between their barbarism and their world-historical prominence – which seems to prove this point.) The whole question does not matter too much, in as far as it is obvious that the spans of ability occurring within given 'ethnic' or 'racial' groups are far greater than the differences between the averages of such diverse groups.

Something very important follows from all this. The blues are concentrated at the bottom, and it may even be that their performance is, on average, inferior to that of groups more randomly distributed. No-one knows whether this is due to genetic differences or to social factors. But one thing is certain: *within* the blue population, there will be many who are much abler, much more fit in terms of whatever criteria of performance may currently be relevant and applied, than very many members of non-blue segments of the total population.

What will now happen, in the situation as described and defined? The association of blueness with low position will have created a prejudice against blues. When those at the bottom appear to be, chromatically or in whatever way you choose, a random sample of the population, then the prejudice against them cannot spread to some other specific trait, for occupancy of the lowest position is not specifically connected with any other trait, *ex hypothesi*. But if so many of those at the bottom are blue, then the prejudice which is engendered among slightly higher strata against those below them by the fear of being pushed downwards, inevitably spreads to blueness. In fact, non-blue groups low down the scale will be specially prone to anti-blue feelings, for they will have precious little else to be proud of, and they will cling to their only and pathetic distinction, non-blueness, with special venom.

However, very many of the blues will be on the way up, in spite of prejudice against them. The concentration of the blues at the bottom is only statistical, and many blues (even if they are themselves but a minority within their own blue sub-population) will, by dint of hard work, ability or luck be on the way up and have achieved a higher position. What happens to them?

We have assumed that blueness is, for one reason or another, ineradicable. So the condition of the ascending blues will be painful and fraught with tension. Whatever their individual merits, to their random non-blue acquaintances and encounters (and it is of the essence of a mobile complex industrial society that so many human contacts are random, fleeting, but nonetheless significant), they will still be the dirty, lazy, poor, ignorant blues; for these traits, or similar ones, are associated with the occupancy of positions low down on the social scale.

In all this, the rising blue is perhaps not much worse off than the rising Ruritanian migrant worker in our previous example; but there is one overwhelmingly important difference. Ruritanian culture can be shed; blueness cannot. We have also assumed that the Ruritanians had a territorial base: there is an area, the Ruritanian heartland, where peasants speaking some version of Ruritanian were in a majority. So, once again, Ruritanians had two ways out: assimilation into Megalomanian language or culture, or the establishment of a glorious independent Ruritania, where their patois would be turned into an official and literary language. Each of the two alternatives has been successfully tried in different places and by different people. *Ex hypothesi*, however, the blues are devoid of the first of these two options. Their give-away blueness stays with them, do what they will. Moreover, Megalomanian culture is old and has a well-established self-image, and blueness is excluded from it.

What about the second option, the establishment of national independence? As a matter of historical and contemporary fact, populations finding themselves in the kind of situation corresponding to those of our blues sometimes do, and sometimes do not, possess a territorial base of their own. In the former case, they thereby do have at least one of the two options available to the Ruritanians, and if it is politically and militarily feasible they may take it. If, however, the hypothetical blues possess no territorial base in which they can plausibly hope to establish an independent blue land, or alternatively, if they do have one, but this blue homeland is, for one reason or another, too exiguous and unattractive to secure the return to it of the blues dispersed in other regions, then the plight of the blues is serious indeed.

In this kind of situation grave sociological obstacles, not easily removable by mere good will and legislation or by political irredentism and activism, block the way to that cultural homogeneity and social entropy which is not merely the norm of advanced industrial society, but also, it seems, a condition of its smooth functioning. Where this systematic entropy-inhibition occurs, it may well constitute one of the gravest dangers that industrial society must face. Conversely, while the blue populations are blocked in both directions, neither smooth assimilation nor independence being easily available to them, some other populations may be doubly blessed. In a federal state, populations such as our hypothetical Ruritanians may simultaneously possess an autonomous Ruritania in which Ruritanian is the official language, and yet also, at the same time, thanks to the small cultural distance between them and other cultures in the federal state, and to the non-identifiability of assimilated Ruritanians, be able to move smoothly, frictionlessly, in an entropic way, in the wider state. It is, I suppose, for Ruritanians to decide whether this double advantage is worth the price they pay; namely, that the Ruritanian canton or federal autonomous republic is not fully independent. Some cases which fit this general description remain within the wider federal state voluntarily, and some have been deprived of this option by force. Quebec would seem to exemplify the first situation; Iboland, in Nigeria, the second.

The question then arises: what are the kinds of attribute in the real world which resemble the 'blueness' of our hypothetical example? Genetically transmitted traits are one specimen of such blueness, but one specimen only; and the other, non-genetic species of it are at least as important. One must also add that not *any* genetically transmitted trait will have the effect of producing a fissure in society. Ginger-headedness, for example, causes some people to be teased as children; and on the other hand, redheads among women are sometimes deemed specially attractive. Moreover, some ethnic groups are said to have a disproportionate number of red-headed members; but despite these facts and/or folk beliefs, red hair does not, all in all, generate conflicts or social problems.

Part of the explanation must be, to use the term previously introduced for this purpose, that red hair is fairly entropic, notwithstanding any alleged ethnic correlation. Physical traits which, though genetic, have no strong historic or geographical associations tend to be entropic; and even if they do mildly correlate with social advantage or disadvantage, this tends to remain socially unperceived. By contrast, in Ruanda and Urundi physical height related to ethnic affiliation and political status in a very marked way, both in fact and in ideology, the conquering pastoralists being taller than the local agriculturalists, and both being taller than the pygmies. But in most other societies, this correlation is loose enough not to become socially significant. Etonians, it appears, are on average taller than others; but tall guardsmen in the ranks are not deemed upper class.

Physical or genetically transmitted traits are but one kind of 'blueness'. What of the others? It is a supremely important and interesting fact that some deeply engrained religious-cultural habits possess a vigour and tenacity which can virtually equal those which are rooted in our genetic constitution. Language and formal doctrinal belief seem less deep rooted and it is easier to shed them; but that cluster of intimate and pervasive values and attitudes which, in the agrarian age, are usually linked to religion (whether or not they are so incorporated in the official high theology of the faith in question) frequently have a limpet-like persistence, and continue to act as a diacritical mark for the populations which carry them. For instance, at the time when Algeria was legally counted as a part of France, the assimilation of Algerian migrant workers in France was not hampered by any physical, genetic difference between, say, a Kabyle and a southern French peasant. The generally impassable fissure between the two populations, precluding an assimilationist solution, was cultural and not physical. The deeply rooted communal conflict in Ulster is not based, obviously, on any communications gap between the two communities, but on an identification with one of two rival local cultures which is so firm as to be comparable to some physical characteristic, even if, in reality, it is socially induced. Terrorist organizations whose nominal doctrine, or rather verbiage, is some kind of loose contemporary revolutionary Marxism, are in fact exclusively recruited from a community once defined by a religious faith, and continuing to be defined by the culture which had been linked to that faith.

A fascinating and profoundly revealing event recently occurred in Yugoslavia: in Bosnia the ex-Muslim population secured at long last, and not without arduous efforts, the right to describe themselves as Muslim, when filling in the 'nationality' slot on the census. This did not mean that they were still believing and practising Muslims, and it meant even less that they were identifying as one nationality with other Muslims or ex-Muslims in Yugoslavia, such as the Albanians of Kosovo. They were Serbo-Croat speakers of Slav ancestry and Muslim cultural background. What they meant was that they could not describe themselves as Serb or as Croat (despite sharing a language with Serbs and Croats), because these identifications carried the implications of *having been* Orthodox or Catholic; and to describe oneself as 'Yugoslav' was too abstract, generic and bloodless.

They preferred to describe themselves as 'Muslim' (and were now at last officially allowed to do so), meaning thereby Bosnian, Slav ex-Muslims who feel as one ethnic group, though not differentiable linguistically from Serbs and Croats, and though the faith which does distinguish them is now a lapsed faith. Justice Oliver Wendell Holmes once observed that to be a gentleman one does not need to know Latin and Greek, but one must have forgotten them. Nowadays, to be a Bosnian Muslim you need not believe that there is no God but God and that Mohamed is his Prophet, but you do need to have lost that faith. The point of transition from faith to culture, to its fusion with ethnicity and eventually with a state, is neatly illustrated by an exchange in that classic study of the role of the military in a developing country, Anton Chekhov's *Three Sisters*:

> *Tuzenbach*: Perhaps you think – this German is getting over-excited. But on my word of honour, I'm Russian. I cannot even speak German. My father is Orthodox.

The Baron, despite his Teutonic name and presumably ancestry, defends his Slav status by reference to his Orthodox religion.

To say this is not to claim that each and every pre-industrial religion will tend to make a new appearance as an ethnic loyalty in the industrial melting-pot. Such a view would be absurd. For one thing, as in the case of languages and of cultural differentiations, the agrarian world is often far too well provided with religions. There were too many of them. Their number was too large, when compared with the number of ethnic groups and national states for which there can possibly be room in the modern world. So they simply could not all survive (even in transmogrified form, as ethnic units), however tenacious they might be. Moreover, as in the case of languages, many of them are not really so very tenacious. It is the high religions, those which are fortified by a script and sustained by special-ized personnel, which sometimes, but by no means always, become the basis of a new collective identity in the industrial world, making the tran-sition, so to speak, from a culture-religion to a culture-state. Thus in the agrarian world, high culture co-exists with low cultures, and needs a church (or at least a clerkly guild) to sustain it. In the industrial world high cultures prevail, but they need a state not a church, and they need a state *each*. That is one way of summing up the emergence of the nation-alist age.

High cultures tend to become the basis of a new nationality (as in Algeria) when before the emergence of nationalism the religion defined fairly closely *all* the under-privileged as against the privileged, even or especially if the under-privileged had no other positive shared character-istic (such as language or common history). There had previously been no Algerian nation prior to the nationalist awakening in this century, as Ferhat Abbas, one of the principal early nationalist leaders in that country, observed. There had been the much wider community of Islam, and a whole set of narrower communities, but nothing corresponding even remotely to the inhabitants of the present national territory. In such a case a new nation is in effect born, defined as the totality of all the adherents of a given faith, within a given territory. (In the case of the Palestinians today, language and culture and a shared predicament, but not religion, seem to be producing a similar crystallization.) To perform the diacritical, nation-defining role, the religion in question may in fact need to trans-form itself totally, as it did in Algeria: in the nineteenth century, Algerian Islam with its reverence for holy lineages was for all practical purposes co-extensive with rural shrine and saint cults. In the twentieth century it repudiated all this and identified with a reformist scripturalism, denying the legitimacy of any saintly mediation between man and God. The shrines had defined tribes and tribal boundaries; the scripturalism could and did define a nation.

Fissures and Barriers

Our general argument might be re-stated as follows. Industrialization engenders a mobile and culturally homogeneous society, which consequently has egalitarian expectations and aspirations, such as had been generally lacking in the previous stable, stratified, dogmatic and absolutist agrarian societies. At the same time, in its early stages, industrial society also engenders very sharp and painful and conspicuous inequality, all the more painful because accompanied by great disturbance, and because those less advantageously placed, in that period, tend to be not only relatively, but also absolutely miserable. In that situation – egalitarian expectation, non-egalitarian reality, misery, and cultural homogeneity already desired but not yet implemented – latent political tension is acute, and becomes actual if it can seize on good symbols, good diacritical marks to separate ruler and ruled, privileged and underprivileged.

Characteristically, it may seize on language, on genetically transmitted traits ('racism'), or on culture alone. It is very strongly impelled in this direction by the fact that in industrializing societies communication and hence culture assumes a new and unprecedented importance. Communication becomes important because of complexity, interdependence and mobility of productive life, within which far more numerous, complex, precise and context-free messages need to be transmitted than had ever been the case before.

Among cultures, it is the ones linked to a high (literate) faith which seem most likely to fill the role of crystallizer of discontent. Local folk faiths and cultures, like minor dialects, are less likely to aspire so high. During the early period of industrialization, of course, low cultures are also liable to be seized on and turned into diacritical markers of the disadvantaged ones, and be used to identify and unite them, if they look politically promising, notably if they define large and territorially more or less compact populations. During that early stage, several contrasts are liable to be super-imposed on privilege and underprivilege: ease of access to the new style of life and its educational precondition, as opposed to hampered access (easy or inhibited communication), a high and low culture.

This is the type of fissure-generation where the lack of actual communication is crucial, because it marks out and highlights an objective difference. Later, when owing to general development the communication barrier and the inequalities are no longer so great, and when a shared industrial style enables people to communicate even across diverse languages, it is rather the persistent unevenly distributed ('counter-entropic') traits which become really crucial, whether they be genetic or deep-cultural. At that stage, the transformation of erstwhile low cultures into a new high one, in the interests of providing a banner for a whole wide category of the underprivileged who may previously have lacked any way of hailing each other and uniting, is no longer quite so probable; the period of acute misery, disorganization, near-starvation, total alienation of the lower strata is over. Resentment is now engendered less by some objectively intolerable condition (for deprivation now is, as the phrase goes, relative); it is now brought about above all by the non-random social distribution of some visible and habitually noticed trait.

The difference between the two stages, early and late, can be put as follows. In the early stage there is a terrible difference between the life chances of the well-off and the starving poor, those who can swim in the new industrial pool and those who are only painfully learning to do so. Even then, the conflict will seldom become acute or escalate indefinitely, contrary to Marxist predictions, unless the privileged and the others can identify themselves and each other culturally, 'ethnically'. But if they can so tell each other apart, then, generally speaking, a new nation (or nations) is born; and it can organize itself around either a high or a previously low culture. If a high culture is not ready-made and available, or has already been taken over by a rival group, why then a low one is transformed into a high one. This is the age of the birth (or allegedly 'rebirth') of nations, and of the transmuting of low cultures into newly literate high ones.

The next stage is different. It is no longer the case that an acute objective social discontent or a sharp social differentiation is seeking out any old cultural differentiation that may be to hand, and will use it if it can to create a new barrier, indeed eventually a new frontier. Now it is only a genuine prior barrier to mobility and equality which will, having inhibited easy identification, engender a new frontier. The difference is considerable.

A Diversity of Focus

Some special cases deserve specific comment. Islamic civilization in the agrarian age conspicuously illustrated our thesis that agrarian societies are *not* prone to use culture to define political units; in other words, that they are not given to being nationalistic. The loose guild of *ulama*, of scholars-lawyers-theologians,[2] who set the tone and morally dominated the traditional Muslim world, was trans-political and trans-ethnic, and not tied to any state (once the Khalifate with its monopolistic pretensions to providing the unique political roof for the entire community had dis-integrated), nor to any 'nation'. The folk Islam of shrine and holy lineage, on the other hand, was sub-ethnic and sub-political (as far as major units, resembling historic and 'national' states, are concerned), serving and rein-forcing instead the vigorous local self-defence and self-administration units (tribes). So Islam was internally divided into a high and a low culture, the two flowing into each other, of course, and intimately related and intertwined, but also periodically erupting into conflict, when 'remembrancers' revived the alleged pristine zeal of the high culture, and united tribesmen in the interests of purification and of their own enrich-ment and political advancement. But the changes produced in this way did not, in the traditional order (though they occurred quite often) produce any deep, fundamental structural change. They only rotated the personnel, they did not fundamentally alter the society.[3]

With the coming of the travail of modernization, things turned out quite differently. We have argued that in general this means, among other things, the replacement of diversified, locality-tied low cultures by stan-dardized, formalized and codified, literacy-carried high cultures. But Islamic society was ever ideally prepared, by an accident of history, for this development. It possessed within itself both a high and low culture. They had the same name, and were not always carefully distinguished, and were often deliberately conflated and fused; they were linked to each other. Both, in the past, could be and were the means of a whole-hearted, passionate identification with a (supposedly unique) Islam, as an absolute, uncompromising and final revelation. Islam had no church perhaps, but the church it did not have was a broad one. In the modern world, the low or folk variant can be and is disavowed, as a corruption, exploited if not actually invented or instigated by the alien colonialist enemy, while the high variant becomes the culture around which a new nationalism can crystallize. This is particularly easy in the case of the one linguistic group whose language is linked to that of the unique revelation; it is also easy in those cases in which the entire nation is identified with

---

[2]   N. Keddie (ed.), *Scholars, Saints and Sufis* (Berkeley, Calif.: University of California Press, 1972); E. Gellner, *Muslim Society* (1981).

[3]   Ibn Khaldun, *The Muqaddimah*, transl. F. Rosenthal (London: Routledge & K. Paul, 1958).

Islam and is surrounded by non-Muslim neighbours (Somalis, Malays); or when the entire discriminated-against population, though not linguistically homogenous, is Muslim and opposed to non-Muslim privileged power-holders (Algeria), or when the nation is habitually defined in terms of one Muslim sect, and its resentment directed against a provocatively secularized and Westernized ruling class and against non-Muslim foreigners (Iran).

The uniqueness of Islam can perhaps be brought out best if we recapitulate our general theme. The agrarian age of mankind is a period in which some can read and most cannot, and the industrial age is one in which all can and must read. In the agrarian age, literate high cultures co-exist with illiterate low or folk cultures. During the period of transition between the two ages, some erstwhile low cultures become new high cultures; and on occasion a new high culture can be invented, re-created by political will and cultural engineering, based on elements drawn from a distant past, and reassembled to create something in effect quite new, as in Israel.

But the high cultures which survive the period of transition cease to be the medium and hallmark of a clerisy or a court and become instead the medium and emblem of a 'nation', and at the same time undergo another interesting transformation. When they were carried by a court or courtly stratum or a clerisy, they tended to be trans-ethnic and even trans-political, and were easily exportable to wherever that court was emulated or that clerisy respected and employed; and on the other hand, they were liable to be closely tied to the usually rigid, dogmatic theology and doctrinal corpus, in terms of which the clerisy in question was defined, and the court legitimated. As is the way of literate ideologies of the agrarian age, that corpus of doctrine had absolutist pretensions, and was reinforced by claiming on its own behalf not merely that it was true (what of that?) but that it was the very *norm* of truth. At the same time it issued virulent imprecations against all heretics and infidels, whose very doubts about the unique manifest truth was evidence of their moral turpitude, of 'corruption on earth', in the vivid phrase used in death sentences by the agrarian-faith-reviving regime at present in control of Iran. These ideologies are like fortresses – *Eine feste Burg ist mein Gott* – which retain all sources of water within their bastion and thus deny them to the enemy. They hold not merely a monopoly of truth (a trivial matter, that), but above all, of the very sources and touch-stones of truth. The wells are all located within the ramparts, and that settles the matter, for the enemy cannot reach them.

This was all very well, and a great advantage to them in the agrarian age, when they only encountered enemies at worst similar to themselves, and often feebler, unsophisticated, unfortified folk religions. The industrial age is based on economic growth. This in turn hinges on cognitive growth, which was ratified (and perhaps even significantly aided) by Cartesian and empiricist philosophies. Their essence was to de-absolutize all substantive conviction about the world, and to subject all assertions, without exception, to neutral scrutiny by criteria ('experience', 'the light of reason') located beyond the bounds and the ramparts of any one belief system. That puts paid to their absolutist pretensions, for they must bow to a judge outside their control. Evidence becomes king, or at least king-maker. The wells of truth are henceforth located in neutral territory, and no one can claim to own them.

That, at any rate, is the purely intellectual, doctrinal aspect of a complex story, the whole of which cannot be pursued here, by which the absolutist high cultures of the agrarian age are obliged to shed their absolutism, and allow the wells of truth to pass into public, neutral control. In brief, the price these high cultures pay for becoming the idiom of entire territorial nations, instead of appertaining to a clerkly stratum only, is that they become secularized. They shed absolutist and cognitive pretensions, and are no longer linked to a doctrine. Spain was one of the most retarded exceptions to this, having retained at a remarkably late date a nationalist regime which incorporated the endorsement of absolutist Catholic claims in its image of the nation. During the earlier and timid stages of Francoist liberalization, the legalization of public Protestant worship was opposed as a kind of provocative disturbance of Spanish unity and identity. An absolute doctrine for all and a high culture for *some*, becomes an absolute culture for *all*, and a doctrine for some. The Church must surrender and dissolve itself if it is to capture the entire society. The Great Tradition must throw off its erstwhile legitimating doctrine, if it is to become the pervasive and universal culture.

In general, what had once been an idiom for some and an obligatory prescribed faith for all, becomes an obligatory idiom for all, and a watered-down, non-serious, Sunday-suit faith for some. That is the generic fate of high cultures, if they survive the great transition. In the classical North-West European case, one may say that the process had two stages: the Reformation universalized the clerisy and unified the vernacular and the liturgy, and the Enlightenment secularized the now universalized clerisy and the now nation-wide linguistic idiom, no longer bound to doctrine or class.

It is interesting to reflect what would have happened in Western Europe had industrialization and all it involves begun during the High Middle Ages, before the development of vernacular literatures and the emergence of what was eventually destined to become the basis of the various national high cultures. There would clearly have been the prospect of a clerkly-led Latin, or perhaps Romance, nationalism, as opposed to the relatively more local nationalisms which did eventually crystallize, secularizing no longer a trans-political clerkly high culture, but a half-clerkly, half-courtly one. Had it all happened earlier, a pan-Romance nationalism would have been as plausible as the pan-Slavism which was taken seriously in the nineteenth century, or the pan-Arab nationalism of the twentieth, which were also based on a shared clerkly high culture, co-existing with enormous differences at the low or folk level.

Islam is precisely in this condition, experiencing a number of transformations simultaneously. The most protestant of the great monotheisms, it is ever Reformation-prone (Islam could indeed be described as Permanent Reformation). One of its many successive self-reformations virtually coincided with the coming of modern Arab nationalism, and can only with great difficulty be disentangled from it. The emergence of the nation and the victory of the reform movement seem parts of one and the same process. The dissolution of the vigorous old local and kin structures, whose strong and sometimes deadly shadows survive as pervasive patronage networks dominating the new centralized political structures, goes hand in hand with the elimination of the saint cults which had ratified the mini-communal organization, and their replacement by a reformed individualist unitarian theology, which leaves the individual believer to relate himself, singly, to one God and one large, anonymous, mediation-free community – all of which is virtually the paradigm of the nationalist requirement.

Other high cultures which make the transition need to pay the price of abandoning their erstwhile doctrinal underpinning and support. The bulk of the doctrines they had carried so long are so utterly absurd, so indefensible in an age of epistemic (evidence-revering) philosophies, that they become an encumbrance rather than the advantage which they had been. They are gladly, willingly shed, or turned into 'symbolic' tokens meant to indicate a link to the past, the continuity of a community over time, and evasively ignored as far as their nominal doctrinal content goes.

Not so with Islam. Islam had been Janus-faced in the agrarian days. One face was adapted to the religiously and socially pluralistic country folk and groupings, the other set for the more fastidious, scholarly, individualist and literate urban schoolmen. Moreover, the dogma made obligatory for the latter was purified, economical, unitarian, sufficiently so to be at least relatively acceptable even in the modern age, when the baroque load carried by its rival on the north shore of the Mediterranean is pretty intolerable, and needs to be surreptitiously toned down and cast away, bit by bit. Little of this underhand purification is required south of the Mediterranean – or rather, the purification had *already* been carried out, loud and clear, in the name of freeing the true faith from ignorant, rural, if not alien-inspired superstition and corruption. Janus has relinquished one of his two faces. So, within the Muslim world, and particularly of course within the Arab part of it (but also among what might be called the Arab-surrogate nations, who happen locally to define themselves as *the* Muslims of a given area), a nationalism based on a generalized anonymous territorial community can perpetuate the specific doctrines previously carried by a clerkly stratum, proudly and without disavowing them. The ideal of the *ulama* comes closer to reality, at least within various nation-size territories, than it had been in the days of the kin-defined fragmentation.

Doctrinal elegance, simplicity, exiguousness, strict unitarianism, without very much in the way of intellectually offensive frills: these helped Islam to survive in the modern world better than do doctrinally more luxuriant faiths. But if that is so, one might well ask why an agrarian ideology such as Confucianism should not have survived even better; for such a belief system was even more firmly centred on rules of morality and the observance of order and hierarchy, and even less concerned with theological or cosmological dogma. Perhaps, however, a strict and emphatic, insistent unitarianism is better here than indifference to doctrine coupled with concern for morality. The moralities and political ethics of agro-literate polities are just a little too brazenly deferential and inegalitarian for a modern taste. This may have made the perpetuation of Confucianism implausible in a modern society, at least under the same name and under the same management.

By contrast, the stress on the pure unitarianism of Islam, jointly with the inevitable ambiguity of its concrete moral and political precepts, could help to create the situation where one and the same faith can legitimate both traditionalist regimes such as Saudi Arabia or Northern Nigeria, and socially radical ones such as Libya, South Yemen or Algeria. The political conjurers could build their patter around the strict theology, while they shuffled the cards dealing with political morality according to their own preference, without attracting too much attention. The unitarianism, the (sometimes painful) forswearing of the solaces of spiritual mediation and middlemen, took the believers' minds away from the intellectual trans-formations, which were turning a faith that had once dealt with the inher-itance of camels into one prescribing or proscribing, as the case might be, the nationalization of oil wealth.

If Islam is unique in that it allows the use of a pre-industrial great tra-dition of a clerisy as the national, socially pervasive idiom and belief of a new-style community, then many of the nationalisms of sub-Saharan Africa are interesting in that they exemplify the opposite extreme: they often neither perpetuate nor invent a local high culture (which could be difficult, indigenous literacy being rather rare in this region), nor do they elevate an erstwhile folk culture into a new, politically sanctioned literate culture, as European nationalisms had often done. Instead, they persist in using an *alien*, European high culture. Sub-Saharan Africa is one of the best, and certainly the most extensive, testing grounds for the attribution of great power to the principle of nationalism, which requires ethnic and political boundaries to converge. Sub-Saharan political boundaries defy this principle almost without exception. Black Africa has inherited from the colonial period a set of frontiers drawn up in total disregard (and gen-erally without the slightest knowledge) of local cultural or ethnic borders.

One of the most interesting and striking features of the postcolonial history of Africa has been that nationalist, irredentist attempts to remedy this state of affairs, though not totally absent, have nevertheless been astonishingly few and feeble. The efforts either to replace the use of European languages as the state administrative medium, or to adjust inter-state boundaries so as to respect ethnicity, have been weak and infrequent. What is the explanation? Is nationalism not a force in black Africa after all?

We have suggested a dichotomy between 'early' or communication-gap nationalisms (in which the additional disadvantage a dislocated ex-rural population incurs through not sharing the dominant culture exac-erbates its resentment over its other, 'objective' deprivations), and a 'late' nationalism, engendered by obstacles other than those of communication. In terms of this important contrast, African nationalism on the whole belongs to the latter or counter-entropic type. At its core we do not find labour migrants maltreated at the factory gate by foremen speaking a different language; what we do find is intellectuals capable of fluent communication, but debarred as a category from positions of real power by a shared distinctive trait: colour. They are united by a shared exclusion, not a shared culture. The phenomena associated with other early and communication-gap types of nationalism are of course not absent, and are often very important. The flashpoint of the South African conflict is obviously the condition of the African industrial proletariat; and the role of the urban lower classes in, for instance, the rise of Nkrumah was conspicuous.

The typical situation created by European domination in Africa was this: effective administrations, political units controlling and maintaining the peace in extensive and well-defined, stable areas, were set up. These administrations were extremely, conspicuously and indeed paradig-matically counter-entropic. The rulers and a few others were white, and everyone else was black. It could hardly have been simpler or more conspicuous. Seldom has there been a political system whose guiding principle was so easily intelligible, so easy to read.

In the traditional agrarian world this could have been counted a positive advantage, a great aid in the avoidance of status-ambiguity and all the ills of obscure, uncertain power-relations which that can bring in its train. It would have augured well for the stability and survival-worthiness of the system. The principle was not alien to Africa, and some indigenous political structures had indeed used variants of it. The Azande were a conquering aristocracy supper-imposed on ethnically distinct subjects. A Fulani aristocracy ruled many of the northern Nigerian city states.

But this was no longer the traditional agrarian order. The Europeans in Africa, though occasionally respectful of local custom and endorsing its authority, were there to set up a market- and trade-oriented, educated ('civilized') and eventually industrial type of society. But, for reasons which we have stressed at length and need not now repeat, industrial or industrializing society is profoundly allergic to counter-entropic institu-tions. Here there was an outstandingly clear, conspicuous example of just that! This was not a case, as in our earlier example, of a category of 'blues' being statistically too frequently located in the lower layers of society, as in the European irredentist nationalisms. Here there was a case of a small number of whites ruling large, occasionally enormous black populations. The nationalism which this engendered was simply the summation of all the blacks, the non-whites of a given historically accidental territory, now unified by the new administrative machinery. The adherents of the new nationalism did not necessarily share any positive traits.

After Independence, in the struggle for control of the newly won states, the contestants generally had their power-base in this or that traditional, pre-existing ethnic group. Nevertheless, the striking fact remains the stability of the ethnicity-defying frontiers that had been arbitrarily drawn up by the colonialists, and the perpetuation of the colonial languages as the media of government and education. It is perhaps too soon to speculate whether these societies will reach the age of internal homogeneity, mobility and generalized education while continuing to use the colonial language, or whether at some point they will brave the ardours of cultural self-transformation involved in modernizing, adapting and imposing one of the indigenous languages. This process has been pioneered, for instance, in Algeria, with its extremely painful 'Arabization', which in practice means imposing a distant literary language on local Arab and Berber dialects.[4] In black Africa, the linguistic indigenization is hampered not merely by the conveniences of the alien language, with its textbooks and international links, and with the heavy time-investment in it on the part of the ruling elite, but also by the local linguistic fragmentation, far more extreme than that which had prevailed in Europe; and by the fact that the selection of any one of the rival local languages would be an affront to all those to whom it is not a native tongue – and this residue generally constitutes a majority, often an overwhelmingly large one.

For these reasons those African ethnic groups that were linked to a literate high culture through conversion to a world religion, Islam or Christianity, were better equipped to develop an effective nationalism than the others. The region in which the struggle between these two faiths had traditionally gone on without a decisive victory for either, the Horn of Africa, is also the area with the best examples of what may be called classical nationalisms. It has been said of the Boers that the only things which really distinguished them from their Bantu enemies, when both were entering South Africa from different directions, was the possession of the Book, the wheel and the gun. In the Horn of Africa both the Amharas and the Somalis possessed both gun and Book (not the same Book, but rival and different editions), and neither bothered greatly with the wheel. Each of these ethnic groups was aided in its use of these two pieces of cultural

---

[4]   Hugh Roberts, 'The Unforeseen Development of the Kabyle Question in Contemporary Algeria', in *Government and Opposition*, 17 (1982), no. 3. The emergent Kabyle nationalism is interesting in that it expresses the feeling of an erstwhile small-holding peasantry which has done well out of urban migration, without losing its rural base. A similar case may be that of the Basques. See Marianne Heiberg, 'Insiders/outsiders: Basque nationalism', in *European Journal of Sociology*, 16 (1975), no. 2.

equipment by its links to other members of the wider religious civilization which habitually used them, and were willing to replenish their stock. Both the Somalis and the Amharas were aided by these bits of equipment in state-formation. The Somalis created a few of those characteristic Muslim formations based on urban trade and tribal pastoral cohesion, brought together by some religious personage; the Amharas created in Ethiopia the one really convincing African specimen of a feudalism, a loose empire with local territorial power-holders, linked to a national Church.

The gun and the Book, with their centralizing potential, enabled these two ethnic groups to dominate the political history of this large region, though neither of them was numerically predominant. Other ethnic groups without the same advantages, even when far more numerous – notable the Oromo (more commonly known as the Galla) – were unable to stand up to them. At the time of the temporarily successful Somali advance against the Ethiopians in the 1970s, it was plausible, and from the Somali viewpoint attractive, to present the Oromo as a kind of human population without a set form, a pre-ethnic raw material, waiting to be turned either into Amharas or into Somalis by the turn of political fortune and religious conversion. This would make sense of their Somalization, should it come to pass. The Oromo were to be seen as an enormous population of Adams and Eves, from whom the apple of ethnicity had as yet been withheld, and who were familiar only with the rudimentary fig leaf of age-set organization. When incorporated in the Amhara state, their local chiefs would become its officials and eventually go Christian and Amhara; but if brought into the Somali sphere, Islamization in the name of the great local saint cults would eventually mean Somalization. Since the Somali defeat in the war, however, the prospects of resisting Amhara domination in the Horn hinge largely on stimulating the various national liberation fronts at long last emerging within the Ethiopian empire, including that of the Oromo, who as the largest group are also emerging as the most important; and hence we are now less likely to hear of their pre-cultural status as ethnic raw material.

The Amhara empire was a prison-house of nations if ever there was one. When the old Emperor was toppled in 1974, the new rulers promptly announced, as new rulers are liable to do, that henceforth all ethnic groups were equal, and indeed free to choose their own destiny. These admirable liberal sentiments were followed fairly soon by a systematic liquidation of intellectuals drawn from the non-Amharic group, a regrettably rational policy from the viewpoint of inhibiting the emergence of rival nationalisms within the empire.[5]

In brief, both these vigorous and, for the present, dominant nationalisms illustrate the advantage of the availability of an old high culture, once an invaluable asset for state-formation, but now also crucial for the attaining of an early political sense of ethnicity. In each of these cases the ethnic group in question seems, within the local area, co-extensive with its own faith, thus greatly aiding self-definition.

The Somalis are also interesting in that they are one of the examples (like the Kurds) of the blending of old tribalism based on social structure with the new, anonymous nationalism based on shared culture. The sense of lineage affiliation is strong and vigorous (notwithstanding the fact that it is officially reprobated, and its invocation actually proscribed), and it is indeed crucial for the understanding of internal politics. This does not, I think, contradict our general theory, which maintains that the hold of a shared literate culture ('nationality') over modern man springs from the erosion of the old structures, which had once provided each man with his identity, dignity and material security, whereas he now depends on education for these things. The Somalis possess a shared culture, which, when endowed with its own state (as indeed it is), can ensure for each Somali access on good terms to bureaucratic employment. The life chances and psychic comfort of an individual Somali are manifestly better within such a state, based on his culture, than they are within a neighbouring state not so based. At the same time, however, many Somalis remain pastoralists with an interest in the pasture rights defined in the old terms, and retain reciprocal links with kinsmen, links which appear not to be altogether forgotten in the give and take of political life.

What it all amounts to is this: in most cases, the appeal of the new, education-transmitted ethnicity comes from both push and pull: the attraction of the new employment opportunities and the repulsion arising from the erosion of the old security-giving kin groupings. The Somali case is not unique, even if it is particularly conspicuous. Persistence of pastoralism and certain kinds of labour migration or of trade networks may cause extensive kin organization to survive in the modern world. When this happens, we get a juxtaposition of tribal loyalty to structure and of

---

[5] Ioan Lewis, 'The Western Somali Liberation Front (WSLF) and the legacy of Sheikh Hussein of Bale', in J. Tubiana (ed.), *Modern Ethiopia* (Rotterdam: Balkema, 1980); and I.M. Lewis (ed.), *Nationalism and Self-determination in the Horn of Africa* (Indiana: Ithaca, 1983).

national loyalty to culture (and a literate culture at that). But it is scarcely conceivable that the modern world could have emerged had the structural, mini-organizational rigidities remained strong *everywhere*. The great stories of successful economic development were about societies whose wealth and power had the demonstration effect which pointed humanity towards the new style of life; and those stories or paradigms were not and could not be of that kind. The general emergence of modernity hinged on the erosion of the multiple petty binding local organizations and their replacement by mobile, anonymous, literate, identity-conferring cultures. It is this generalized condition which made nationalism normative and pervasive; and this is not contradicted by the occasional superimposition of both of these types of loyalty, the occasional use of kin links for a kind of interstitial, parasitic and partial adaptation to the new order. Modern industry can be paternalistic, and nepotistic at the top; but it cannot recruit its productive units on the basis of kin or territorial principles, as tribal society had done.

The contrast I am here drawing between culture-mediated nationalism and structure-mediated tribalism is, of course, meant to be a genuine analytical distinction between two objectively distinguishable kinds of organization; it must not be confused with the relativistic or emotive opposition between *my* nationalism and *your* tribalism. That is merely the language of praise and invective by means of which rival potential nationalisms combat each other, in which 'I am a patriot, you are a nationalist and he is a tribalist', and that remains so whoever happens to be speaking. In this sense nationalisms are simply those tribalisms, or for that matter any other kind of group, which through luck, effort or circumstance succeed in becoming an effective force under modern circumstances. They are only identifiable *ex post factum*. Tribalism never prospers, for when it does, everyone will respect it as a true nationalism, and no one will dare call it tribalism.

7

A Typology of Nationalisms

A useful typology of nationalisms can be constructed by simply working out the various possible combinations of the crucial factors which enter into the making of a modern society. The first factor to be introduced into this deductively established model is that of *power*. Here there is no need to play with binary or any other alternatives. There is no point in considering the possibility of the absence or diffusion of centralized power in a modern society. Modern societies are always and inevitably centralized, in the sense that the maintenance of order is the task of one agency or group of agencies, and not dispersed throughout the society. The complex division of labour, the complementarity and interdependence and the constant mobility: all these factors prevent citizens from doubling up as producers and participants in violence. There are societies – notably some pastoral ones – where this is feasible: the shepherd is simultaneously the soldier, and often also the senator, jurist and minstrel of his tribe. The entire culture, or very nearly, of the whole society seems encapsulated in each individual rather than distributed among them in different forms, and the society seems to refrain from specialization, at least in its male half, to a very remarkable degree. The few specialists whom this kind of society tolerates it also despises.

Whatever may be feasible among near-nomadic pastoralists, it is not remotely possible in complex modern industrial society. The specialists who compose it cannot take time off to shoot their way from home to office, take precautionary measures against a surprise raid by members of a rival corporation, or join in a nocturnal reprisal raid themselves. Bootleggers may have done this, but they did not become the model for the modern Organization Man. Mafia-type business flourishes on the whole only in areas where illegality makes the invocation of official enforcement agencies difficult. There would seem to be more movement from this kind of enterprise into legitimate business, than the other way. In fact, members of modern societies have little training or practice in applying or resisting violence. Some sectors of modern society on occasion escape this generalization, like those who must live with urban violence in decaying urban centres; and there is at any rate one economically complex society, namely Lebanon, which so far seems to have survived the disintegration of effective central authority with astonishing resilience and success.

But these relatively minor exceptions do not undermine the basic contention that in a modern society the enforcement of the social order is not something evenly diffused throughout society – as is characteristically the case among tribesmen with segmentary social organization – but is concentrated in the hands of some of the members of society. In simpler terms, it is always the case that some wield this power and some do not. Some are closer to the command posts of the enforcement agencies than others. This engenders the admittedly loose, but nevertheless useful distinction between the power-holders and the rest, a contrast which provides us with the first element in our simplified model of modern society, which is to generate, through diverse combinations of the further elements, the various possible types of nationalism.

The next element in the model is access to education or to a viable modern high culture (the two here being treated as equivalent). The notion of education or a viable modern high culture is once again fairly loose but nonetheless useful. It refers to that complex of skills which makes a man competent to occupy most of the ordinary positions in a modern society, and which makes him, so to speak, able to swim with ease in this of cultural medium. It is a syndrome rather than a strict list: no single item in it is, perhaps, absolutely indispensable. Literacy is no doubt central to it, though on occasion skilful and *débrouillard* individuals can get by in the modern world, or even amass fortunes, without it. The same goes for elementary numeracy and a modicum of technical competence, and a kind of non-rigid, adaptable state of mind often encouraged by urban living, and inhibited by rural traditions. By and large, one can say – and this is, of course, important for our argument – that suitably gifted individuals or well-placed sub-communities can sometimes acquire this minimal syndrome independently, but that its wide and effective diffusion presupposes a well-maintained and effective centralized educational system.

In connection with this access to education (in this sense), there are alternatives and different possible situations. With regard to power there are none: it is always the case, in an industrial society, that some have it and some do not. This provided us with our baseline situation, a society loosely divided into power-holders and the rest. But in connection with access to education, there is no such predetermined distinction. In terms of the given power-bifurcated society, there are now four distinct possibilities: it may be that *only* the power-holders have access, that they use their power-privilege to preserve for themselves the monopoly of this access; or alternatively, that both the power-holders and the rest have this access; or again, *only* the rest (or some of them) have such access, and the power-holders do not (a situation not as absurd, implausible or unrealistic as might appear at first sight); or finally, as sometimes happens, that *neither* party enjoys the benefits of such access, or to put it in simpler terms, that the power-holders, and those over whom the power is exercised, are both of them packs of ignoramuses, sunk, in Karl Marx's phrase, in the idiocy of rural life. This is a perfectly plausible and realistic situation, not uncommon in the course of past human history, and not totally unknown even in our age.

The four possibilities envisaged or, rather, generated by our assumptions (each with two sub-alternatives in figure 2, to be explained) do correspond to realistic historic situations. When the category of those who have power roughly corresponds to those who also have access to the kind of educational training fitting them for the new life, we have something corresponding, all in all, to early industrialism. The powerless new migrants, newly drawn in from the land, are politically disenfranchised and culturally alienated, helpless *vis-à-vis* a situation in which they have no leverage and which they cannot understand. They constitute the classical early proletariat, as described by Marx and Engels (and quite wrongly attributed by them to the subsequent stages of industrial society), and such as is often reproduced in the shantytowns of lands which were submerged by the wave of industrialism later.

The second combination, on the other hand, corresponds to late industrialism as it actually is (and not as was erroneously predicted): great power inequality persists, but cultural, educational, life-style differences have diminished enormously. The stratification system is smooth and continuous, not polarized, nor consisting of qualitatively different layers. There is a convergence of life-style and a diminution of social distance, and the access to the new learning, to the gateway of the new world, is open to virtually all, and if by no means on terms of perfect equality, at least without seriously debarring anyone eager to acquire it. (Only possessors of counter-entropic traits, as described, are seriously hampered.)

The third and seemingly paradoxical situation, in which those who wield power are at a disadvantage when it comes to acquiring the new skills, does in fact occur, and represents a by no means unusual historic constellation. In traditional agrarian societies ruling strata are often imbued with an ethos which values warfare, impulsive violence, authority, land-owning, conspicuous leisure and expenditure, and which spurns orderliness, time or other budgeting, trade, application, thrift, systematic effort, forethought and book learning. (The manner in which some of these traits could nevertheless become fashionable and dominant, and come to characterize the dominant strata of society, is after all the subject matter of the most famous of all sociological speculations, namely Weber's account of the origin of the capitalist spirit.) In consequence, these latter traits are then normally found only among more or less despised urban, commercial, learning-oriented groups, which may be tolerated and intermittently persecuted by their rulers. So far so good: within the traditional order, the situation acquires a certain stability. Personnel may change, the structure remains. The thrifty work-oriented accumulators are not normally permitted to displace the leisured class oriented to conspicuous consumption, because the latter regularly fleece and occasionally massacre them. (In the Indian case those who acquired a surplus tended to put all their money in temples to mitigate or to avoid fleecing.)

But with the coming of the industrial order, in the form of the diffusion of market relations, new military and productive technologies, colonial conquest and so forth, the erstwhile stability is lost forever. And within this new unstable and turbulent world it is the values and style and orientation of those despised urban commercial groups which provide a great advantage and easy access to new sources of wealth and power, while the old compensatory mechanisms of expropriation may no longer be available or effective.[1] The counting house becomes more powerful than the sword. The single-minded use of the sword no longer takes you very far.

---

[1] Albert O. Hirschman, *The Passions and the Interests* (Princeton, N. J.: Princeton University Press, 1977). It is, of course, possible that the individualist, mobile spirit preceded by many centuries, in one society at any rate, the coming of industrial order: see Alan Macfarlane, *The Origins of English Individualism* (Oxford: Blackwell, 1978). That would not contradict our thesis, though it might throw light on the early emergence of national sentiment in England. For a summary of the way in which the present theory of nationalism fits into a wider social philosophy, see John A. Hall, *Diagnoses of Our Time* (London: Heinemann Educational, 1981).

The old rulers may, of course, sense the wind of change and mend their ways. They did so in Prussia and Japan. But it is not at all psychologically easy for them to do it quickly (or, sometimes, to do it at all), and quite often they may not do it fast enough. The result then is the situation envisaged: it is now the *ruled*, or at least some of them, who are at a positive advantage, when it comes to access to the new education and skills.

Finally, there is the fourth scenario: neither rulers nor ruled may have any access to the relevant skills. This is the standard situation in any stagnant agrarian society, unaffected by the industrial world, in which both rulers and ruled are sunk in whatever combination of conspicuous display, superstition, ritualism, alcoholism or other diversion may be locally favoured, and when neither of them wish or are able to take the new way out.

By combining the (ever-present) inequality of power with the various possible patterns of the distribution of the access to education, we have obtained four possible situations: equal access, equal lack of access, and access tilted either in favour of or against the power-holders. But we have as yet not introduced the element which is most crucial from the viewpoint of nationalism: identity or diversity of culture.

It goes without saying here that the term 'culture' is being used in an anthropological, not a normative sense: what is meant by the term is the distinctive style of conduct and communication of a given community. The term 'culture' on its own is never used in this discussion in its other sense, as *Kultur*, high culture or great tradition, a style of conduct and communication endorsed by the speaker as superior, as setting a norm which should be, but alas often is not, satisfied in real life, and the rules of which are usually codified by a set of respected, norm-giving specialists within the society. 'Culture' without qualification means culture in the anthropological, non-normative sense; *Kultur* appears as high culture. The relationship between the two kinds of 'culture' is of course a matter of central importance for our subject. The high (normative) cultures or traditions which specially concern us are, of course, literate ones. Hence the problem of access to them appears, in the present discussion, as access to education. The phrase 'access to a culture' consequently means access to culture (anthropological sense) which is denied to a person in virtue of his membership of *another* culture, and not in virtue of lack of 'education'. This perhaps pedantic clarification was essential if misunderstanding of the argument was to be avoided.

To avoid premature complications, the diversity of cultures is introduced in the simplest possible form. Emulating the economists who sometimes discuss worlds containing only one or two commodities, we assume that in each case our society is either mono-cultural (everyone endowed with the same culture, in the anthropological sense), or alternatively, that there are *two* such cultures, the power-holders being a different culture from the rest. The complications in the real world arising from the simultaneous presence in one sphere of three, four or more cultures, does not very seriously affect the argument.

The imposition of this further binary opposition 'cultural unity/cultural duality' on our already established four-fold typology, immediately generates eight possible situations (see figure 2). Note first of all that lines 1, 3, 5 and 7 correspond to situations where, whatever inequalities of power or access to education may prevail, nationalism has no grip, for lack of (*ex hypothesi*) cultural differentiation. Other conflicts may occur, and it is an interesting question whether indeed they do. The evidence seems to indicate that the classes engendered by early industrialism (let alone the smoother, milder stratification produced by its later form), do not take off into permanent and ever-escalating conflict, unless cultural differentiation provides the spark, the line-up as it were, the means of identifying both oneself and the enemy. Clearly there was a good deal of straight class conflict in, say, 1848: Tocqueville, who did not like it, saw it as unambiguously as did Marx, who did. But it did not go on becoming ever sharper and more uncontrollable.

Marxism, on the other hand, likes to think of ethnic conflict as camouflaged class conflict, and believes that humanity would somehow benefit if the mask were torn off, if only people became clear-sighted and thereby freed from nationalist prejudice and blinkers. This would seem to be a misreading both of the mask and of the reality beneath it. 'Anti-Semitism is the socialism of the stupid', the phrase once went, though it was not conspicuously echoed in the days of the Slansky trial or of the Polish purges of 1968, when a socialist regime fomented anti-Semitism. The workers, allegedly, have no country; nor, presumably, a native culture separating them from other workers, especially immigrants; nor, it would seem, any skin colour. Unfortunately the workers generally appear to be unaware of these interesting and liberating sensitivity-deprivations – though not for any lack of being told of them. In fact, ethnicity enters the political sphere as 'nationalism' at times when cultural homogeneity or continuity (not classlessness) is required by the economic base of social life, and when consequently culture-linked class differences become noxious, while ethnically unmarked, gradual class differences remain tolerable.

	P	~ P	
	E	~ E	
1	A	A	early industrialism without ethnic catalyst
2	A	B	'Habsburg' (and points east and south) nationalism
	E	E	
3	A	A	mature homogeneous industrialism
4	A	B	classical liberal Western nationalism
	~ E	E	
5	A	A	Decembrist revolutionary, but not nationalist situation
6	A	B	diaspora nationalism
	~ E	~ E	
7	A	A	untypical pre-nationalist situation
8	A	B	typical pre-nationalist situation

Figure 2 A typology of nationalism-engendering and nationalism-thwarting social situations
~ stands for negation, absence. P stands for power, E for access to modern-style education, and A and B for names of individual cultures. Each numbered line represents one possible situation; a line containing both A and B shows a situation in which two cultures co-exist in a single territory, and a line with A and A stands for cultural homogeneity in a similar territory. If A or B stand under an E and/or a P, then the cultural group in question does have access to education or power; if it stands under ~E or ~P, it lacks such access. The situation of any group is indicated by the *nearest* E and P *above* it.

Line 1 corresponds to classical early industrialism, where both power and educational access are concentrated in the hands of some; but in line 1 the deprived ones are not culturally differentiated from the privileged ones, and consequently nothing, or at least nothing very radical, happens in the end. The conflict and cataclysm predicted by Marxism do not occur. Line 3 corresponds to late industrialism, with generalized access to education, *and* absence of cultural difference; and here there is even less reason to expect conflict than in line 1. We shall yet have to discuss the difficult and important question whether advanced industrialism as such in any case constitutes a shared culture, overruling the – by now – irrelevant differences of linguistic idiom. When men have the same concepts, more or less, perhaps it no longer matters whether they use different words to express them, you might say. If this is so, line 3 might characterize the shared future of mankind, after the general consummation of industrialism, if and when it comes. This question will be discussed later. Line 5, once again, gives rise to no *nationalist* problems and conflicts. A politically weak sub-group is economically or educationally privileged, but being indistinguishable from the majority, is capable of swimming in the general pool without detection, and, like the proverbial Maoist guerrilla, it does not attract hostile attention.

Lines 7 and 8 are jointly exempt from the nationalist *Problematik* for quite another reason: because the question of access to a new high culture, which is a pre-condition of entry into and benefits from the new style of life, simply doesn't arise. Here, no one has it, so no one has it more than anyone else. This, of course, is the element which is crucial and central to our theory: nationalism is about entry to, participation in, identification with, a literate high culture which is co-extensive with an entire political unit and its total population, and which must be of this kind if it is to be compatible with the kind of division of labour, the type or mode of production, on which this society is based. Here, in l ines 7 and 8, this mode is absent, even in the form of any awareness of it or aspiration towards it. There is no high culture, or at any rate none which possesses a tendency and capacity to generalize itself throughout the whole of society and to become the condition of its effective economic functioning. Line 7 is excluded from the nationalist issue twice over; once for the reasons just given, and once because it also lacks cultural differentiation which could give bite to its other problems, whatever they might be. Line 8 is more typical of complex agrarian societies than line 7: the ruling stratum is identifiable by a distinct culture, which serves as a badge of rank, diminishing ambiguity and thus strain. Line 7, with its cultural continuity, is untypical for the agrarian world.

Note a further difference between the picture underlying this typology, and the one customarily offered by Marxism. As already indicated, our model expects and predicts vertical conflict, between diverse horizontal layers, in a way which is quite different from Marxism. It anticipates it only in those cases where 'ethnic' (cultural or other diacritical marks) are visible and accentuate the differences in educational access and power, and, above all, when they inhibit the free flow of personnel across the loose lines of social stratification.[2] It also predicts conflict *sooner* rather than later in the development of industrialism (with the proviso that without ethnic/cultural differention virulent and decisively explosive conflict will not arise at all, early or late). But these differences in prediction are best seen not in isolation, but as consequences of the differences in underlying interpretation.

At this level there are at least two very important differences between the two viewpoints. One concerns a theme well explored and much commented on among critics of Marxism: its views on the social stratification engendered by industrialism (or, in its own terms, 'capitalism'). Our model assumes that a sharp polarization and social discontinuity does indeed occur in early industrialism, but that this then becomes attenuated by social mobility, diminution of social distance, and convergence of life-styles. It is not denied that great differences in ownership persist, but it suggests that the effective social consequences of this, both hidden and perceived, become very much less important.

Even more significant is the nature of the polarization that occurs in industrial society. What distinguishes our model from the Marxist one is that control or ownership of capital wasn't even mentioned. Identity of culture, access to power, and access to education were the only elements fed as premises into the model, and used for generating our eight possible situations. Capital, ownership and wealth were simply ignored, and deliberately so. These once so respected factors were replaced by another one, generically designated as access to education, by which was meant, as explained, possession or access to the acquisition of the bundle of skills which enable men to perform well in the general conditions of an industrial division of labour, as defined. I hold this approach to be entirely justified. The point is one much invoked by economists of development of a *laisser faire* persuasion. Quite impecunious populations (indentured transplanted Chinese coolies, for example) do astonishingly well when endowed with the apposite attitudes; while capital poured into

---

[2]   This fact about the crucial fissures in society seems to have been recognized by an author who nevertheless continues to class himself as a Marxist. See Nairn 1977.

unsuitable human contexts as an aid to development achieves nothing. Capital, like capitalism, seems an overrated category.

The Varieties of Nationalist Experience

Our model was generated by the introduction of the three factors that alone really matter: power, education, and shared culture, in the senses intended. Of the eight possible situations which the model generates, five are as it were non-nationalist, four of them because there is no cultural differentiation, and two because the question of access to a centrally sustained high culture does not arise (and one of the specimens, of course, is included both in the four and in the two). That leaves us with three forms of nationalism.

Line 2 corresponds to what one may call the classical Habsburg (and points south and east) form of nationalism. The power-holders have privileged access to the central high culture, which indeed is their own, and to the whole bag of tricks which makes you do well under modern conditions. The powerless are also the education-deprived. They share, or groups of them share, folk cultures which, with a good deal of effort and standardized and sustained propaganda, can be turned into a rival new high culture, whether or not sustained by the memory, real or invented, of a historical political unit allegedly once built around that same culture or one of its variants. The required effort is, however, very energetically put into this task by the intellectuals-awakeners of this ethnic group, and eventually, if and when circumstances are propitious, this group sets up a state of its own, which sustains and protects the newly born, or reborn as the case might be, culture.

The resulting situation is of immediate and immense advantage to the said awakeners, and eventually may also be of some advantage to the other speakers of the culture, although it is hard to say whether they might not have done just as well out of assimilation into the culture of the original power-holders. Non-speakers of the new culture who happen to live in the territory now controlled by the new state themselves in turn now face the options of assimilation, irredentist effort, emigration, disagreeable minority status and physical liquidation. This model has been emulated in other parts of the world, with occasionally the significant modification of what one may call the 'African' type (though it is not restricted to Africa), which arises when the local folk cultures are incapable of becoming the new high culture of the emergent state, either because they are too numerous or too jealous of each other, or for some other reason.

This has already received some discussion in connection with the pseudo-hypothetical Ruritania, above (chapter 5). But at that stage of the discussion I was concerned primarily with the difference between this Ruritanian (or line 2) type, and a special problem facing advanced industrial societies through the presence of mobility-resisting, counter-entropic traits in their populations: the contrast between brakes on mobility due to difficulties of communication, and brakes due to difficulties of cultural identification, or if you like, due to the *facility* of the identification of inequality, the tar-brushing effect or the giving-a-dog-a-bad-name effect.

The barrier on mobility due to persistent clustering of some traits in underprivileged strata is a very serious problem, particularly for developed industrial societies, and the distinction is an important one; but it is not identical with the one which concerns us now; namely, the difference between lines 2 and 4. The situation symbolized by line 4 is interesting: some have power and some do not. The difference correlates with, and can be seized in terms of, differences of culture. But when it comes to access to education, there is *no* significant difference between the relevant populations. What happens here?

The historic reality to which this model corresponds is the unification nationalisms of nineteenth-century Italy and Germany. Most Italians were ruled by foreigners, and in that sense were politically underprivileged. The Germans, most of them, live in fragmented states, many of them small and weak, at any rate by European great power standards, and thus unable to provide German culture, as a centralized modern medium, with its political roof. (By a further paradox, multi-national great power Austria was endeavouring to do something of that kind, but much to the displeasure of some of its citizens.)

So the political protection of Italian and German culture was visibly and, to the Italians and Germans offensively, inferior to that which was provided for, say, French or English culture. But when it came to access to education, the facilities provided by these two high cultures, to those who were born into dialectal variants of it, were not really in any way inferior. Both Italian and German were literary languages, with an effective centralized standardization of their correct forms and with flourishing literatures, technical vocabularies and manners, educational institutions and academies. There was little if any cultural inferiority. Rates of literacy and standards of education were not significantly lower (if lower at all) among Germans than they were among the French; and they were not significantly low among the Italians, when compared with the dominant Austrians. German in comparison with French, or Italian in comparison with the German used by the Austrians, were not disadvantaged cultures, and their speakers did not need to correct unequal access to the eventual benefits of a modern world. All that needed to be corrected was that inequality of power and the absence of a political roof over a culture (and over an economy), and institutions which would be identified with it and committed to its maintenance. The Risorgimento and the unification of Germany corrected these imbalances.

There is a difference, however, between this kind of unificatory nationalism, on behalf of a fully effective high culture which only needs an improved bit of political roofing, and the classical Habsburg-and-east-and-south type of nationalism. This difference is the subject of a fascinating and rather moving essay by the late Professor John Plamenatz, an essay which might well have been called 'The Sad Reflections of a Montenegrin in Oxford'.[3] Plamenatz called the two kinds of nationalism the Western and the Eastern, the Western type being of the Risorgimento or unificatory kind, typical of the nineteenth century and with deep links to liberal ideas, while the Eastern, though he did not stress it in so many words, was exemplified by the kind of nationalism he knew to exist in his native Balkans. There can be no doubt but that he saw the Western nationalism as relatively benign and nice, and the Eastern kind as nasty, and doomed nastiness by the conditions which gave rise to it. (It would be an interesting question to ask him whether he would have considered the markedly un-benign forms taken by these once-benign or relatively liberal and moderate Western nationalisms in the twentieth century, as accidental and avoidable aberrations or not.)

The underlying logic of Plamenatz's argument is clear. The relatively benign Western nationalisms were acting on behalf of well-developed high cultures, normatively centralized and endowed with a fairly well-defined folk clientele: all that was required was a bit of adjustment in the political situation and in the international boundaries, so as to ensure for these cultures, and their speakers and practitioners, the same sustained protection as that which was already enjoyed by their rivals. This took a few battles and a good deal of sustained diplomatic activity but, as the making of historical omelettes goes, it did not involve the breaking of a disproportionate or unusual number of eggs, perhaps no more than

[3] John Plamenatz, 'Two Types of Nationalism', in Kamenka 1973.

would have been broken anyway in the course of the normal political game within the general political framework and assumptions of the time.

By way of contrast, consider the nationalism designated as Eastern by Plamenatz. Its implementation did, of course, require battles and diplomacy, to at least the same extent as the realization of Western nationalisms. But the matter did not end there. This kind of Eastern nationalism did not operate on behalf of an already existing, well-defined and codified high culture, which had as it were marked out and linguistically pre-converted its own territory by sustained literary activities ever since the early Renaissance or since the Reformation, as the case might be. Not at all. This nationalism was active on behalf of a high culture not as yet properly crystallized, a merely aspirant or in-the-making high culture. It presided, or strove to preside, in ferocious rivalry with similar competitors, over a chaotic ethnographic map of many dialects, with ambiguous historical or linguo-genetic allegiances, and containing populations which had only just begun to identify with these emergent national high cultures. Objective conditions of the modern world were bound, in due course, to oblige them to identify with one of them. But till this occurred, they lacked the clearly defined cultural basis enjoyed by their German and Italian counterparts.

These populations of Eastern Europe were still locked into the complex multiple loyalties of kinship, territory and religion. To make them conform to the nationalist imperative was bound to take more than a few battles and some diplomacy. It was bound to take a great deal of very forceful cultural engineering. In many cases it was also bound to involve population exchanges or expulsions, more or less forcible assimilation, and sometimes liquidation, in order to attain that close relation between state and culture which is the essence of nationalism. And all these consequences flowed, not from some unusual brutality of the nationalists who in the end employed these measures (they were probably no worse and no better than anyone else), but from the inescapable logic of the situation.

If the nationalist imperative was to be implemented in what Plamenatz generically designated as Eastern conditions, then these consequences followed. A modern type of society cannot be implemented without the satisfaction of something pretty close to the nationalist imperative, which follows from the new style of division of labour. The hunger for industrial affluence, once its benefits and their availability are known and once the previous social order has in any case been disrupted, is virtually irresistible. The conclusion to which this series of steps leads us cannot be avoided. With luck, understanding and determination, the price can be mitigated; but its payment cannot be altogether avoided.

Diaspora Nationalism

Our discussion of the difference between lines 2 and 4 of figure 2 in a way repeats Plamenatz's distinction between Western and Eastern nationalisms; but it claims certain advantages over his treatment. For one thing, the contrast is not simply asserted as a contingently, historically encountered distinction, but is a derived consequence of a simple model into which, by way of hypothesis, certain very basic and elementary factors have been fed. This constitutes an advantage at any rate for those who, like myself, believe that such model-building should at least be attempted.

But there is further benefit: this 'constructive' approach engenders a further, third variant of nationalism, left out by Plamenatz altogether, but cogently generated by a further combination of those self-same elements which also account, in different combinations, for the two species which did preoccupy him. This third species can best be called diaspora nationalism, and it is, as a matter of historical fact, a distinctive, very conspicuous and important sub-species of nationalism.

Traditional agrarian society, we have stressed, uses culture or ethnicity primarily to distinguish privileged groups, thus underscoring their distinctiveness and legitimacy, enhancing their aura, and diminishing the danger of status ambiguity. If the rulers speak one kind of language or have one kind of accent and wear one kind of habit, it would be a solecism, or much worse, for non-members of the ruling stratum to use the same mode of communication. It would be a presumption, *lèse-majesté*, pollution or sacrilege, or ridiculous. Ridicule is a powerful sanction. It constitutes a most powerful social sanction against which reason is specially powerless, even or particularly when the verdict is passed by the least qualified of juries. Other and possibly more brutal punishments can also be deployed.

But the same social marker device of culture or ethnicity is used to identify and separate off not merely privileged, but also underprivileged, ambivalently viewed or pariah groups. And it is socially most useful to have such groups. As we have noted, in pre-industrial societies bureaucratic functions can best be performed by eunuchs, priests, slaves and foreigners. To allow free-born native citizens into such key positions is too dangerous. They are far too much subject to pressures and temptations from their existing local and kin links to use their position to benefit their kinsmen and clients, and to use their kinsmen and clients in turn to strengthen their own positions further. It is not till the coming of our own modern society, when everyone becomes both a mamluk and a clerk, that everyone can also perform reasonably as a bureaucrat, without needing to be emasculated, physically or socially. Now men can be trusted to honour what had been the politically awkward and untypical norms of agrarian society, but have become the pervasive and acceptable ones in ours. We are now all of us castrated, and pitifully trustworthy. The state can trust us, all in all, to do our duty, and need not turn us into eunuchs, priests, slaves or Mamluks first.

But the manning of posts in an administrative structure is not the only reason for having pariahs in the agrarian order. Pariah bureaucracies are not the only form of exemption from full humanity, and bureaucracy is not the only source of social power. Magic, the forging of metals, finance, elite military corps, various other such mysteries and in some circumstances *any* kind of key specialism may confer dangerous power on the specialist who has access to it. One way of neutralizing this danger, while at the same time tolerating the specialism and possibly confirming the monopoly of the guild or caste, is to insist that this social niche may be occupied only by a group easily identifiable culturally, destined for avoidance and contempt, and excluded from political office, from the ultimate control of the tools of coercion, and from honour.

Clear examples of such positions, often too dangerous to be given to locals and full citizens, and consequently reserved for foreigners, are palace guards and the providers of financial services. The handling of large sums of money obviously confers great power, and if that power is in the hands of someone precluded from using it for his own advancement, because he belongs to a category excluded from high and honourable office and from being able to command obedience, then so much the better. In the traditional order, groups occupying these positions take the rough with the smooth, accepting with resignation the benefits, the perils and the humiliations of their situation. They are generally born into it and have little choice in the matter. Sometimes they may suffer a great deal, but often there are benefits as well as losses involved in their position.

The situation changes radically and profoundly with the coming of mobile, anonymous, centralized mass society. This is particularly true for minorities specializing in financial, commercial, and generally urban specialist occupations. With pervasive mobility and occupational change, it is no longer feasible to retain the monopoly of some activity for a particular cultural group. When so many members of the wider society aspire to these often comfortable, and in themselves (if not subject to confiscation) lucrative occupations, they can hardly be reserved for a minority, and still less for a stigmatized one.

At the same time, however, these previously specialized and segregated populations are liable to have a marked advantage when it comes to the new pursuits and the new style. Their urban style of life, habits of rational calculation, commercial probity, higher rates of literacy and possibly a scriptural religion, all fit them better than either the members of the old ruling class, or the old peasantry, for the new life-style.

It is often asserted, even by sophisticated sociologists such as Max Weber, that these minorities have a double standard, one for their own group, and another, instrumental and amoral, for outsiders. They do indeed have a double standard, but it is exactly the other way round. Their entire standing with the outside world previously hinged on performing some specific service or supplying some specific good. Their name and revenue depended entirely on doing this *reliably*, and they were indeed known for such professional reliability. This was quite different from the relations prevailing inside a *moral* community, where a commercial deal between two individuals was inevitably always far more than a mere commercial deal. The two partners in it were also kinsmen, clansmen, allies, enemies, and so forth; hence the deal was never restricted to a simple delivery of *this* good at *this* price. There was always a promise or a fear of greater advantages or possible betrayal. Both sides were involved in bargains and calculations far more long-term and intangible, and thus had to try to deliver more. If on the other hand they were dissatisfied with the deal, powerful considerations operated to inhibit complaints, lest all the other strands in the relationship were thereby also put at risk.

The advantage on the other hand of dealing with a minority, one with whom you could not eat, marry, or enter into political or military alliance, was that both parties could concentrate on a rational cost-benefit analysis of the actual specific deal in question, and expect, on the whole, to get what they bargained for, neither more nor less. Within the minority community, of course, relationships were once again many-stranded, and hence deals were less rational and reliable, and more many-sided. But in the wider society, those who lack status can honour a contract. Those on the other hand who enjoyed a social station, and had to respect its rights and duties, were thereby deprived of much of the elbow-room required for negotiating and observing specific contracts. Status and honour deprive a man of options, by imposing too many obligations and commitments. Deprivation of status enables a man to attend to the business at hand, negotiate a rational deal, and observe its terms.

So it is indeed true that the minority community had a double standard, but in the opposite sense from what is normally supposed. To the outsider they displayed that reliability which is the presupposed anticipation of single-stranded modern relations. It was with their fellows that their dealings had that rich many-stranded quality which, to our modern sensibility, smacks of corruption. But, of course, with the coming of anonymous mobile mass society, single-stranded, one-shot deals have become quite normal, and not a special feature of dealings between non-commensal groups.

Under conditions of modernization the erstwhile specialized minority groups lose their disabilities, but *also* alas their monopoly and their protection. Their previous training and orientation often make them perform much more successfully than their rivals in the new economic free-for-all. Their background fits them for it so much better. But at the same time their background also contains a tradition of political impotence, and of the surrender of the communal right of self-defence. That, after all, had been the price of their entering the profession in the first place: they had to make themselves politically and militarily impotent, so as to be allowed to handle tools that could be, in the wrong hands, so very powerful and dangerous. But even without such a tradition, the political and military weakness of such a group follows from its minority status and, very often, from its dispersal among a variety of urban centres, and its lack of a compact defensible territorial base. Some economically brilliant groups of this kind have behind them a long tradition of dispersal, urbanization and minority status: this is clearly the case of the Jews, Greeks, Armenians or Parsees. Other groups come to occupy similar positions only as a result of recent migrations and aptitudes (or educational opportunities) only acquired or deployed in modern times. Such is the situation of overseas Chinese and Indians, or the Ibos in Nigeria.

The disastrous and tragic consequences, in modern conditions, of the conjunction of economic superiority and cultural identifiability with political and military weakness, are too well known to require repetition. The consequences range from genocide to expulsion. Sometimes a precarious and uneasy balance is maintained. The main point is that the central power now finds itself in a very different situation, and subject to very different temptations and pressures from those which prevailed in the days of the agrarian division of labour. Then, there was no question of *everyone* becoming mobile, educated, specialized or commercial-minded; who would then have tilled the land?

> When Adam delved and Eve span,
> Who was then the businessman?

Well, there were some. But they could not constitute the majority or the norm. An almost universally embourgeoised society was inconceivable.

The general population then did not covet the minority role, which was in any case stigmatized. The rulers welcomed a defenceless, fairly easily taxable, economically specialized group, tied to the rulers by its strictly sustained and reinforced defencelessness. But now, the national 'development' requires precisely that everyone should move in the direction which was once open only to a minority and stigmatized group. Once the state had an interest in protecting the minority, which was easy to milch. Now the state has more interest in depriving the minority of its economic monopolies, and, because of the minority's visibility and wealth, it can buy off a great deal of discontent in the wider population by dispossessing and persecuting it; and so the inevitable happens. This provides a most enjoyable (except for its victims) and pathetic theatre of humiliation, inflicted on the once-envied group, to the delectation of the majority. This pleasure can be savoured by a far larger category than just the restricted group of inheritors of the positions vacated by the persecuted minority, and that too is a politically important consideration, making this course a politically attractive option for the state.

Under these circumstances the minority is faced with the same kind of options (though under different circumstances) as those which faced our Ruritanian labour migrants. It can assimilate; and sometimes indeed the entire minority, or some considerable parts of it, succeed in doing just that. Alternatively, it can endeavour to shed both its specialization and its minority status, and create a state of its own, as the new protector of a now un-specialized, generic, newly national culture. For a dispersed urban population the major problem is, of course, the acquisition of the required territorial base. The Ruritanian peasants, being peasants, inevitably had a territorial base, destined soon to become the kingdom of Ruritania, and later to become the Socialist People's Republic of Ruritania. But what was an urban, specialized and dispersed group, with few or no rural links, to do?

For these kinds of nationalism, the acquisition of territory was the first and perhaps the main problem. The Hellenes initially thought not so much in terms of secession from the Ottoman Empire, as of inverting the hierarchy within it and taking it over, thereby reviving Byzantium. The first Greek rising took place not in Greece, but in what is now Romania, where the Greeks were a minority, and moreover one doing rather well out of the Ottoman system. The use of what is now southern Greece as a territorial basis only came later.

The most famous and dramatic case of a successful diaspora nationalism is Israel. It is also the 'last, least typical of European nationalisms', in Hugh Trevor-Roper's words.[4] (It solved a European problem by creating an Asian one, about which the Israelis have barely begun to think. In the diaspora, the Jewish religion referred to Jerusalem; once back in Jerusalem, semi-secular Zionism for a time used the dated socialist or populist clichés of nineteenth-century Europe.) Nearly two thousand years of history had left no Jewish territorial base whatever, least of all in the land of Israel, and had moreover left Jews as a set of discontinuous and fairly highly specialized strata within the structures of other societies, rather than the kind of balanced population which can be the base of a more or less autarchic modern state, of a *geschlossener Handelstaat*. Nevertheless, this extraordinary transformation was achieved, no doubt thanks in large part to the incentive provided by the persecutions, first in Eastern Europe and then throughout Europe during the period of the Holocaust. These persecutions illustrate, better than any others, the kind of fate which is likely to befall culturally distinguishable, economically privileged and politically defenceless communities, at a time when the age of specialized communities, of the traditional form of organic division of labour, is over.

The human transformation involved in the Jewish case went counter to the global trend: an urban, highly literate and sophisticated, cosmopolitan population was at least partly returned to the land and made more insular. Normally the nationalist process is inversely related to its own verbiage, talking of peasants and making townsmen. Here it was really necessary to make a few surrogate peasants. In fact, they turned out to be peasants with certain crucial tribal traits: a form of local organization which was made up of units that were simultaneously productive and military in their effective role. The manufacture of such tribesmen-peasants from an urban background could not conceivably be an easy matter, and the surrogate peasant-soldiers were in fact formed by a species of secular monastic order. This needed an ideology, and by a

[4] Hugh Trevor-Roper, *Jewish and Other Nationalisms* (London: Weidenfeld and Nicolson, 1962).

historic accident the suitable mixture of socialism and populism was indeed available and pervasive in the intellectual milieux in which the order did its recruiting. The pro-rural, anti-division-of-labour, collectivist themes in this ideology were ideally suited for the purpose. Whether the kibbutzim do indeed provide the good life for modern man, as their founders believed and hoped, remains an open question; but as a piece of machinery for effectively re-settling the land by people drawn from heavily urbanized and embourgeoised populations, *and* effectively defending it in a military crisis with minimal and exiguous means, they proved to be quite outstanding, and indeed unequalled.

The problems of social transformation, cultural revivification, acquisition of territory, and coping with the natural enmity of those with previous claims on the territory in question, illustrate the quite special and acute problems faced by diaspora nationalisms. Those of them which retain some residue of an ancient territory may face problems which are correspondingly less acute. But the problems which face a diaspora culture which does not take the nationalist option may be as grave and tragic as those which face it if it does adopt nationalism. In fact, one may say that it is the extreme peril of the assimilationist alternative which makes the adherents of the nationalist solution espouse their cause in this situation.

The gravity of the situation faced by diaspora populations if they do not choose nationalism, and the manner in which the whole situation can be deduced from the very general characteristics of the transition from an agrarian to an industrial order, show that it is quite wrong to invoke diaspora nationalisms as counter-examples to our theory of nationalism:

> Greek and Armenian nationalism arose among populations which were generally more prosperous and better able to understand the wealth-generating economies of modern Europe than their Ottoman Muslim overlords.[5]

---

[5] Kedourie 1970, p. 20. In the same volume (p. 132) Professor Kedourie challenges the doctrine that industrial social organization makes for cultural homogeneity: 'Large industrial enterprises have taken root and flourished in multi-lingual societies: in Bohemia and the United States in the nineteenth century; in Hong Kong, Israel, French Algeria, India, Ceylon, and Malaya in the twentieth.'

It has never been claimed that you can only have industrial enterprise in a society which is *already* culturally homogeneous. What the theory does claim is that if an industrial economy is established in a culturally heterogeneous society (or if it even casts its advance shadow on it), *then* tensions result which *will* engender nationalism. With the possible and temporary exception of Hong Kong, whose population is recruited from Chinese not

In our Ruritanian case, nationalism was explained in terms of an economically and politically disadvantaged population, able to distinguish itself culturally, and thus impelled towards the nationalist option. But the intolerable position, once the process of industrialization begins, of culturally distinguishable populations which are not at an economic disadvantage (quite the reverse), only at a *political* disadvantage which is inherent in their minority status, follows from the same general premisses, and points to the same conclusion, though naturally by its own specific path. To concentrate exclusively on economic disadvantage, which admittedly is prominent in the most typical cases, is to travesty our position. The industrial order requires homogeneity within political units, at least sufficient to permit fairly smooth mobility, and precluding the 'ethnic' identification of either advantage or disadvantage, economic or political.

---

wishing to live under the present mainland Chinese regime, so that the very principle of recruitment of the community selects for absence of irredentist longing, every single other country cited in Kedourie's list, far from constituting a counter-example to the theory, in fact illustrates it, and indeed provides veritable paradigms of the model which the theory proposes. Bohemia was the source of much of the early nationalist activity and theory, both German and Czech; the educational system of the United States was notoriously geared to turning a heterogeneous immigrant population into an ethnically homogeneous one, with the warm concurrence of the population so processed. All the other countries listed illustrate the story of nationalism, some of them in extreme and tragic form. It is true that in India, cultural homogeneity *sometimes* cuts across linguistic diversity: Hindus 'speak the same language' even when they do not speak the same language. But the theory does not preclude that.

8

The Future of Nationalism

Our general diagnosis of nationalism is simple. Of the three stages of human history, the second is the agrarian, and the third is the industrial. Agrarian society has certain general features: the majority of the population is made up of agricultural producers, peasants. Only a minority of the society's population are specialists, whether military, political, religious or economic. Most agrarian populations are also affected by the two other great innovations of the agrarian age: centralized government and the discovery of writing.

Agrarian society – unlike, it would seem, both its predecessor and successor societies – is Malthusian: both productive and defence necessities impel it to seek a growing population, which then pushes close enough to the available resources to be occasionally stricken by disasters. The three crucial factors operating in this society (food production, political centralization and literacy) engender a social structure in which cultural and political boundaries are seldom congruent.

Industrial society is quite different. It is not Malthusian. It is based and dependent on cognitive and economic growth which in the end both outstrips and discourages further dramatic population growth. Various factors in it – universal literacy, mobility and hence individualism, political centralization, the need for a costly educational infrastructure – impel it into a situation in which political and cultural boundaries are on the whole congruent. The state is, above all, the protector, not of a faith, but of a culture, and the maintainer of the inescapably homogeneous and standardizing educational system, which alone can turn out the kind of personnel capable of switching from one job to another within a growing economy and a mobile society, and indeed of performing jobs which involve manipulating meanings and people rather than things. For most of these men, however, the limits of their culture are the limits, not perhaps of the world, but of their own employability and hence dignity.

In most of the closed micro-communities of the agrarian age the limits of the culture were the limits of the world, and the culture often itself remained unperceived, invisible: no-one thought of it as the ideal political boundary. Now, with mobility, it has become visible and is the limit of the individual's mobility, circumscribing the newly enlarged range of his employability; and thus it becomes the natural political boundary. To say this is not to reduce nationalism to mere anxiety about the prospects for social mobility. Men really love their culture, because they now perceive the cultural atmosphere (instead of taking it for granted), and know they cannot really breathe or fulfil their identity outside it.

The high (literate) culture in which they have been educated is, for most men, their most precious investment, the core of their identity, their insurance, and their security. Thus a world has emerged which in the main, minor exceptions apart, satisfies the nationalist imperative, the congruence of culture and polity. The satisfaction of the nationalist principle was not a precondition of the first appearance of industrialism, but only the product of its spread.

A transition has to be made from a world which does not encourage even the formulation of the nationalist ideal, let alone remotely make possible its implementation, to an age which makes it seem (erroneously) a self-evident ideal valid for all times, thus turning it into an effective norm, which in most cases is implemented. The period of this transition is inevitably a period of nationalist activism. Mankind arrived in the industrial age with cultural and political institutions which generally contradicted the nationalist requirements. Bringing society into line with the new imperatives was inevitably a turbulent process.

The most violent phase of nationalism is that which accompanies early industrialism, and the diffusion of industrialism. An unstable social situation is created in which a whole set of painful cleavages tend to be superimposed on each other: there are sharp political, economic and educational inequalities. At the same time, new culture-congruent polities are emerging. In these conditions, if these multiple and superimposed inequalities also coincide, more or less, with ethnic and cultural ones, which are visible, conspicuous and easily intelligible, they impel the new emerging units to place themselves under ethnic banners.

Industrialization inevitably comes to different places and groups at different times. This ensures that the explosive blend of early industrialism (dislocation, mobility, acute inequality *not* hallowed by time and custom) seeks out, as it were, all the available nooks and crannies of cultural differentiation, wherever they be. Few of those that can be effectively activated for nationalism, by coinciding however loosely with the septic inequalities of the time, and defining viable potential industrial states, fail so to be activated. As the tidal wave of modernization sweeps the world, it makes sure that almost everyone, at some time or other, has cause to feel unjustly treated, and that he can identify the culprits as being of another 'nation'. If he can also identify enough of the victims as being of the same 'nation' as himself, a nationalism is born. If it succeeds, and not all of them can, a nation is born.

There is a further element of economic rationality in the political system of 'lateral boundaries' which nationalism engenders in the modern world. Territorial boundaries are drawn and legally enforced, while differences of status are neither marked nor enforced, but rather camouflaged and disavowed. Notoriously, advanced economies can swamp and inhibit newly emerging ones, unless these are effectively protected by their own state. The nationalist state is not the protector only of a culture, but also of a new and often initially fragile economy. (It generally loses interest in protecting a faith.) In those cases where a modern nation is born of what had previously been a mere stratum – peasants only, or urban specialists only – the state's concerns with making its ethnic group into a balanced nation, and with developing its economy, become aspects of one and the same task.

The question now arises whether nationalism will continue to be a major force or a general political imperative in an age of advanced, perhaps even in some sense completed industrialism. As the world is not yet too close to a satiation of the craving for economic growth, any answer to this question will inevitably be speculative. The speculation is nevertheless well worth attempting. The implications of growth for occupational and social mobility were prominent in our argument. Constant occupational changes, reinforced by the concern of most jobs with communication, the manipulation of meaning rather than the manipulation of things, makes for at least a certain kind of social equality or diminished social distance, and the need for a standardized, effectively shared medium of communication. These factors underlie both modern egalitarianism and nationalism.

But what happens if a satiated industrial society becomes once again stabilized, un-mobile? The classical imaginative exploration of this occurs in Aldous Huxley's *Brave New World*. A satiated industrial society is indeed conceivable: though there is no reason to suppose that all possible technological innovations will one day be exhausted, there is reason to suppose that beyond a certain point further technical innovations may cease to have any significant further impact on social structure and society generally, on the analogy of a man who, beyond a certain point of wealth, can no longer in any way alter his life-style in response to further enrichment. This analogy may or may not be valid, and it is difficult to be confident about the answer to this question. The age of wealth-saturation for mankind at large still seems fairly distant, and so the issue does not affect us too urgently at present.

But it is worth stating that much of our argument did hinge on the implications of continuing commitment to global economic growth, and hence to innovation and occupational change; it also presupposed the persistence of a society based on the promise of affluence and on generalized Danegeld. These assumptions, though valid now, cannot be expected to remain so indefinitely (even if we exclude the possibility of the termination of this kind of society by some nuclear or similar disaster). Our culturally homogeneous, mobile and, in its middle strata, fairly unstructured society may well not last for ever, even if we disregard the possibility of cataclysms; and when this kind of society no longer prevails, then what we have presented as the social bases of nationalism will be profoundly modified. But that is not something which will be visible in our lifetimes.

In the shorter run, without looking ahead so far, we can expect nationalism to become modified. Its acute stage arose, as stated, at the time of the maximal gap between the industrially incorporated, politically and educationally enfranchised populations, and those at the gate of the new world but not yet inside it. As economic development proceeded, this gap narrowed (pessimistic assertions to the contrary notwithstanding). The gap may even continue to increase in absolute terms, but once both the privileged and the underprivileged are above a certain level, it is no longer felt and perceived to be so acute. The difference between starvation and sufficiency is acute; the difference between sufficiency with more, or with fewer, largely symbolic, artificial frills, is not nearly so great, especially when, in an at least nominally egalitarian industrial society, those frills are all made in the same style.

The diminution of the acuteness of nationalist fervour does not mean, however, that counter-entropic minorities will necessarily fare well. Their fate in the modern world has often been tragic, and to be confident that these tragedies will not be repeated would be an indulgence or facile, unwarranted optimism. A mature industrial society requires smooth communication and smooth mobility for its members. Attainment of the former is the condition of maturity; the latter seems to be more elusive. Obstruction of mobility, where it occurs, is one of the most serious and intractable problems of industrial society. The gap in prosperity may also increase between nations, but when a frontier *already* exists between the haves and have-nots, the tension between them cannot, as it were, create it twice over, so from the viewpoint of nationalism this is irrelevant. (I leave aside for the time being the possibility of some collective hostility by an entire class of 'proletarian nations', politically sovereign, towards the rich nations. If this occurs, it will in any case be something other than nationalism. It would manifest an international solidarity of the poor.)

So what happens to later nationalism, if disparities of wealth between populations diminish with the extension of the industrial system? The answer to this question is not yet clear, but it does concern us far more closely than the more distant vistas; for a fair number of countries already at least approach this condition. We can look both at the implications of our theoretical premises, and at the concrete empirical, historical evidence. A fair amount of it is already available. It all hinges, in effect, on the nature of industrial culture.

Industrial Culture – One or Many?

There are two possible visions of the future of culture in industrial societies, and any number of intermediate compromise positions between the poles which they represent. My own conception of world history is clear and simple: the three great stages of man, the hunting-gathering, the agrarian and the industrial, determine our problems, but not our solution. In other words, Marxism was wrong twice over, not merely in multiplying the stages beyond the elegant, economical and canonical three (trinitarians such as Comte, Frazer or Karl Polanyi were right, whether or not they had correctly identified the elements of the trinity), but above all in suggesting that the solution as well as the problem was determined for each stage:

> The mode of production of material life determines the general character of the social, political and spiritual processes of life. . . . In broad outline we can designate the Asiatic, the ancient, the feudal and the modern bourgeois

modes of production can be indicated as progressive epochs in the economic formation of society.[1]

But, in general, the determination of society by the available economic base does not seem to hold. Neither hunting nor agrarian societies are all alike. What is specifically disastrous for the Marxist philosophy of history is that the crucial superstructural features (the state and literacy) do *not* correlate with the appearance of the really decisive infrastructure change, namely the beginning of food production. If James Woodburn is right, a crucial structural change occurs already *within* the category of hunting societies, which can be divided into those practising immediate return, and those with delayed return hunting and gathering economies. The latter, by acquiring the moral and institutional basis for long-term obligation, already possess the organizational pre-conditions for developing agriculture, if and when the pressures in that direction operate and the technical means become available.[2] Division of tasks over time engenders the habits of thought and action which then make possible the permanent specialization of roles between individuals involved in food production. If this is so, then one great socio-structural change *precedes* the past great leap to food production; while there is no doubt but that the other great structural change, state-formation, follows it, and is not in any immediate or single way linked to it.[3] Mankind moved from a hunting-gathering state when all had leisure, to an agrarian one when only some (the ruling elite) had it, to an industrial age governed by the work ethic, when none have it. Or you might say we moved from no delay in gratification to some delay and finally to eternal delay.

So the idea of the material determination of society would seem to be out, in general. But is it also out for industrial society, in the long run? Is the general form of industrial society, at least, uniquely determined by its productive infrastructure? The answer is not obvious, and certainly not predetermined by the clear evidence to the contrary for hunting and

[1] K. Marx, Introduction to *A Contribution to the Critique of Political Economy*, in numerous editions and translations.

[2] James Woodburn, 'Hunters and gathers today and reconstruction of the past', in E. Gellner (ed.), *Soviet and Western Anthropology* (London and New York: Duckworth, 1980).

[3] The problems, empirical and theoretical, which face the doctrine of a regular relation between social base and superstructure in Marxism, and their greater acuteness once a unilineal view of social development is dropped, do receive some attention in Soviet thought. See for instance Eero Loone, *Sovremennaia Filosofia Istorii* (Contemporary Philosophy of History) (Tallin Eesti raamat, 1980), especially part IV.

agrarian societies. It *could* be that industrial man will, in the end, have fewer social options than his hunter and peasant ancestor. It *could* be that the thesis that all industrial societies eventually come to resemble each other is correct, or at any rate will in the long run turn out to be such. With specific reference to culture and nationalism, what may we expect?

It may be convenient to explore first this convergence thesis. Suppose it *were* indeed the case that the industrial mode of production uniquely determines the culture of society: the same technology canalizes people into the same type of activity and the same kinds of hierarchy, and that the same kind of leisure styles were also engendered by the existing techniques and by the needs of productive life. Diverse languages might and probably would, of course, survive: but the social uses to which they were being put, the meanings available in them, would be much the same in any language within this wider shared industrial culture.

In such a world, a man moving from one language to another might indeed need to learn a new vocabulary, new words for familiar things and contexts, and he might also, at worst, have to learn a new grammar, in a more or less purely linguistic sense; but this would be about the limit of the adjustment demanded of him. No new thought styles would be required of him. He could all in all comport himself like a tourist with a phrase book, confident that all he needed was to locate the new phrase for an old and familiar need. The tourist would move from one area to another, knowing that within each of them human requirements are bounded by the want of a room, meal, drink, petrol, tourist office, and a few other things. Likewise, in a world in which the convergence thesis were wholly valid, inter-linguistic adjustment would be a simple matter of exchanging one verbal currency for another, within a well-run international conceptual system in which exchange rates were fairly stable, fixed and reliable.

There is clearly an element of truth in this. Industrial society has a complex division of labour and interdependence internationally as well as internally. Notwithstanding the care national states take not to be too specialized and hence too dependent on others, the amount of international trade is very great, and so is the accompanying conceptual and institutional convergence. It is deeply significant that credit cards are valid across Iron Curtains. You can freely use your credit card in countries where you cannot freely speak your mind. The dollar is quite legally used as currency in at least one socialist system. There is notoriously an international, trans-ideological youth culture.

In the industrial age only high cultures in the end effectively survive. Folk cultures and little traditions survive only artificially, kept going by language and folklore preservation societies. Moreover, the high cultures of industrial societies are a special breed among high cultures in general, and resemble each other more than do agrarian high cultures. They are tied to a shared cognitive base and a consciously global economy. They probably overlap more closely than did the old high cultures that were once deeply pervaded by distinctive theologies, by their culturally private, idiosyncratic cognitive systems.

Is this the whole truth? Should one expect that eventually, with the consummation of effective industrialization, inter-cultural and inter-linguistic differences will degenerate into merely phonetic ones, when only the superficial tokens of communication are variable, while the semantic content and the social context of utterances and actions become universal, non-regional? If that came to be, the communication gap between diverse 'languages' could become negligibly small, and the corresponding social gap, the counter-entropic, mobility-inhibiting effect of diverse linguistic and cultural backgrounds could become correspondingly insignificant. No nationalist inhibitions would then impede inter-cultural amity and internationalism.

To some extent and in some areas, something of this kind does in fact already happen: two equally sophisticated well-trained members of the upper professional layers of developed industrial countries feel little strain and need to adjust when visiting each other's lands, irrespective of how competent they are at speaking each other's language, in the literal sense. They happily co-operate in the multinational corporation. They already 'speak each other's language', even if they do not speak each other's language. At that level something like an international labour market and interchangeability already obtain. But can or will this situation become generalized? It is ironic that intellectuals, the driving force of initial nationalism, are now, in a world of nation-states, often the ones who move with the greatest ease between states, with the least prejudice, as once they did in the days of an international inter-state clerisy.

If this freedom of international movement became general, nationalism would cease to be a problem; or at any rate, communication gaps engendered by cultural differences would cease to be significant and would no longer produce nationalist tensions. Nationalism as a permanent problem, as a Damocles' sword hanging over any polity which dares to defy the nationalist imperative of the congruence of political and cultural boundaries, would be removed, and cease to be an ever-present and acute threat.

In this hypothetical global continuum of a basically homogeneous industrial culture, differentiated by languages which are distinct only phonet-
ically and superficially but not semantically, the age of nationalism would
become a matter of the past.

I do not believe that this will come to pass. I am inclined to follow
J.-F. Revel on this point.

> Les peuples ne sont pas tous les mêmes. Ils ne l'étaient pas dans la misère,
> ils ne le sont pas dans le luxe.[4]
>
> (Nations are not all alike. They weren't alike in poverty, and they are not
> alike in luxury.)

The shared constraints of industrial production, of a unique background science, and of a complex international interdependence and sustained continuous contact and communication, will no doubt produce a
certain measure of global cultural convergence, a fair amount of which
we can see already. This will prevent failure of communication arising
from cultural divergence from being quite such a major factor in exacer-
bating tension between the more and the less privileged. (It will not
prevent other counter-entropic traits from aggravation or provoking tensions.) Within developed countries, countries within which the great
majority of the citizens have reasonably good and not very unequal access
to the dominant economically effective high culture, and where the existing inequalities cannot be dredged to the surface and activated politically
by a cultural or 'ethnic' net, a certain amount of secondary cultural pluralism and diversity may emerge again, and be politically innocuous.
Given generalized development, and something like equal access to social
perks, then related cultures, or those with a shared history, will be able to
cohabit amicably. The linguistic plurality of the Swiss canton of the
Grisons does not seem to have put the political unity of that canton under
stress. The same cannot be said of canton Bern, where the inhabitants of
the Jura were sufficiently discontented with the German-speaking unit to
effect, not without conflict, a reorganization of the Swiss Confederacy.

But it remains difficult to imagine two large, politically viable,
independence-worthy cultures cohabiting under a single political roof,
and trusting a single political centre to maintain and service both cultures
with perfect or even adequate impartiality. The degree of sovereignty

---

[4] J.F. Revel, *En France* (Paris: Juillard, 1965).

which national states will retain in various circumstances can be foreseen – the restrictions on sovereignty by bodies such as the United Nations, regional confederations and alliances and so forth – is not a subject of this study, nor a topic which absolutely needs to be discussed here; but it would seem overwhelmingly likely that differences between cultural styles of life and communication, despite a similar economic base, will remain large enough to require separate servicing, and hence distinct cultural-political units, whether or not they will be wholly sovereign.

How about the other extreme possibility? The alternative pole corresponds to a situation in which distinct cultures would remain just as incommensurate and incompatible as they are alleged to have been among pre-industrial cultures, if not more so. This question is complicated by the fact that it is by no means clear, among anthropologists or others, just *how* totally incommensurate and self-sufficient pre-industrial cultures were.

In its extreme form, the (recently quite fashionable) incommensurability thesis runs something as follows: each culture or way of life has its own standards not merely of virtue, but also of reality itself, and no culture may ever legitimately be judged, let alone condemned, by the standards of another, or by standards pretending to be universal and above all cultures (for there are no such higher and external norms). This position is usually urged by romantics, using it as a premiss for defending archaic beliefs and customs from rational criticism, and insisting that the idea of extraneous, universally rational standards is a myth. In this form, such a position would seem to entail a virulent nationalism, in as far as it clearly entails that the subjection of one culture to the political management administered by members of another must always be iniquitous.

I am deeply sceptical about the applicability of the incommensurability thesis even to agrarian societies. I do not believe it can legitimately be used to deny the possibility of inter-cultural communication, or of the comparative evaluation of agrarian and industrial cultures. The incommensurability thesis owes some of its plausibility to a tendency to take too seriously the self-absolutizing, critic-anathematizing official faiths of late agrarian societies, which indeed are generally so constructed as to be logically invulnerable from outside and perpetually self-confirming from inside. Despite these notorious traits, which have now become repellent to men of liberal inclinations, the adherents of these faiths have, in practice, known how to transcend their own much advertised blinkers. They are and were conceptually bilingual, and knew how to switch from commensurate to incommensurate idioms with ease and alacrity. Functionaries of nominally exclusive, truth-monopolizing faiths nonetheless participate amicably in discussions at the World Council of Churches. The question concerning just *how* we manage to transcend relativism is interesting and difficult, and certainly will not be solved here. What is relevant, however, is that we somehow or other do manage to overcome it, that we are not helplessly imprisoned within a set of cultural cocoons and their norms, and that for some very obvious reasons (shared cognitive and productive bases and greatly increased inter-social communication) we may expect fully industrial man to be even less enslaved to his local culture than was his agrarian predecessor.

On this issue the truth seems to me to lie somewhere in the middle. The shared economic infrastructure of advanced industrial society and its inescapable implications will continue to ensure that men are dependent on culture, and that culture requires standardization over quite wide areas, and needs to be maintained and serviced by centralized agencies. In other words, men will continue to owe their employability and social acceptability to sustained and complex training, which cannot be supplied by kin or local group. This being so, the definition of political units and boundaries will not be able to ignore with impunity the distribution of cultures. By and large, ignoring minor and innocuous exceptions, the nationalist imperative of the congruence of political unit and of culture will continue to apply. In that sense, one need not expect the age of nationalism to come to an end.

But the sharpness of nationalist conflict may be expected to diminish. It was the social chasms created by early industrialism, and by the unevenness of its diffusion, which made it acute. Those social chasms were probably no worse than those which agrarian society tolerates without batting an eyelid, but they were no longer softened or legitimated by longevity and custom, and they occurred in a context which in other ways encouraged hope and the expectation of equality, and which required mobility. Whenever cultural differences served to mark off these chasms, then there was trouble indeed. When they did not, nothing much happened. 'Nations', ethnic groups, were not nationalist when states were formed in fairly stable agrarian systems. Classes, however oppressed and exploited, did not overturn the political system when they could not define themselves 'ethnically'. Only when a nation became a class, a visible and unequally distributed category in an otherwise mobile system, did it become politically conscious and activist. Only when a class happened to be (more or less) a 'nation' did it turn from being a class-in-itself into a class-for-itself, or a nation-for-itself. Neither nations nor classes seem to be political catalysts: only nation-classes or class-nations are such.

An interesting author who attempts to salvage Marxism, or unearth or invent a new viable form of it, recognizes this fact.[5] Late industrial society no longer engenders such deep social abysses, which could then be activated by ethnicity. (It will continue to encounter difficulties, sometimes tragic ones, from counter-entropic traits such as 'race' which visibly contradict its overt egalitarianism.) It will have to respect cultural differences where they survive, provided that they are superficial and do not engender genuine barriers between people, in which case the barriers, not the cultures, constitute a grave problem. Though the old plethora of folk cultures is unlikely to survive, except in a token and cellophane-packaged form, an international plurality of sometimes fairly diverse high cultures will no doubt (happily) remain with us. The infrastructural investment made in them can be relied on to perpetuate them. Partly because many boundaries have already adjusted themselves to the boundaries of these cultures, and partly because the nationalist imperative is now so widely respected that developed societies seldom defy it brazenly, and try to avoid head-on confrontations with it: for these various reasons, late industrial society (if mankind is spared long enough to enjoy it) can be expected to be one in which nationalism persists, but in a muted, less virulent form.

[5]   Nairn 1977.

9

Nationalism and Ideology

A conspicuous feature of our treatment of nationalism has been a lack of interest in the history of nationalist ideas and the contributions and nuances of individual nationalist thinkers. This is in marked contrast to many other approaches to this subject. This attitude does not spring from any generalized contempt for the role of ideas in history. Some ideas and belief systems do make a very great difference. (It is not necessarily the good ideas which make the greatest impact. Some ideas are good and some bad, and some make a great impact and some make none, and there is no systematic relationship between these two oppositions.) For instance, the belief systems known as Christianity and Marxism, are both of them contingent: each of them consists of a complex of themes, which individually may have been inherent in the situation in which it came into being, but which, as a particular combination endowed with a name and a historic existence and continuity, were only forged into some kind of unity by a set of thinkers or preachers.

This unity in some measure survives the selective use made of them subsequently. Moreover, once they emerged, they came on occasion to dominate societies which happened to take their doctrines with great seriousness, and applied them (or some of them) with great determination. This being so, if we are to understand the fate of these societies, we are sometimes obliged to look carefully at the words, doctrines and arguments of the thinkers who forged the faiths that dominate them. For instance, the particular ethnographic doctrines which happened to influence Marx and Engels in the 1870s, about the survival of the communal spirit in villages of backward countries and the conditions of its perpetuation, are incorporated in a crucial manner in Marxism, and probably had a decisive and disastrous effect on Soviet agrarian policy.

But this does not seem to me to be the case with nationalism. (This incidentally may help to explain why nationalism, notwithstanding its indisputable importance, has received relatively little attention from academic political philosophers: there was not enough in the way of good doctrines and texts, which is the kind of material they used to like, for them to get their teeth into.)[1] It is not so much that the prophets of nationalism were not anywhere near the First Division, when it came to the business of thinking: that in itself would not prevent a thinker from having an enormous, genuine and crucial influence on history. Numerous examples prove that. It is rather that these thinkers did not really make much difference. If one of them had fallen, others would have stepped into his place. (They liked saying something rather like this themselves, though not quite in the sense intended here.) No-one was indispensable. The quality of nationalist thought would hardly have been affected much by such substitutions.

Their precise doctrines are hardly worth analysing. We seem to be in the presence of a phenomenon which springs directly and inevitably from basic changes in our shared social condition, from changes in the overall relation between society, culture and polity. The precise appearance and local form of this phenomenon no doubt depends a very great deal on local circumstances which deserve study; but I doubt whether the nuances of nationalist *doctrine* played much part in modifying those circumstances.

Generally speaking, nationalist ideology suffers from pervasive false consciousness. Its myths invert reality: it claims to defend folk culture while in fact it is forging a high culture; it claims to protect an old folk society while in fact helping to build up an anonymous mass society. (Prenationalist Germany was made up of a multiplicity of genuine communities, many of them rural. Post-nationalist united Germany was mainly industrial and a mass society.) Nationalism tends to treat itself as a

---

[1]   The disproportion between the importance of nationalism and the amount of thought given to it is noted by Professor Eric Hobsbawm in his 'Some Reflections on Nationalism', in *Imagination and Precision in the Social Sciences, Essays in Memory of Peter Nettl*, eds. T.J. Nossiter, A.H. Hanson, Stein Rokkan et al. (Atlantic Heights, N.J.: Faber, 1972). He quotes from D. Mack Smith's *Il Risorgimento* (Bari: Laterza, 1968), some truly bizarre views of Mazzini on the proper nationalist organization of Europe, which would have included Slovenia in a kind of Greater Switzerland, and joined up Magyars, Romanians and Czechs with, for some reason, Herzegovina. All in all Mazzini, outside Italy, seemed to have more sense of the political economies of scale and of territorial compactness than of cultural sensibilities.

manifest and self-evident principle, accessible as such to all men, and violated only through some perverse blindness, when in fact it owes its plausibility and compelling nature only to a very special set of circumstances, which do indeed obtain now, but which were alien to most of humanity and history. It preaches and defends continuity, but owes everything to a decisive and unutterably profound break in human history. It preaches and defends cultural diversity, when in fact it imposes homogeneity both inside and, to a lesser degree, between political units. Its self-image and its true nature are inversely related, with an ironic neatness seldom equalled even by other successful ideologies. Hence it seems to me that, generally speaking, we shall not learn too much about nationalism from the study of its own prophets.

Shall we learn more from studying its enemies? A little more, but we need to be cautious. Their main merit seems to me that they teach us not to take nationalism at its own valuation, on its own terms, and as something self-evident. The temptation to do so is so deeply built into the modern condition, where men simply assume that culturally homogeneous units, with culturally similar rulers and ruled, are a norm whose violation is inherently scandalous. To be shocked out of this pervasive assumption is indeed something for which one must be grateful. It is a genuine illumination.

But it would be just as disastrous to follow a declared enemy of nationalism such as Elie Kedourie all the way, and treat nationalism as a contingent, avoidable aberration, accidentally spawned by European thinkers. Nationalism – the principle of homogeneous cultural units as the foundations of political life, and of the obligatory cultural unity of rules and ruled – is indeed inscribed neither in the nature of things, nor in the hearts of men, nor in the pre-conditions of social life in general, and the contention that it *is* so inscribed is a falsehood which nationalist doctrine has succeeded in presenting as self-evident. But nationalism as a phenomenon, not as a doctrine presented by nationalists, is inherent in a certain set of social conditions; and those conditions, it so happens, are the conditions of our time.

To deny this is at least as great a mistake as to accept nationalism on its own terms. There is something bizarre in the suggestion that a force so widespread and pervasive, a flame that springs up so strongly and spontaneously in so many disconnected places, and which needs so very little fanning to become a devouring forest blaze, should spring from nothing more than some extremely abstruse lucubrations of philosophers. For better or for worse, our ideas seldom have quite such power.

In an age of cheap paper, print, and widespread literacy and easy communication, any number of ideologies are spawned and compete for our favour; and they are often formulated and propagated by men with greater literary and propagandist gifts than those which nature chose to bestow on the prophets of nationalism. Yet these other forms of nonsense have never had a remotely comparable impact on mankind. This was not due to lesser literary merit on their part. Nor can it be a matter of luck; the experiment has been repeated in so many parts of the globe that, if chance were the king here, one might confidently expect a far more motley overall pattern, with one kind of doctrine prevailing in one place and quite another kind somewhere else. But it is not so: the trend of events points much the same way in most places. And as we *can* trace a clear and manifest connection between the general social conditions of our age and this overwhelmingly predominant trend, then surely we are justified in invoking that link, rather than the accidental appeal of an arbitrary idea, thrown up by the play of European intellectual fancy at the turn of the eighteenth and nineteenth centuries!

In the case of nationalism (though the same is not always true of other movements), the actual formulation of the idea or ideas, the question concerning who said or wrote precisely what, doesn't matter much. The key idea is in any case so very simple and easy that anyone can make it up almost at any time, which is partly why nationalism can claim that nationalism is *always* natural. What matters is whether the conditions of life are such as to make the idea seem compelling, rather than, as it is in most other situations, absurd.

In this connection it is worth saying something about the role of communication in the dissemination of the nationalist idea. This term plays a crucial part in the analysis of nationalism of at least one noted author.[2] But the usual formulation of the connection between nationalism and the facility of modern communications is somewhat misleading. It gives the impression that a given idea (nationalism) happens to be there, and then the printed word and the transistor and other media help this notion to reach audiences in distant valleys and self-contained villages and encampments, audiences which in an age not blessed with mass media would have remained untouched by it.

That is altogether the wrong way to see it. The media do not transmit an idea which happens to have been fed into them. It matters precious little what has been fed into them: it is the media themselves, the

---

[2]   Deutsch 1966.

pervasiveness and importance of abstract, centralized, standardized, one to many communication, which itself automatically engenders the core idea of nationalism, quite irrespective of what in particular is being put into the specific messages transmitted. The most important and persistent message is generated by the medium itself, by the role which such media have acquired in modern life. That core message is that the language and style of the transmissions is important, that only he who can understand them, or can acquire such comprehension, is included in a moral and economic community, and that he who does not and cannot, is excluded. All this is crystal clear, and follows from the pervasiveness and crucial role of mass communication in this kind of society. What is actually *said* matters little.

The manner in which conditions have changed, turning an idea which was once bizarre into one which is compelling and seemingly self-evident, can perhaps best be conveyed by invoking Kedourie's own concluding and crucial words:

> The only criterion capable of public defence is whether the new rulers are less corrupt and grasping, or more just and merciful, or whether there is no change at all, but the corruption, the greed, and the tyranny merely find victims other than those of the departed rulers. (Kedourie 1960, p. 140)

The question which Professor Kedourie asks with such eloquence is indeed one which a typical burgher in an agrarian society would ask himself, if one morning he just heard that the local Pasha had been overthrown and replaced by an altogether new one. If, at that point, his wife dared ask the burgher what language the new Pasha spoke in the intimacy of his home life – was it Arabic, Turkish, Persian, French or English? – the hapless burgher would give her a sharp look, and wonder how he would cope with all the new difficulties when, at the same time, his wife had gone quite mad. Probably he would send her to a shrine that specialized in acute mental aberration.

The question commended by Kedourie did indeed make sense in societies in which government on the one hand, and economy and society on the other, were distinct, where cultural continuity between the two was an irrelevancy, and where, as the quotation clearly implies, one may hope at best for merciful and just government, but not for an accountable, participatory and representative one. (Are these totally illusory aspirations among us, then?) But something other than the dissemination of the words of obscure European scribblers must have happened to make the wife's query, once so manifestly mad, become the question which is now upper-most in almost everyone's mind. And something has indeed happened. The economy is now such as to require sustained and precise communication between all those who take part in it, *and* between them and government, and the maintenance of the educational and cultural infrastructure has become one of the central tasks of government. Hence the home idiom of the new Pasha, once so irrelevant, is now the crucial sign as to whom the new power will favour and whom it will exclude.

In a later book, *Nationalism in Asia and Africa*, Kedourie does indeed ask questions about the European colonial domination of the world which are, quite rightly, totally and significantly different from the question recommended at the end of *Nationalism*. He comments at length on the failure of the European conquerors to accept as equals those members of the conquered populations who had acquired the necessary qualifications and skills, and he evidently considers this exclusiveness to be at least part of the explanation of why European rule produced the nationalist reaction which in fact it elicited. It is not entirely clear whether this is a criticism or merely a neutral diagnosis, though it is difficult not to feel that the former element is present; and if so, it would seem that a question *is* now being asked about rulers which is not only about their mercy and rapacity!

The new question is whether the rulers are willing and able to run a mobile society, one in which rulers and ruled can merge and form a cultural continuum. This, in my argument, is indeed the crucial question which under modern conditions is bound to be asked of all rulers, and to complement and largely overshadow the older question. But without these special modern conditions, why should their exclusiveness have been a demerit or a weakness? Some past rulers (Romans and Greeks) may at times have been open and receptive (though the Romans did not exactly rush about offering free Roman citizenship to any newly conquered area); but many others were not, without necessarily suffering for it. On the contrary, under traditional conditions, easy identifiability and seclusion of rulers must often have been a great asset, conducive to stability. The Mamluks did not benefit, as a class, when they intermarried with the market. Why should exclusiveness suddenly have become so disastrous and why should it have provoked such a virulent, widespread and shared reaction?

Kedourie himself provides the answer:

There is no gainsaying the fact that Europe has been the origin and centre of a deep radical disturbance spreading over the world in everwidening ripples and bringing unsettlement and violence to the traditional societies of Asia and Africa, whether these societies did or did not experience direct European rule . . . This pulverization of traditional societies, this bursting open of self-sufficient economies . . .

If one supplements this account, with which one could hardly disagree, with the question of what kind of new re-organization is feasible, given modern productive methods and the society which they imply, then, I contend, one comes out with an answer which makes modern nationalism more than either an ideological accident or the fruit of mere resentment, and which shows it, in its general forms if not in its details, to be a necessity.

It may be worth giving a short, no doubt incomplete, list of false theories of nationalism:

1   It is natural and self-evident and self generating. If absent, this must be due to forceful repression.

2   It is an artificial consequence of ideas which did not need ever to be formulated, and appeared by a regrettable accident. Political life even in industrial societies could do without it.

3   The Wrong Address Theory favoured by Marxism: just as extreme Shi'ite Muslims hold that Archangel Gabriel made a mistake, delivering the Message to Mohamed when it was intended for Ali, so Marxists basically like to think that the spirit of history or human consciousness made a terrible boob. The awakening message was intended for *classes*, but by some terrible postal error was delivered to *nations*. It is now necessary for revolutionary activists to persuade the wrongful recipient to hand over the message, and the zeal it engenders, to the rightful and intended recipient. The unwillingness of both the rightful and the usurping recipient to fall in with this requirement causes the activist great irritation.

4   Dark Gods: Nationalism is the re-emergence of the atavistic forces of blood or territory. This is the view shared often by both lovers and haters of nationalism. The former think of these dark forces as life-enhancing, the latter as barbarous. In fact, man of the age of nationalism is neither nicer nor nastier than men of other ages. There is some slight evidence that he may be nicer. His crimes are equalled by those of other ages. They are more conspicuous only because, precisely, they have become more shocking, and because they are executed with more powerful technological means.

Not one of these theories is remotely tenable.

Who is for Nuremberg?

An author committed to the view that the ideological or doctrinal history of nationalism is largely irrelevant to the understanding of it should not perhaps indulge in debates about its intellectual ancestry. If it has no doctrinal ancestry worth discussing, why should we argue about who does and who does not figure in its genealogy? Nevertheless, some remarks seem called for by Kedourie's influential account of its ideal origins.

Leaving aside the strange implicit exculpation of Hegel, what seems both perplexing and unfair is the inculpation of Kant. Certainly the notion of self-determination is absolutely central to Kant's thought. Kant's main problem was the validation (*and* circumscription) of both our scientific and our moral knowledge. The main philosophic device he employs for the attainment of this end is the contention that our guiding cognitive and moral principles are self-generated, and inescapably so. As there is no final authority or validation to be found outside, it must be inside.

That is the core of his thought. The authority of the principles we live by resides in the fact that our minds necessarily have a certain structure, which inescapably engenders them. This gives us, among other things, an ethic of impartiality, and also the justified hope of finding exceptionless regularities in nature. An orderly ethic and an orderly science are thus, both of them, underwritten. The fact that the structure of our minds is *given* and rigid frees us from the fear that these bases of science and morality might be at the mercy of caprice, that they might turn out to be quicksands. Though they are based on us only, yet, on this view, we can be trusted, and provide a reliable base. The fact that it is we, or rather, each single one of us individually (though mutually respectful of each other) who assumes responsibility for these principles, frees Kant from the fear of a regression which was repellent both to the logician and to the protestant within him: if the authority and the justification were outside us, (however elevated it might be), how could that authority in turn be justified?

The authority of the self, unsusceptible to caprice, final and absolute, terminates the regression. It avoids the scandal, intolerably repugnant both to the logician and the moralist in Kant, of accepting some outside authority, however elevated: the scandal of heteronomy, as he himself called it, which is the antithesis of self-determination. At the same time, the fortunate rigidity of the self makes its authority reliable and usable.

That is the essence of Kant's philosophy, the picture contained in *his* notion of 'self-determination'. What connection, other than a purely verbal one, does it have with the self-determination of nations, which so concerns the nationalists? None. It is individual human nature which is really sovereign for Kant – the transference of sovereignty to it constituted his Copernican revolution – and it is universal and identical in all men. It is the universal in man which he revered, not the specific, and certainly not the *culturally* specific. In such a philosophy, there is no place for the mystique of the idiosyncratic culture. There is in fact hardly any room for culture in the anthropological sense at all. A person's identity and dignity is for Kant rooted in his universal humanity, or, more broadly, his rationality, and not in his cultural or ethnic specificity. It is hard to think of a writer whose ideas provide less comfort for the nationalist.

On the contrary: Kant's identification of man with that which is rational and universal in him, his fastidious and persistent, highly characteristic distaste for basing anything of importance on that which is merely contingent, historical or specific, makes Kant a very model for that allegedly bloodless, cosmopolitan, emaciated ethic of the Enlightenment, which romantic nationalists spurned and detested so much, and which they so joyously repudiated in favour of a more earthy, shamelessly specific and partial commitment to kin or territory or culture.

This point is of some general interest. Kant is the very last person whose vision could be credited with having contributed to nationalism. Nevertheless, this accusation is not simply an error, but springs from something deeper which deserves note. What *is* true is that Kant felt an acute need to base our central values on ideas, on something less fragile, less contingent, less world-bound than the mere tradition which happens to prevail in this land or that. His whole philosophical strategy reflects this need and the acuteness with which he felt it. He thought he could satisfy it by invoking the universal structure of the human mind.

From the viewpoint of a crypto-romantic traditionalism which spurns such pursuit of external, 'rational' bases for the practices of life, which wishes to teach men to stay content within the limits of concrete *praxis*, to accept the contingency of history, and to refrain from seeking the illusory comfort and support of extraneous and abstract ideas, Kant is certainly a deeply misguided figure. He was most certainly a 'rationalist' in the sense in which Professor Michael Oakeshott pejoratively uses the term, and *Nationalism in Asia and Africa* seems to be argued within this general framework. In other words, Kant most certainly does belong to the Promethean strand in European thought, which perhaps reached its apogee in the eighteenth century, which strives to steal the divine fire and will not be content with the makeshift accidental compromises contained in specific traditions. Kant makes his deep contempt for such attitudes, for allowing oneself to be satisfied with merely contingent, historic foundations, utterly plain.

Kant's insistence on individual self-determination as the only genuinely valid morality was neither wilful nor romantic. It was, on the contrary, a despairing attempt to preserve a genuine, objective, binding, universal ethic (and knowledge). Kant accepted Hume's argument that necessity and universality simply were not there to be found in the empirical data; hence, he reasoned, they could only be rooted in the ineluctably imposed structure of the individual mind. Admittedly, this *faute de mieux* solution also fitted in neatly with a kind of protestant individualist pride, which scorns to find authority outside. But the main reason why authority had to be inside the individual was because it simply could not be found anywhere else.

Nationalists, when they invoke the abstract principle of nationalism against the traditional local institutions which had once worked tolerably well, are indeed fellow-Private Prometheans. In fact, nationalism has a Janus-like quality. It is Promethean in its contempt for political compromise which ignores the nationalist imperative. But it is also anti-Promethean, when it sees the nation and its cultural development as something which, just because it is concrete and historically specific, rightly overrides the abstract morality of the internationalists and humanists.

In this very, *very* generic, and above all *negative* sense, Kant and the nationalists can perhaps be classed together. Neither of them are, in the required sense, respecters of tradition. (Or rather, nationalism is opportunistically selective in the respect which it accords to tradition.) Both are, in this wide sense, 'rationalists', seeking the bases of legitimacy in something beyond that which merely *is*.

Nationalists, in fact, might well acclaim conservative traditionalists as brothers, as fellow-repudiators of the abstract rationalism of the Enlightenment, and very often do so. Both of them wish to respect or revere the concrete realities of history, and refuse to subject them to the verdict of a bloodless abstract pan-human reason. Far from revelling in the defiant individual will, nationalists delight in feelings of submission or incorporation in a continuous entity greater, more persistent and more legitimate than the isolated self. In a curious way, Kedourie not only credits nationalism with a theory of wilful self-determination, but also (erroneously in my view) concedes the historical success of such a nationalism. A theory sprang from the heads of certain philosophers, and those who became converted to it succeeded, by sheer will, in imposing the theory on hapless humanity! This stark version of his view, which initially makes few concessions to the social circumstances which favoured nationalism, would make its success seem a veritable triumph of the will.

It just so happens, it seems to me, that nationalists or conservatives select different parts of the concrete for their reference: in the one case, continuous institutions, and in the other, allegedly continuous communities of speech, race, or some other notion. But is that not a disagreement on detail rather than principle? This affinity of underlying attitude does not, of course, prove either of these positions to be necessarily in error. I only invoke it to show that one man's sense of concrete historical reality is another man's *trahison des clercs*. How are we to choose our realists?

So not all those who spurn a given position (traditionalism) therefore necessarily resemble each other in any other way. This mistaken inference, reinforced by the homonym 'self-determination', seems to be at the base of the accusation of Kant. Kant did indeed speak of self-determination (autonomy). But then, he also spoke a great deal about the synthetic *a priori* status of our categories. It is well-established history that no bombs have been ever thrown on behalf of Kant's doctrine of the *a priori* status of categories. But the same is just as true of his views on self-determination. If a connection exists between Kant and nationalism at all, then nationalism is a reaction against him, and not his offspring.

One Nation, One State

Nationalist sentiment is deeply offended by violations of the nationalist principle of congruence of state and nation; but it is not equally offended by all the various kinds of violation of it. It is most acutely offended by ethnic divergence between rulers and ruled. As Lord Acton put it

> Then began a time when the text simply was, that nations would not be governed by foreigners. Power legitimately attained, and exercised with moderation, was declared invalid.[3]

Note that Acton shows that this time *began*, whereas nationalists pretend it was ever present in a latent, suppressed form. But when it comes to the arithmetical non-correspondence between nation and state, it is more offended if, so to speak, the state is too few, than if it is too many.

---

[3]   Quoted in Kohn 1955, pp. 122–3.

A culturally homogeneous population which has no state at all to call its own is deeply aggrieved. (Its members are obliged to live in a state, or in states, run by other and alien cultural groups.) A group which, on the other hand, has more than one state associated with its culture, though it is also technically violating the national principle, yet has less grievance, except perhaps in special circumstances. What are they?

Most New Zealanders and most citizens of the United Kingdom are so continuous culturally that without any shadow of doubt the two units would never have separated, had they been contiguous geographically. Distance made the effective sovereignty of New Zealand convenient and mandatory, and the separation does not provoke resentment in anyone's breast, notwithstanding the technical violation of the national principle. Why not? There are Arabs who deplore the failure of the Arabs to unite, though Arabs of different countries differ culturally far more than Englishmen and New Zealanders. The obvious answer seems to be that the international standing and general position of the English and of the New Zealanders does not suffer significantly from their failure to present themselves to the world as one unit. In fact, their standing does not suffer from this fact at all, and the inconveniences of the alternative arrangement would be very considerable. By contrast, it is arguable that the political strength of Arabs, Latin Americans,[4] and pre-unification nineteenth-century Italians and Germans did suffer from the fragmentation of their political roofs.

Nevertheless, this particular violation of the national principle, the one nation-many states case, is clearly the least septic, the least irritant of all the possible violations. The obstacles lying in the way of its correction are obvious and powerful. If a given nation is blessed with n states, it follows rigorously that the glorious unification of the nation will mean the diminution of the number of its prime ministers, chiefs of staff, presidents of the academy, managers and skippers of its football team, and so on, by a factor of n. For every person occupying a post of this kind after unification, there will be $n-1$ who will have lost it. In anticipation, all those $n-1$ stand to lose by unification, even if the nation as a whole benefits.

Admittedly the one fortunate enough to have retained or acquired the post in question is now laureate, director of the national theatre, and so on, of something bigger, more glorious, and associated with far greater

---

[4] The continued complaisance of Latin Americans in the face of this situation is cogently invoked against our theory by José Merquior in 'Politics of Transition', *Government and Opposition*, 16 (1981), no. 2, p. 230.

resources than before. All the same, there can be little doubt that while it is better to be head of a big 'un than a little 'un, the difference is not so drastic as that between being a head, never mind of how much, and not being a head at all. Even allowing for the effect of the illusion which may have encouraged a lot more than one of the little 'uns to expect that *they* will be the big 'un when the day comes, the fact remains that on balance, the rational opposition to unification must be considerable. Unification succeeds, nevertheless, only in those cases where the external disadvantages of fragmentation are very great and visible, and those who suffer from them can make their interests felt against those who will lose out in the n-fold diminution of political jobs, and when the new leaders of the larger unity somehow succeed in imposing themselves on the others, by force or by political glamour.

10

Conclusion

A book like this, which argues a simple and sharply defined case, never-theless (or perhaps all the more) risks being misunderstood and mis-represented. Attempts to present earlier and simpler versions of this argument on previous occasions have convinced me of the reality of this danger. On the one hand, the very simplicity and starkness of the posi-tion may lead readers to add to it their own associations, which were not intended by the author. On the other hand, any new position (which is what I fondly believe this one to be) can be articulated only if the frame for asserting it is first set up, however quietly. No original assertion can be made, I think, by simply drawing on the cards already available in the language pack that is in use. The pack has been dealt too often, and all simple statements in it have been made many times before. Hence a new contribution to a topic is possible only by re-designing a pack so as to make a new statement possible in it. To do this very visibly is intolerably pedantic and tedious. The overt erection of a new scaffolding is tolerable in mathematics, but not in ordinary prose. Good presentation consists in fairly unobtrusively loosening the habitual associations, setting up new ones on principles which become evident from the context, until at last the context *has* been set up in which an assertion can be made which is simple, and yet not a trite repetition of the old wisdom.

What is not being Said

Only others can judge whether I have succeeded in this endeavour. But experience has taught me that one is seldom if ever wholly successful in this. Hence I wish to list a few assertions which have *neither* been asserted *nor* are in any way required for the views which have been propounded.

It is no part of my purpose to deny that mankind has at all times lived in groups. On the contrary, men have always lived in groups. Usually these groups persisted over time. One important factor in their persistence was the loyalty men felt for these groups, and the fact that they identified with them. This element in human life did not need to wait for some distinctive kind of economy. This was, of course, not the only factor helping to perpetuate these groups, but it was one among others. If one calls this factor, generically, 'patriotism', then it is no part of my intention to deny that some measure of such patriotism is indeed a perennial part of human life. (How strong it was in relation to other forces is something we need not try to decide here.)

What is being claimed is that nationalism is a very distinctive species of patriotism, and one which becomes pervasive and dominant only under certain social conditions, which in fact prevail in the modern world, and nowhere else. Nationalism is a species of patriotism distinguished by a few very important features: the units which this kind of patriotism, namely nationalism, favours with its loyalty, are culturally homogeneous, based on a culture striving to be a high (literate) culture; they are large enough to sustain the hope of supporting the educational system which can keep a literate culture going; they are poorly endowed with rigid internal sub-groupings; their populations are anonymous, fluid and mobile, and they are unmediated; the individual belongs to them directly, in virtue of his cultural style, and not in virtue of membership of nested sub-groups. Homogeneity, literacy, anonymity are the key traits.

It is not claimed that cultural chauvinism was generally absent from the pre-industrial world, but only that it did not have its modern political clout or aspirations. It is not denied that the agrarian world occasionally threw up units which may have resembled a modern national state; only that the agrarian world *could* occasionally do so, whilst the modern world is *bound* to do so in most cases.

It is not claimed that, even in the modern world, nationalism is the only force operating, or an irresistible one. It is not. It is occasionally defeated by some other force or interest, or by inertia.

It is not denied that one may on occasion have an overlay of pre-industrial structures and national sentiment. A tribal nation may for a time be tribal internally and national externally. It is in fact easy to think of one or two marked cases of this kind (for example, Somalis and Kurds). But a man may now claim to belong to one of these national units simply in virtue of his culture, and he need not disclose (and eventually, need not even *have*) a mediating sub-group membership. It is not claimed that the present argument can explain why some nationalisms, notably those of the Hitler and Mussolini period, should have become so specially virulent. It only claims to explain why nationalism has emerged and become pervasive.

All these disclaimers are not an insurance against counter-examples, which would at the same time covertly reduce the content of the central thesis to something approaching naught. They are only the recognition that in a complex world, at the macro-level of institutions and groupings, exceptionless generalizations are seldom if ever available. This does not prevent overall trends, such as nationalism, from being conspicuous – or being sociologically explicable.

Summary

In this matter as in some others, once we describe the phenomenon we are interested in with precision, we come close to explaining it correctly. (Perhaps we can only describe things well when we have already understood them.) But consider the history of the national principle; or consider two ethnographic maps, one drawn up before the age of nationalism, and the other after the principle of nationalism had done much of its work.

The first map resembles a painting by Kokoschka. The riot of diverse points of colour is such that no clear pattern can be discerned in any detail, though the picture as a whole does have one. A great diversity and plurality and complexity characterizes all distinct parts of the whole: the minute social groups, which are the atoms of which the picture is composed, have complex and ambiguous and multiple relations to many cultures; some through speech, others through their dominant faith, another still through a variant faith or set of practices, a fourth through administrative loyalty, and so forth. When it comes to painting the political system, the complexity is not less great than in the sphere of culture. Obedience for one purpose and in one context is not necessarily the same as obedience for some other end or in some other season.

Look now instead at the ethnographic and political map of an area of the modern world. It resembles not Kokoschka, but, say, Modigliani. There is very little shading; neat flat surfaces are clearly separated from each other, it is generally plain where one begins and another ends, and there is little if any ambiguity or overlap. Shifting from the map to the reality mapped, we see that an overwhelming part of political authority has been concentrated in the hands of one kind of institution, a reasonably large and well-centralized state. In general, each such state presides over, maintains, and is identified with, one kind of culture, one style of communication, which prevails within its borders and is dependent for its perpetuation on a centralized educational system supervised by and often actually run by the state in question, which monopolizes legitimate culture almost as much as it does legitimate violence, or perhaps more so.

And when we look at the society controlled by this kind of state, we also see why all this must be so. Its economy depends on mobility and communication between individuals, at a level which can only be achieved if those individuals have been socialized into a high culture, and indeed into the same high culture, at a standard which cannot be ensured by the old ways of turning out human beings, as it were on the job, as part of the ordinary business of living, by the local sub-communities. It can only be achieved by a fairly monolithic educational system. Also, the economic tasks set these individuals do not allow them to be both soldiers and citizens of local petty communities; they need to delegate such activities so as to be able to do their jobs.

So the economy needs both the new type of central culture and the central state; the culture needs the state; and the state probably needs the homogeneous cultural branding of its flock, in a situation in which it cannot rely on largely eroded sub-groups either to police its citizens, or to inspire them with that minimum of moral zeal and social identification without which social life becomes very difficult. Culture not community provides the inner sanctions, such as they are. In brief, the mutual relationship of a modern culture and state is something quite new, and springs, inevitably, from the requirements of a modern economy.

What has been asserted is very simple. Food-producing society was above all a society which allowed some men *not* to be food-producers, but (excepting parasitic communities) nevertheless obliged the majority of men to remain such. It is industrial society which has succeeded in dispensing with this need.

It has pushed the division of labour to a new and unprecedented level, but, more important still, it has engendered a new *kind* of division of labour: one requiring the men taking part in it to be ready to move from one occupational position to another, even within a single life-span, and certainly between generations. They need a shared culture, and a literate sophisticated high culture at that. It obliges them to be able to communicate contextlessly and with precision with all comers, in face-to-face ephemeral contacts, but also through abstract means of communication. All this – mobility, communication, size due to refinement of specialization – imposed on the industrial order by its thirst for affluence and growth, obliges its social units to be large and yet culturally homogeneous. The maintenance of this kind of inescapably high (because literate) culture requires protection by a state, a centralized order-enforcing agency or rather group of agencies, capable of garnering and deploying the resources which are needed both to sustain a high culture, and to ensure its diffusion through an entire population, an achievement inconceivable and not attempted in the pre-industrial world.

The high cultures of the industrial age differ from those of the agrarian order in a number of important and conspicuous ways. Agrarian high cultures were a minority accomplishment carried by privileged specialists, and distinguished from the fragmented, uncodified majority folk cultures over which they presided and which they strove to dominate. They defined a clerkly stratum seldom tied to a single political unit or linguistically delimited folk catchment area. On the contrary, they tended and strove to be trans-ethnic and trans-political. They frequently employed a dead or archaic idiom, and had no interest whatever in ensuring continuity between it and the idiom of daily and economic life. Their numerical minority and their political dominance were of their essence; and it is probably of the essence of agrarian society that its majority is constituted by food-producers excluded both from power and from the high culture. They were tied to a faith and church rather than to a state and pervasive culture. In China a high culture linked more to an ethic and a state bureaucracy than to a faith and church was perhaps untypical, and in that way, but that way only, anticipated the modern linkage of state and culture. There the high literate culture co-existed, and continues to co-exist, with a diversity of spoken languages.

By contrast, an industrial high culture is no longer linked – whatever its history – to a faith and a church. Its maintenance seems to require the resources of a state co-extensive with society, rather than merely those of a church superimposed on it. A growth-bound economy dependent on cognitive innovation cannot seriously link its cultural machinery (which it needs unconditionally) to some doctrinal faith which rapidly becomes obsolete, and often ridiculous.

So the culture needs to be sustained *as* a culture, and not as the carrier or scarcely noticed accompaniment of a faith. Society can and does worship itself or its own culture directly and not, as Durkheim taught, through the opaque medium of religion. The transition from one kind of high culture to the other is visible outwardly as the coming of national-ism. But, whatever the truth about this complex and crucial issue, the emergence of the industrial world was somehow intimately linked to a Protestantism which happened to possess some of the important traits that were to characterize the newly emerging world, and which also engender nationalism. The stress on literacy and scripturalism, the priest-less unitarianism which abolished the monopoly of the sacred, and the individualism which makes each man his own priest and conscience and not dependent on the ritual services of others: all foreshadowed an anony-mous, individualistic, fairly unstructured mass society, in which relatively equal access to a shared culture prevails, and the culture has its norms publicly accessible in writing, rather than in the keeping of a privileged specialist. Equal access to a scripturalist God paved the way to equal access to high culture. Literacy is no longer a specialism, but a pre-condition of all the specialisms, in a society in which everyone is a spe-cialist. In such a society, one's prime loyalty is to the medium of our literacy, and to its political protector. The equal access of believers to God eventually becomes equal access of unbelievers to education and culture.

Such is the world of modern state-sustained, pervasive and homo-geneous high cultures, within which there is relatively little ascription of status and a good deal of mobility, presupposing a well-diffused mastery of a shared sophisticated high culture. There is a profound irony in Max Weber's celebrated account of the origins of this world: it was engendered because certain men took their vocation so very seriously, and it produced a world in which rigidly ascribed vocations have gone, where specialisms abound but remain temporary and optional, involving no final commit-ment, and where the important, identity-conferring part of one's educa-tion or formation is not the special skill, but the shared generic skills, dependent on a shared high culture which defines a 'nation'. Such a nation/culture *then* and then only becomes the natural social unit, and cannot normally survive without its own political shell, the state.

Select Bibliography

This select bibliography contains all the items given by Gellner in the first edition but where appropriate they have been updated to take note of later editions or translations into English. In addition, I have tried to include most post-1983 general surveys or critiques, some readers and works of reference, some wide-ranging collections of essays and works that have opened up new concerns such as multiculturalism, the normative dimensions of nationalism, gender and discourse, as well as work that continued to explore 'classical' issues. I have not sought to include books dealing with particular countries or regions unless they also had a more general interpretative ambition. Even so, the sheer amount of relevant publications makes this a somewhat arbitrary selection.

John Breuilly

Readers and Works of Reference

Hutchinson, John and Anthony D. Smith (eds), *Nationalism*, Oxford and New York: Oxford University Press, 1994

Hutchinson, John and Anthony D. Smith (eds), *Ethnicity*, Oxford and New York: Oxford University Press, 1996

Hutchinson, John and Anthony D. Smith (eds), *Nationalism: Critical Concepts*, 5 vols, London: Routledge, 2000

Motyl, Alexander J. (general ed.), *Encyclopaedia of Nationalism*, 2 vols, San Diego and London: Academic, 2000

Spencer, Philip and Howard Wollman (eds), *Nations and Nationalism: A Reader*, Edinburgh: Edinburgh University Press, 2005

General Studies

Alter, Peter, *Nationalism*, London: Edward Arnold, 1989

Anderson, B., *Imagined Communities: Reflections on the Origin and Spread of Nationalism*, second edn, London: Verso, 1991 [1983]

Armstrong, John A., *Nations Before Nationalism*, Chapel Hill, N.C.: University of Carolina Press, 1982

Avineri, Shlomo, *The Making of Modern Zionism: The Intellectual Origins of the Jewish State*, London: Weidenfeld and Nicolson, 1981

Balakrishnan, Gopal (ed.), *Mapping the Nation*, London: Verso, 1996

Banton, Michael, *Rational Choice: Theory of Racial and Ethnic Relations*, Bristol: Social Science Research Unit on Ethnic Relations, 1977

Barth, Fredrik (ed.), *Ethnic Groups and Boundaries: The Social Organization of Culture Difference*, London: Allen and Unwin, 1969

Bendix, Reinhard, *Max Weber: An Intellectual Portrait*, London: Heinemann, 1960

Bhabha, Homi (ed.), *Nation and Narration*, London: Routledge, 1990

Billig, Michael, *Banal Nationalism*, London: Sage, 1995

Brass, Paul, *Ethnicity and Nationalism*, London: Sage, 1991

Breuilly, J.J., *Nationalism and the State*, second edn, Manchester & Chicago: Manchester University Press, 1993 [1982]

Bromley, Yu. V., et al., *Sovremennye Etnicheskie Protsessy v SSSR* (Contemporary Ethnic Processes in the USSR), Moscow: Nauka, 1975

Brubaker, Rogers, *Nationalism Reframed: Nationhood and the National Question in the New Europe*, Cambridge and New York: Cambridge University Press, 1996

Brubaker, Rogers, *Ethnicity without Groups*, Cambridge, Mass., and London: Harvard University Press, 2004

Buchanan, Allen, *Secession. The Morality of Political Divorce from Fort Sumter to Lithuania and Quebec*, Boulder, Colo., and Oxford: Westview Press, 1991

Calhoun, Craig, *Nationalism*, Buckingham: Open University Press; Minneapolis: University of Minnesota Press, 1997

Chatterjee, Partha, *The Nation and Its Fragments: Colonial and Post-colonial Histories*, Princeton, N. J., and Chichester: Princeton University Press, 1993

Cohen, Abner, *Two-Dimensional Man*, London: Routledge and Kegan Paul, 1974

Cohen, Percy, *Jewish Radicals and Radical Jews*, London: Academic Press, 1980

Cole, J.W. and E.R. Wolf, *The Hidden Frontier, Ecology and Ethnicity in an Alpine Valley*, New York: Academic Press, 1974

Connor, Walker, *Ethno-Nationalism, the Quest for Understanding*, Princeton N.J.: Princeton University Press, 1994

Day, Graham and Andrew Thompson, *Theorizing Nationalism*, Basingstoke: Palgrave Macmillan, 2004

Deutsch, K., *Nationalism and Social Communication*, second edn, New York: MIT Press, 1966

Emerson, R., *From Empire to Nation*, Boston: Harvard University Press, 1960

Eriksen, T.H., *Ethnicity and Nationalism: Anthropological Perspectives*, second edn, London: Pluto, 2002 [1993]

Fromkin, David, *The Independence of Nations*, New York: Praeger, 1981

Geertz, C. (ed.), *Old Societies and New States*, New York: Free Press, 1962

Giddens, Anthony, *The Nation-State and Violence: Volume II of A Contemporary Critique of Historical Materialism*, Polity: Cambridge, 1985

Glazer, N. and D. Moynihan (eds), *Ethnicity: Theory and Experience*, Cambridge, Mass.: Harvard University Press, 1975

Goldmann, Kjell, et al. (eds), *Nationalism and Internationalism in the Post-Cold War Era*, London: Routledge, 2000

Grillo, P., *Nation and State in Europe: Anthropological Perspectives*, London: Academic Press, 1981

Guibernau, Montserrat and John Hutchinson (eds), *Understanding Nationalism*, Cambridge: Polity, 2001

Haim, Sylvia, *Arab Nationalism, An Anthology*, Berkeley: University of California Press, 1962

Hall, John A., *Powers and Liberties: The Causes and Consequences of the Rise of the West*, Oxford: Blackwell, 1985

Hall, John A. (ed.), *The State of the Nation: Ernest Gellner and the Theory of Nationalism*, Cambridge: Cambridge University Press, 1998

Hall, John A. and Ian Jarvie (eds), *The Social Philosophy of Ernest Gellner*, Amsterdam and Atlanta: Rodopi, 1996

Hastings, Adrian, *The Construction of Nationhood: Ethnicity, Religion and Nationalism*, Cambridge: Cambridge University Press, 1997

Hechter, M., *Internal Colonialism*, London: Transaction Publishers, 1975

Hechter, Michael, *Containing Nationalism*, Oxford: Oxford University Press, 2000

Hobsbawm, Eric, *Nations and Nationalism since 1780: Programme, Myth, Reality*, Cambridge: Cambridge University Press, 1990

Hobsbawm, Eric and Terence Ranger (eds), *The Invention of Tradition*, Cambridge: Cambridge University Press, 1983

Horowitz, Donald L., *Ethnic Groups in Conflict*, Berkeley and London: University of California Press, 1985

Hroch, Miroslav, *Social Preconditions of National Revival in Europe: A Comparative Analysis of the Social Composition of Patriotic Groups among the Smaller European Nations*, transl. Ben Fowkes, Cambridge: Cambridge University Press, 1985. (Originally published in German as *Die Vorkämpfer der nationalen Bewegung bei den kleinen Völkern Europas*, Prague: Univ. Karlova, 1968.)

Hutchinson, John, *Modern Nationalism*, London: Fontana, 1994

Hutchinson, John, *Nations as Zones of Conflict*, London: SAGE, 2004

Ichijo, Atsuko and Gordana Uzelac (eds), *When Is the Nation?: Towards an Understanding of Theories of Nationalism*, London: Routledge, 2005

Kamenka, E. (ed.), *Nationalism*, corrected edn, London: Edward Arnold, 1976 [1973]

Kaufmann, Eric (ed.), *Rethinking Ethnicity*, London: Routledge, 2004

Kedourie, Elie, *Nationalism*, fourth edn, Oxford: Blackwell, 1993 [1960]

Kedourie, Elie (ed.), *Nationalism in Asia and Africa*, London: Frank Cass, 1970

Kohn, Hans, *The Idea of Nationalism: A Study in its Origins and Background*, third edn, New Brunswick: Transaction Publishers, 2005 [1944]

Kohn, Hans, *Nationalism, Its Meaning and History*, Princeton, N.J.: Van Nostrand, 1955

Kohn, Hans, *The Age of Nationalism*, New York: Harper, 1962

Kymlicka, Will, *Politics in the Vernacular: Nationalism, Multiculturalism and Citizenship*, Oxford, 2001

Lawrence, Paul, *Nationalism: History and Theory*, Harlow: Pearson Education, 2005

Llobera, J.L., *The God of Modernity: The Development of Nationalism in Western Europe*, Oxford and Providence, R.I.: Berg, 1994

Loizos, P., *Heart Grown Bitter: Chronicle of Cypriot War Refugees*, Cambridge: Cambridge University Press, 1981

Lukes, Steven, *Emile Durkheim, His Life and Work: A Historical and Critical Study*, London: Allen Lane, 1973

Mayall, James, *Nationalism and International Society*, Cambridge and New York: Cambridge University Press, 1990

McGarry, John and Brendan O'Leary (eds), *The Politics of Ethnic Conflict Regulation: Case Studies of Protracted Ethnic Conflicts*, New York and London: Routledge, 1993

Miller, David, *On Nationality*, Oxford: Clarendon Press, 1995

Minogue, K.R., *Nationalism*, London: Batsford, 1969

Moore, Margaret, *The Ethics of Nationalism*, Oxford: Oxford University Press, 2001

Nairn, Tom, *The Break-Up of Britain*, London: NLB, 1977

Nimni, Ephraim (ed.), *National Cultural Autonomy and its Contemporary Critics*, London: Routledge, 2005

Olsen, Mancur, *The Rise and Decline of Nations*, New Haven: Yale University Press, 1982

Özkirimli, Umut, *Theories of Nationalism: A Critical Introduction*, Basingstoke: Palgrave, 2000

Özkirimli, Umut, *Contemporary Debates on Nationalism: A Critical Engagement*, Basingstoke: Palgrave Macmillan, 2005

Periwal, S. (ed.), *Notions of Nationalism*, Budapest, London and New York: CEU Press, 1995

Scales, Len and Oliver Zimmer (eds), *Power and the Nation in European History*, Cambridge: Cambridge University Press, 2005

Schöpflin, George, *Nations, Identity, Power*, New York: New York University Press, 2000

Seton-Watson, Hugh, *Nations and States*, London: Methuen, 1977

Smith, Anthony D., *Theories of Nationalism*, London: Duckworth, 1971

Smith, Anthony D. (ed.), *Nationalist Movements*, London: Macmillan, 1976

Smith, Anthony D., *Nationalism in the Twentieth Century*, Oxford: M. Robertson, 1979

Smith, Anthony D., *The Ethnic Revival*, Cambridge: Cambridge University Press, 1981

Smith, Anthony D., *The Ethnic Origins of Nations*, Oxford: Basil Blackwell, 1986

Smith, Anthony D., *Nationalism and Modernism*, London: Routledge, 1998

Spencer, Philip and Howard Wollman, *Nationalism: A Critical Introduction*, London: SAGE, 2002

Sugar, P. (ed.), *Ethnic Diversity and Conflict in Eastern Europe*, Santa Barbara, Calif.: ABC-Clio, 1980

Suny, Ronald Grigor, *The Revenge of the Past: Nationalism, Revolution, and the Collapse of the Soviet Union*, Stanford, Calif.: Stanford University Press, 1993

Tilly, C. (ed.), *The Formation of National States in Western Europe*, Princeton, N.J.: Princeton University Press, 1975

Wallman, S., *Ethnicity at Work*, New York: Holmes and Meier, 1979

Weber, Eugen, *Peasants into Frenchmen: The Modernization of Rural France, 1870–1914*, London: Chatto and Windus, 1979

Weber, Max, *The Protestant Ethic and the Spirit of Capitalism*, transl. Talcott Parsons, second edn, London: Allen and Unwin, 1976

Yuval-Davis, Nira, *Gender and Nation*, London: SAGE, 1997

Zimmer, Oliver, *Nationalism in Europe, 1890–1940*, Basingstoke: Palgrave Macmillan, 2003

Bibliography of Ernest Gellner's Writings on Nationalism

Compiled by Ian Jarvie

This bibliography of Gellner's publications on nationalism is taken from a complete bibliography of his works compiled by Ian Jarvie. This bibliography can be accessed at www.arts.york.ca/phil/jarvie/ErnestGellner. The date-letter string identifying a item is its unique number in that complete bibliography. Asterisks after an item indicate that it was reprinted in a volume of selected essays (i.e. * = vol. 1). The titles and their assigned asterisks are listed at the head of the complete bibliography.

1954b 'Reflections on Violence' (review-article on Stanislaw Andrzejewski, *Military Organization and Society*), *British Journal of Sociology*, vol. 5, no. 3 (September), pp. 267–71.

1957f 'Independence in the Central High Atlas', *Middle East Journal*, vol. 11, no. 3 (Summer), pp. 236–52.

1957m 'Contemporary Thought and Politics' (article-review on P. Laslett and W.G. Runciman (eds), *Philosophy, Politics and Society*), *Philosophy*, vol. 32, no. 123 (October), pp. 336–57.**

1960a 'The Middle East Observed', *Political Studies*, vol. 8, no. 1 (February), pp. 66–70.

1960b Review of J.N.D. Anderson, *Islamic Law in the Modern World*, *British Journal of Sociology*, vol. 11, no. 1 (March), pp. 98–9.

1960f 'Allah and Caesar', *The Hibbert Journal*, vol. 59 (October), pp. 54–8.

1961g 'From Ibn Khaldun to Karl Marx' (review of Donald E. Ashford, *Political Change in Morocco*), *The Political Quarterly*, vol. 32, no. 4 (October/December), pp. 385–92.

1961*h* 'The Struggle for Morocco's Past', *Middle East Journal*, vol. 15, no. 1 (Winter), pp. 79–90; reprinted in I.W. Zartman (ed.), *Man, State and Society in the Contemporary Maghrib*, New York: Praeger 1973, pp. 37–49.

1961*i* 'Morocco', in Colin Legum (ed.), *Africa, A Handbook of the Continent*, London: Anthony Blond, pp. 43–60.

1962*e* 'Patterns of Rural Rebellion in Morocco: Tribes as Minorities', *European Journal of Sociology*, vol. 3, no. 2, pp. 297–311; reprinted in 1973*b*, pp. 361–74.*****

1963*a* 'Going Into Europe', *Encounter*, vol. 20 (January), pp. 54–5.

1963*b* 'A Tunisian Visit', *New Society*, vol. 1 (3 January), pp. 15–17.

1963*c* Review of Rom Landau, *Morocco Independent*, *Middle East Journal*, vol. 17, nos 1 and 2 (Winter–Spring), pp. 174–5.

1963*d* 'Sanctity, Puritanism, Secularisation and Nationalism in North Africa', *Archives de sociologie des religions*, no. 15, pp. 71–86; also in J.G. Peristiany (ed.), *Contributions to Mediterranean Sociology: Mediterranean Rural Communities and Social Change*, Acts of the Mediterranean Sociology Conference, July 1963, Paris: Mouton, 1965, pp. 31–48.*****

1963*e* 'Thy Neighbour's Revolution', *New Society*, vol. 1 (16 May), pp. 20–1.

1965*a* *Thought and Change*, London: Weidenfeld & Nicolson; Chicago: University of Chicago Press (with the imprint 1964). pp. viii + 224.

1965*b* 'The Day the Pendulum Stood Still' (review of Sylvia G. Haim (ed.), *Arab Nationalism*), *New Society*, vol. 5 (15 April), pp. 30–1.

1980*a* *Spectacles and Predicaments, Essays in Social Theory*, Cambridge: Cambridge University Press. pp. viii + 385. Contains: 1980*b*, 1976*e*, 1975*p*, 1975*e*, 1975*m*, 1977*i*, 1978*m*, 1974*c*, 1978*g*, 1976*h*, 1975*o*, 1975*h*, 1981*e*, 1978*c*, 1975*d*, 1979*h*, 1976*g*, 1979*a*, 1977*d*, 1975*l*.

1980*p* 'Ethnicity Between Culture, Class and Power', in Peter F. Sugar (ed.), *Ethnic Diversity and Conflict in Eastern Europe*, Santa Barbara: ABC-Clio, pp. 237–77. (Edited version of 1981*j*.)

1980*s* 'As raizes sociais de nacionalismo e a diversidede de suas formas', in *Alternatives politicas, economicas, e sociais ao final do século*, Brazilia: Editore Universided do Brazilien.

1981*c* *Muslim Society*, Cambridge: Cambridge University Press. pp. x + 264. Contains: 1981*d*, 1975*b*, 1973*a*, 1972*g*, 1963*d*, 1974*h*, 1978*a*, 1976*b*, 1962*e*, 1976*c*, 1977*f*, 1979*b*; paperback edition, 1983.

1981*j* 'Nationalism', *Theory and Society*, vol. 10, pp. 753–76.

1981*k* *Nacionalismo e Democracia*, Brasilia: Editore Universede de Brasilia.

1982*f* 'The Individual Division of Labour and National Cultures', *Government and Opposition*, vol. 17, no. 3 (Summer), pp. 268–78.

1983*c* 'Nationalism and the Two Forms of Cohesion in Complex Societies', The Radcliffe-Brown Memorial Lecture, *Proceedings of the British Academy*, vol. 58, pp. 165–87.*******

1983*e* *Nations and Nationalism*, Oxford: Basil Blackwell. pp. x + 150.

1983*j* 'Personal communication' about nationalism, quoted and discussed in Anthony D. Smith, *Theories of Nationalism*, second edn, London: Duckworth 1983, Appendix C, pp. 265–7.

1984*i* Foreword to Eva Schmidt-Hartmann, *Thomas G. Masaryk's Realism: Origins of a Czech Political Concept*, Munich: R. Oldenbourg Verlag, pp. 7–8.

1985*c* *Nazioni e Nazionalismo*, Rome: Editore Rinniti. (Italian translation of 1983*e*.) New edition 1992.

1987*j* 'Nationalism', in Vernon Bogdanor (ed.), *Encyclopaedia of Political Institutions*, Oxford: Blackwell, pp. 382–3.

1987*r* 'Il Nazionalismo, la Democrazia e la Storia', *Quaderni Storici*, new series vol. 66, no. 3 (December), pp. 945–59. (Italian translation by Maria Luisa Pesante.)

1988*j* *Naciones y nacionalismo* (Spanish translation by Javier Setó of 1983*e*), Madrid: Alianza Editorial.

1988*p* *Plough, Sword and Book*, London: Collins Harvill. pp. 288. Paperback editions, University of Chicago and Paladin Grafton Books, London, 1990.

1989*g* 'Natsii i Natsionalism', *Voprosy Filosofi*, no. 7, pp. 119–31. (Russian translation of the opening passages of 1983*e*.)

1989*l* *Nations et nationalisme*, Paris: Bibliothèque [historique] Parpot. (French translation of 1983*e*.)

1989*m* 'The Sacred and the National', essay review of Conor Cruise O'Brien, *Godland: Reflections on Religion and Nationalism*, *LSE Quarterly*, vol. 3, no. 4 (Winter), pp. 357–69.*********

1989*o* 'Nationalism Today: Its Origins and Nature', transcript of a discussion with Igor Kon, *Social Sciences* [USSR], vol. 20, no. 4, pp. 183–95.

1989*r* 'Natsionalizm vozvrashchaietsa' (Nationalism returns) in *Novaia i novieishiya Istoria* (Modern and Recent History), no. 5, pp. 55–62.*********

1990*c* 'The Dramatis Personae of History', review of Roman Szporluk, *Communism and Nationalism: Karl Marx versus Friedrich List*, *East European Politics and Societies*, vol. 4, no. 1, pp. 116–33.*********

1990*o* Interview with V. Borshchev, 'O Prirode Natsionalisma' ('About the Nature of Nationalism'), *Znanie Sila* (Moscow), vol. 7, no. 7 (757), pp. 0–5.

1990*u* 'Nationen Imperium und Ubernationale Gemeinschaft' ('Nations, Empire and the Transnational Community'), in *Transit, Europäische Revue*, vol. 1 (Autumn), pp. 143–5.

1991*b* 'Nationalisme et politique en Europe de l'Est', *Le débat*, no. 63 (January–February), pp. 78–84.

1991*c* 'An interview with Ernest Gellner by John Davis', *Current Anthropology*, vol. 32, no. 1 (February), pp. 63–71.

1991*d* 'Two Escapes from History or the Hapsburg Impact on British Thought', in Alfred Bohnen and Alan Musgrave (eds), *Wege der Vernunft, Festschrift zum siebzigsten Geburstag von Hans Albert*, Tübingen: J.C.B. Mohr (Paul Siebeck), pp. 227–44.

1991*i* *Nationalismus und Moderne*, Berlin: Rotbuch. (German translation of 1983*e*.)

1991*j* *Narodny i Nacjonalizm*, Warsaw: Paustwowy Institut Wydawniczy. (Polish translation of 1983*e*.)

1991*v* 'Le nationalisme en apesanteur', *Terrain*, no. 17, October, pp. 7–16. (French version of 1992*i*.)

1991*w* 'Nationalism in Eastern Europe', *New Left Review*, no. 189 (September/October), pp. 127–36.

1991*ab* 'Nationalism in the New Central Europe', in Working Papers of the Institute of Sociology of the Czechoslovak Academy of Sciences, 'Prague in the New Central Europe', transcript of an international conference, 2–4 June 1990, pp. 24–7. Gellner also contributes to the discussion of his own and other papers.

1991*af* 'Nacionalizem', in Rudi Rizman (ed.), *O Etnonacionalizmn*, Ljubljana (Slovenia): Zbornik Studije, Kujiznica revolucionaruc teorije, pp. 239–66. (Slovenian translation of 1981*j*.)

1991*ah* 'Etnicità, sentimento nazionale e industrialismo', in *Identità culturali*, special issue of *Problemi di Socialismo* (no. 3), Milan: Franco Agnelli, pp. 45–54.

1992*a* 'Alle Radici delle nazioni. Tre etnie e Fondamentalismi', interview with Nicole Janigro, *Il Manifesto*, 3 March.

1992*c* 'Nationalismus und rassenwahn' ('Nationalism and Racial Madness'), *Süddeutsche Zeitung*, no. 6 (7 February), pp. 26–7.

1992*i* 'Nationalism in the Vacuum', in Alexander J. Motyl (ed.), *Thinking Theoretically About Soviet Nationalities*, New York: Columbia University Press, pp. 243–54.

1992*n* 'Prishestvie Natsionalisma. Mify Natsii i Klassa' (The Coming of Nationalism. Myths of Nation and Class.), *Put'* (The Way), no. 1, pp. 9–61.*********

1992*s* *Uluslar ve Ulusculuk*, translated by B.E. Behar and G.F. Özdogan, Istanbul: Insan Yazinlari. (Turkish translation of 1983*e*.)

1992*v* 'Nationalismus und Politik in Osteuropa', *Prokla 87*, issue 22, no. 2, Berlin: Rotbuch Verlag, pp. 242–52. (German translation of 1991*w*.)

1992*x* 'Beyond Nationalism?' (in German as 'Jenseits des Nationalismus?'), *IKUS Lectures*, Nr. 3+4, Wien: Institut fur Kulturstudien 1992, pp. 31–44, discussion pp. 45–52.

1992*aa* 'Nationalism Reconsidered and E.H. Carr', *Review of International Studies*, vol. 18, pp. 285–93.*********

1992*ae* 'C'è il nazionalismo non le nazioni', interview with Annamaria Guadefni, *L'Unità* (Roma), 20 September.

1992*ai* Articles 'Linguistic Philosophy' (pp. 339–40), 'Nation' (pp. 402–3), 'Nationalism' (pp. 409–11), 'Psychoanalysis' (pp. 524–7), 'Unconscious' (pp. 682–3), in William Outhwaite, Tom Bottomore, E. Gellner, R. Nisbet and A. Touraine (eds), *The Blackwell Dictionary of Twentieth-Century Social Thought*, Oxford: Blackwell.

1993*b* *Národy a Nacionalismus* (Nations and Nationalism), transl. Jirí Markus, with a new preface by the author, written in Czech, Praha: Hríbal. (Czech translation of 1983*e*.)

1993*f* *Nacoes e Nacionalismo*, transl. Inez vaz Pinto, Lisbon: Gradiva. (Portuguese translation of 1983*e*.)

1993*i* 'Reborn from below. The forgotten beginnings of the Czech national revival', review of Jan Patocka, *Co Jsou Cesi? Was Sind die Tschechen?*, *Times Literary Supplement*, no. 4702 (14 May), pp. 3–5.*********

1993*j* 'Nationalism in a Post-Marxist World: Contemporary Reflections', in Mario Buttino (ed.), *In a Collapsing Empire*, Milano: Feltrinelli, pp. 83–8.

1993*k Natsii i Natsionalism*, transl. T.V. Berdikova, M.K. Tynnkine, post-word by I.I. Krupnik, Moscow: Progress [dated 1991]. (Russian translation of 1983*e* with a new preface by the author.)

1993*l* 'Nationalizem in politika v Vzhodni Europi', *Teorije in Praksa*, vol. 30, nos 3–4, pp. 191–8. (Slovenian translation of 1991*w*.)

1993*o* 'Nationalisms and the New World Order', in L.W. Reed and C. Keyser (eds), *Emerging Norms of Justified Intervention*, Cambridge, Mass.: Committee on International Security Studies, American Academy of Arts and Sciences, pp. 151–5.

1993*s* 'Il mito della nazione e quello delle classe', in P. Anderson, M. Aymard, P. Bairoch, W. Barberis, C. Ginzburg and G. Einaudi (eds), *Storia d'Europa*, vol. 1, *L'Europa Oggi*, Torino: Editore Giulio Einaudi, pp. 638–89. (Italian translation of 1992*n*.)*********

1993*v* 'Natsionalism v postmarksistskaia Sinat', *Kultura* 15 (October), p. 5. (Bulgarian translation of 1991*w*.)

1993*x* 'Nationalism and Politics in Eastern Europe', *European Review*, vol. 1, no. 4, pp. 341–5.

1993*y* 'Nationalism in Europe', in A. Clesse and A. Kortunov (eds), *The Political and Strategic Implications of the State Crises in Central and Eastern Europe*, Luxembourg: Institute for European and International Studies, pp. 29–32 and discussion pp. 299–335.

1993*ae* Review of Peter Buck, *Folk Cultures and Little Peoples: Aspects of National Awakening in East Central Europe*, *Ethnos*, vol. 58, nos 3–4, p. 406.

1994*a* 'Nationalisms and the New World Order', *Bulletin of the American Academy of Arts and Sciences*, vol. 47, no. 5 (February), pp. 29–36.

1994*e Naties en Nationelisme*, Amsterdam: Wereldbibliotek. (Dutch translation, by Magna van Soest, of 1983*e*.)

1994*f* 'Nacionelizmus a politike ve vychochni Europe' ('Nationalism and Politics in East Europe') in *Mezineroshni vztahy* (*International Relations*) vol. 4, no. 19, pp. 20–9. (Czech translation of 1991*w*.)

1994*h* Interview, 'Natsii i Nationalizm' ('Nations and Nationalism'), with L. Anninskii and I. Mamaladze, *Obshchaia Gazeta*, Moscow, 10/35 (March), pp. 11–17.

1994*k* 'The Marxist Failure', in Geraint Perry (ed.), *Politics in an Interdependent World. Essays Presented to Ghita Ionescu*, Cheltenham: Edward Elgar, pp. 161–72.

1994*n* 'Lawrence of Moravia, Alois Musil, monotheism and the Habsburg Empire', *Times Literary Supplement*, no. 4768 (19 August), pp. 12–14.**********

1994*p* 'Nationalism and Modernization' and 'Nationalism and High Cultures', in John Hutchinson and Anthony D. Smith (eds), *Nationalism*, Oxford Readers,

Oxford: Oxford University Press, pp. 55–62 and 63–9. (Extracts from 1965*a* and 1983*e*.)

1994*s* *Encounters with Nationalism*, Oxford: Blackwell. pp. xvi + 208. Contains: 1990*c*, 1992*aa*, 1989*r*, 1990*q*, 1989*m*, 1987*n*, 1990*l*, 1992*al*, 1993*i*, 1993*u*, 1993*a*, 1992*d*, 1993*s*. Also contains, as chapter 7, 'Kemalism', pp. 81–91, not previously published.

1994*w* 'Rahvused ja rahvuslus' ('Nations and Nationalism'), *Akadeemia*, nos 10, pp. 2207–38 and 11, pp. 2429–62. (Estonian translation by Anneti Andresson of 1983*e*.)

1994*z* *Leumin uLeumit*, Tel Aviv: Open University Press. p. 198. New preface pp. 7–12. (Hebrew translation of 1983*e*.)

1994*aa* 'Mitul natiunnii si mitul claselor' ('Myth of Nations and Myth of Classes'), *Polis*, no. 2. (Romanian version of 1993*s*.)

1994*ad* 'Rahvused ja rahvuslus' ('Nations and Nationalism'), *Akadeemia*, no. 12. (Third instalment of Estonian translation of 1983*e*; see 1994*w*.)

1995*b* 'Rahvused ja rahvuslus' (Nations and Nationalism), *Akadeemia*, no. 7. Aastekëik, no. 1, pp. 197–222. (Fourth instalment of Estonian translation of 1983*e*; see also 1994*w* and 1994*ad*.)

1995*g* 'Rahvused ja rahvuslus', *Akademia*, vol. 7, no. 2, pp. 420–46. (Fifth instalment of Estonian translation of 1983*e*.)

1995*h* 'Rahvused ja rahvuslus', *Akademia*, vol. 7, no. 3, pp. 643–63. (Sixth and final instalment of Estonian translation of 1983*e*, with a biographical note at pp. 665–70 by Eero Loone.)

1995*w* 'Introduction' to Sukumar Periwal (ed.), *Notions of Nationalism*, Budapest: CEU Press, pp. 1–7.

1995*x* *Anthropology and Politics. Revolutions in the Sacred Grove*, Oxford: Blackwell. pp. xvi + 260. Contains: 1992*k*, 1988*b*, 1988*v*, 1989*i*, 1996*a*, 1985*h*, 1994*l*, 1990*v*, 1987*k*, 1993*af*, 1991*z*, 1991*k*, 1991*c*, 1994*n*, 1992*q*, 1995*p*.

1995*y* 'Introduction. Nationalism and Xenophobia', to Bernd Baumgartl and Adrian Favell (eds), *New Xenophobia in Europe*, London: Kluwer Law International, pp. 6–9.

1996*g* 'Reply to Critics', in John A. Hall and Ian C. Jarvie (eds), *The Social Philosophy of Ernest Gellner*, Amsterdam: Rodopi, pp. 623–86.

1996*i* 'The Coming of Nationalism and its Interpretation: the Myths of Nation and Class', in G. Balakrishnan (ed.), *Mapping the Nation*, London: Verso, pp. 98–145. (English version of 1993*s*.)

1997 *Nationalism*, London: Weidenfeld and Nicolson; New York: New York University Press.

1999*a* 'Nations, States, and Religions', in R. English and C. Townshend (eds), *The State: Historical and Political Dimensions*, London: Routledge, pp. 235–47.

Index